Generation
Rent

Chloe
Timperley

First published by Canbury Press 2020
This edition published 2020

Canbury Press
Kingston upon Thames, Surrey, United Kingdom
www.canburypress.com

Printed and bound in Great Britain by CPI Group (UK) Ltd, Croydon
Typeset in Athelas 10pt/13pt
Cover: Cover Kitchen

This is a work of non-fiction.
The events and experiences detailed herein are true and have been
faithfully rendered to the best of the author's ability.

ISBN: Paperback: 978-1-912454-26-6
ePub: 978-1-912454-27-3
PDF: 978-1-912454-28-0

Generation Rent

Chloe Timperley

Preface

Generation Rent is ultimately the story of how the UK turned its youth into an asset class. Over the latter part of the 20th and early 21st centuries, housing went from being a basic good to a financial asset. As it did so, our homes went from being a store of wealth for occupiers, to a store of wealth for landlords and speculators.

This trend goes beyond the behaviour of buy-to-let investors, and begins in the popular imagination. Before we can restore justice and decency, we must change the cultural view of our homes as personal trophies, pension pots and money-making machines, rather than basic necessities for a normal life.

Britain's housing crisis is a vast, sprawling and multi-layered story. In order to make this book concise, some research and case studies had to be left out. I have tried to weave together the most pressing issues faced by today's young (and not so young) renters and parental home dwellers, and place these stories in a wider narrative that affects us all. I have dug out and presented what I believe are the most credible solutions. And I have called for neglected debates to be re-opened – most importantly, on land and credit.

I wrote this book while living and working in Sheffield. Consequently, some of the case studies here are from my home-town, but the outlook is national and the material spans the length and breadth of the country. Many of the trends are found, to a varying degree, in other Western countries.

My hope for *Generation Rent* is that we can break free from the simplistic narratives that dominate the current debate about housing. I want us to leave behind tired binary arguments like 'boost regulation v cut red tape,' 'build more homes v control immigration,' and 'help people get on the ladder v tell them to stop buying avocado toast.' Instead, I want to start talking about what really drives our current shameful situation. I don't profess to have all the answers. But if this book can at least start to change the national conversation on housing, I will consider it a success.

Chloe Timperley

SECTION I. TRYING TO BUY A HOME

1. Can't buy, won't buy

Olivia Lynes and her partner Izaak appear to have everything going for them. Both are 29 years old and have PhDs in chemistry. Both have good jobs: Olivia works in computer programming in Hertfordshire, and Izaak works in the civil service in London. But when Olivia and Izaak talk about the future, they are resigned to a life of constant struggle and compromise, because they rent a home in modern Britain.

Dodgy landlords, security deposit theft, unhygienic plumbing and estate agents' bullying come as standard with membership of 'generation rent.' But these things don't trouble the couple. They have barely any complaint to make about the landlord of their two-bed flat. Instead, they are frustrated by the life-sucking cost of living in the UK private rented sector. For a couple with good educations and jobs, shelling out so much every month makes everyday life more pinched than it should be. It also makes it harder for the couple to save enough money to get their own place, something that was commonplace in the previous generation. 'Both of us earn more than our parents ever have in their entire lives,' Olivia tells me, 'and I'm not sure if we're ever going to be able to afford to buy a house.'

She explains: 'We've worked out we'd need about £35,000 saved up to buy our first home. Small, two-bed homes round here start at about £290k, and when you factor in all the fees associated with buying a house, £35k in cash seems a realistic figure to aim for.'

The couple estimate that, all things equal, it would take at least five years to save the money. Five years is not ideal, but nor is it an eternity. So why does she feel that she may end up being a lifelong renter? Because probably not all things will be equal. 'The thing is,' Olivia says, 'the idea that we can save £35k in five years is based on a lot of assumptions. If we need to relocate for whatever reason, it's a massive setback. Moving here cost us about £4,000 in total – factoring in all the fees, referencing, upfront costs, etc.' Since a ban on tenant fees came into force in June 2019, the upfront cost of moving have reduced. Even so, moving might cost £2,000, three months' worth of savings. And they could be asked to leave their home at any point. Legally, a landlord can ask tenants to leave with two months' notice at the end of a fixed-term contract, without giving a reason. The average tenancy in the UK lasts about four years,[1] and being a good tenant does not prevent eviction.

Even if, against the odds, Olivia and Izaak do manage to stay in the same place, they need all other prices to remain broadly the same. Saving up for five years is only viable if rent and local house prices don't shoot up even further, the car doesn't break down and need replacing, and they continue earning as much as they do now. But their rent probably will rise. According to the housing charity Shelter, on average rents across the UK rose 60 per cent faster than wages between 2011 and 2017.[2] The couple moved out of London to a commuter town to escape the capital's overheating property market. But the figures show that the temperature is rapidly rising across the commuter belt.

'We currently pay £1,000 a month in rent, not including bills,' Olivia says. And while the flat is close to Olivia's job, Izaak must commute to work by train, which costs around £400 a month.

The other problem is that saving for a home entails a long-term austerity drive. For Olivia and Izaak, this means committing themselves to at least five years of '*very* frugal living – no holidays, no luxuries, and constantly counting every penny.' Olivia explains:

'It's not that we're unwilling to make sacrifices, but we at least want to know that the sacrifice is going to be worth it. We've already spent four years living on not very much money. Do we want to spend the next five years living on not very much money, to then realise the goalposts just keep moving – and before you know it five years turns into 25 years?'

For Olivia, opportunities to economise are sparse. Playing devil's advocate, I ask her: does she really *need* two bedrooms? Is a conveniently located flat right next to the train station *absolutely essential*? Were she and Izaak not willing to 'slum it' somewhere less nice to save money? Olivia replies:

'There isn't really a *range* of prices on offer. It's not like we've actively picked somewhere that's expensive – this is pretty much the going rate for a standard two-bed flat in the area. Even one-beds aren't much less. When you look at places far worse than this, they're only slightly cheaper than what we're paying now. If we could save an extra £200-£300 a month by living somewhere a bit gross, we might consider it, but for £50 or even £100 less it's not worth the trouble.'

Plus, moving somewhere less central might cost less in rent, but would probably cost more in transport.

Olivia says: 'Obviously, we've done all the switching we can with things like energy bills and our internet provider.' But the exercise 'almost feels pointless.' Despite shaving '£10 or £20 here and there' off their outgoings, none of it changes the £1,600 they pay out every month in rent, council tax and train fares.

What would Olivia say to someone who suggested that her current situation was a result of too many indulgences – Netflix subscriptions, expensive gadgets and brunch? She laughs: 'My mum tried to pull this one on me the other day! She was saying how, if I cancelled Netflix and Amazon Prime, I could save so much more. I told her, Mum, Netflix costs £9.99 a month and we split it with someone else, and with Amazon Prime we've still got our student subscription, so it's something like £40 for the year.' At a combined saving of £100 per year, it's hard to see how foregoing these 'luxuries' would be worth the self-denial.

'Plus, I need my phone for work. It's not a luxury item – and I'm definitely not on an £80 a month phone contract. It's the same with so much of the advice to young people trying to save – you'll read things like: 'shop at Aldi.' Like, where did you think I was shopping? M&S?!'

I wonder what her parents make of it all? 'My parents are sympathetic, but I don't think they fully get it,' Olivia says. 'I mean, they built their own house. My dad's a farmer so got given a piece of land by my grandpa, and they built a house for about

£4,000. That's the kind of opportunity that gets you on the housing ladder. Not cancelling Netflix.'

While the cost of renting rises year after year in Britain, the homeownership dream demands increasingly heftier sacrifices over expanding periods of time. This, as Olivia can attest, is profoundly demotivating.

'We're coming up to that point where we've got to make a decision: are we going to go for it and hope the sacrifice pays off, or are we going to accept that we'll just be renting forever, and spend our money on having a life instead?'

This is the crux of the matter for generation rent: for the one in three millennials now believed to be locked out of homeownership for good, renting a home is like having a demented money-munching Pac-Man on the loose in your bank account. Not only that, but the goalposts are constantly moving. Even with a decade of strenuous penny pinching, a permanent home may still be out of reach.

If Olivia were an oddball among her friends for having failed to enter the kingdom of homeownership, perhaps a lack of personal responsibility or poor life choices would be to blame. But all of Olivia's friends 'are in the same boat.' 'Some of my friends actually have a 10 per cent deposit gifted from parents, and they still can't get a mortgage, because they don't have the income multiplier.'

In fact, Olivia and Izaak are just two among millions of people – many with excellent jobs – who cannot afford to buy a home in Britain in the 2020s. Instead of being priced at two or three times annual incomes, homes in England and Wales now cost an average of 7.83 times yearly earnings before tax.[3] In Scotland, the picture is almost as grim, with house prices reaching seven times average incomes.[4] The ratio in Northern Ireland is significantly lower at 4.8,[5] however house prices there in late 2019 were growing faster than anywhere else in the UK.[6]

At the peak of the homeownership dream, in 2007, 73 per cent of the population owned their own home. A decade later, in 2016, the figure was 63 per cent, with the steepest decline seen amongst those born in the late 1980s onwards.[7] The difficulty of finding somewhere decent to live in the UK (many rented homes are in poor repair) is not an individual problem. It is generational.

2. 'Refusing to leave home'

Before I began researching this book, I assumed that there would be general agreement about the state of the UK housing market. It was only when I got talking to older family members and their friendship groups, with colleagues, and with friends-of-friends and acquaintances, that I realised that 'young people have been screwed over by the housing crisis' is considered by some to be a controversial opinion rather than a statement of fact.

Media stories often stoke this misinformation. In February 2019, for instance, *The Daily Mail* revealed that three millennials aged under 26 had single-handedly 'debunked' the 'myth' of generation rent by buying property worth £750,000.[1] A few months earlier, *Metro* featured the story of a 29-year-old property tycoon who bought her first home aged 19,[2] right after the financial crash of 2008 (the subtext being if an underprivileged teenager can get on the property ladder, anyone can).

What might be described as housing crisis denialism first began in the early 2000s, when tales appeared about 'kidults' living with parents into their late twenties. Sympathy at this point was next to non-existent, with most of the coverage focussing on the strain being placed on the parents forced to postpone their retirements while they lived in a 'crowded nest.' In 2005, the *Independent* reported that a new wave of young adults had begun to 'lean on their parents for hand-outs and a spare bed,'[3] as if becoming a cash drain on your family was just a trendy new lifestyle choice. After the 2008 crash came the 'Peter Pan' generation: a supposedly infantilised cohort of young adults obsessed with self-pampering and going on 'gap yahs,' while refusing to grow up, find careers and start families.

In 2012, *The Daily Mail* used the findings of a survey to shame under-40s living with their parents for 'refusing to leave home.' These over-stayers, it complained, 'lacked the skills' to cope with adult life and enjoyed the fact that 'someone else cooks and cleans up after them.' Damningly, these wastrels spent £50-£150 a week on 'keeping themselves entertained.'[4] The economic context was absent, but at the time overall unemployment was nearing eight per cent of the economically active population,[5] while youth unemployment stood at 21.9 per cent.[6] In other words, more than one in five young people was not in work, education or training. Despite this, house prices were still in the stratosphere thanks to the Bank of England's emergency base rate cuts and successive rounds of quantitative easing, which we'll explore later.

In my conversations with naysayers of the difficulties faced by generation rent, I've noticed that they invariably have a story to tell about a young person they know who works as a receptionist and has a BMW on finance, the latest iPhone and a predilection for 5-star holidays in Bali. Peruse the MoneySavingExpert forums, and you'll see similar attitudes. During a discussion on how entire age demographics are being priced out of the South East, one person declared: 'My parents bought their home in their late twenties after having lived with my grandparents. They never rented.' They went on to explain: 'Buying a house is not a right – it needs to be earned and sacrifices need to be made.'[7] The implication is that renting is a treat that sensible people resist. And so, the argument comes full-circle. Not only are millennials who move out of the family home and rent just as spoiled and entitled as the boomerang and Peter Pan generations, they are also impatient, imprudent and stuck-up. Either way, the message is clear: if you can't afford to buy a house, it's because of your poor character and decision-making.

Tim Gurner, a 35-year-old property developer, summed up this attitude in 2017 when he told Australia's *60 Minutes* TV show: 'When I was trying to buy my first home I wasn't buying smashed avocados for 19 bucks and four coffees at $4 each.' Gurner, worth an estimated $460 million (about £245 million), warned that wasteful spending was stymying young people from owning a home.[8]

Elle Hunt, a freelance journalist, was set the avocado toast challenge by *The Guardian*: was she being prevented from buying a home because she frittered away too much on luxuries? She kept a money diary for four weeks in December, then enlisted the help of personal finance expert Martin Lewis, founder of Moneysavingexpert.com, to review her spending. Before she met Lewis, Hunt was of the view that, since house-price-to-income-ratios at the time stood at 7.6 in England and Wales and 14-plus in London, owning a home was simply 'out of reach' for her. Despite earning between £35,000-£40,000 a year, she felt that the size of the average deposit needed to get on the property ladder – £32,899 in the UK; £106,577 in London – was so daunting that she had 'resigned [her]self to spending for the now.'

Martin Lewis objected to this 'live for the now' mentality. At the end of the challenge, he concluded that while Hunt had a snowball in hell's chance of buying a property in London without radically changing her ways, homeownership elsewhere could be within her grasp in four to eight years if she went on a serious economy drive. For instance, she could cut out take-away coffee, meals out, drinking alcohol, and buying new clothes. Lewis warned her: 'If you spend £625 a year on coffee but then turn around and say, "I can't save up for a deposit on a house", you start to lose a bit of the moral argument.'[9]

Several months after her piece ran, Hunt wrote a follow-up article. In it she revealed what happened after her money diary went viral. 'The response was immediate and visceral; I have never experienced anything like it,' she wrote. One reader had seen fit to send her a long, typewritten letter to inform her that she had 'brought shame on [her] parents and [her] editor.' The admonishments devolved into dire warnings that Hunt's 'fecklessness' would, if left unchecked, 'cause tension with [her] future husband and [their] hypothetical children, culminating, potentially, in alcoholism.'

The sheer volume of rage led Hunt to regret her openness, not least because she could have avoided being referenced in a lecture at the University of Edinburgh under the heading: *Entitled, spoilt and ridiculous or just youthful play*? She had freely admitted that she earned above the UK average, and that owning a home wasn't a priority.[10] Even so, the vitriol she received for spending her earnings enjoying herself, and not surrendering everything at the altar of homeownership, underlines the current housing hysteria. That people are now expected to prioritise the pursuit of homeownership over the pursuit of happiness only goes to show how warped many views about property and homeownership have become.

For some renters, adopting a 'live for the now' attitude is far from a flippant lifestyle choice; it's a coping mechanism. One I interviewed – who wished to remain anonymous – had arrived at a zen-like acceptance of his poor financial prospects. Before we spoke, 'Joel' sent me a link to his LinkedIn profile. His CV was sparkling: not only was he a highly technically skilled coder who had worked for several blue-chip corporations, he was also a non-executive trustee of a social enterprise, and he was bilingual and could hold a conversation in two other languages.

He and his partner were renting a flat in London from a close friend, and he considered himself lucky that his friend-lord had promised to let him live there for as long as he wanted, so long as he was willing to pay a market rent.

Joel had no wealthy parents to help him escape the rent trap, and when I asked him whether he had a long-term plan for retirement, he nonchalantly declared that he was operating under the assumption that he would never be able to stop working. His situation was somewhat unusual in that his partner was unable to work full-time due to ill-health, so his salary had to cover the costs of two people.

But his reasoning for not beginning to attempt amassing the colossal amount of cash required to see him and his partner through a comfortable post-work life had nothing to do with his personal circumstances. Instead, he wanted to know:

'Who says there'll be a world worth retiring into in 40 years' time? Climate change, rising geopolitical tensions, financial crisis after financial crisis… there's so much uncertainty in modern times; I at least want to enjoy living right now. Why put all your energy into saving for a future that might never happen?'

Joel's stance may seem extreme, but he is not alone in thinking like this. In the last few years we've seen the emergence of the 'YOLO' (an acronym for 'You Only Live Once') hashtag on social media. '#YOLO' signifies a 'screw it, let's do it' attitude, and it has come to characterise young peoples' outlook on life: live the way you want to now, because tomorrow you might not have the chance. It's easy to sneer at this outlook as puerile and self-indulgent, but for people like Joel, it's a rational response to an increasingly insecure and economically hostile world.

Life for Rent

In 2020, renting isn't just a housing tenure. It's becoming an entire lifestyle. The internet has altered the nature of possession, making it more temporary. Increasingly, members of generation rent don't own music, films or digital devices. They have monthly subscriptions with Spotify, Netflix, and mobile phone companies. Personal contract plans are the new model for car 'ownership' – a low-monthly-cost arrangement that suspiciously looks like renting, because at the end of the term, you don't really own the car, you've merely financed its depreciation.

And the reality is that everyday 'luxuries' are much cheaper than they were in the past.[11] For example:

Flights
1990 – return flights from London to Sydney cost £2,150 in today's money.

2019 – the same round trip costs just £686[12]

Cinema
1989 – a single cinema ticket in 1989 cost £2.20.[13] In today's money that's about £5.50

2019 – a monthly Netflix subscription giving access to 5,000 films, TV shows and documentaries is £5.99 – and the cost can be shared by the whole family

Mobile phone
1989 – a Motorola mobile phone cost £1,765,[14] or £4,424 in today's money.

2019 – a brand-new Samsung smartphone costs £250[15]

But that picture of falling prices changes sharply when we look at house prices.

Average home
1985 – £34,700 (£105,932 in today's money)
1995 – £51,334 (£99,430 in today's money)
2019 – £216,805[16]

Broadly, the costs of technology, foreign travel, and everyday food have tumbled in recent decades, but property has become massively more expensive. These figures help explain why generation rent attracts such opprobrium from older housing crisis sceptics. Back in 1989, buying a mobile phone would set back your journey towards homeownership. In 2020, the cost of owning a smartphone is minuscule. As well as this stark change, society itself has changed. The connectivity of modern life makes foregoing a smartphone or other so-called 'luxuries' far more socially alienating and disruptive than it would have been in the eighties. So when you consider all of these factors, the idea of denying yourself a phone to get on the property ladder starts to look facile. Fundamentally, the housing crisis comprises three key issues. These are:

1. Homes are too expensive to buy

The reality is that a person's chances of getting on the housing ladder are largely determined, not by their willingness to drink supermarket own-brand instant coffee instead of takeaway lattes, but by the year of their birth.

According to the Resolution Foundation, between 1990 and 2017, homeownership rates among 25-34-year-olds halved. Over the same period, homeownership levels amongst the next age bracket up – the 35-44s – fell from 70 per cent in 1990 to 52 per cent in 2017. Since 2008, homeownership rates among almost all ages have steadily declined, with only a feeble recovery in the last couple of years. Over the same period, the over-65s were the only age bracket to have experienced a solid increase in homeownership.[17]

Sebastian Burnside, senior economist at NatWest, is confident that private renters will outnumber people with a mortgage by 2025.[18]

2. Private rented homes are often poor quality

Many of those who cannot afford to buy a home or do not wish to do so live in poor quality homes, with little security of tenure. The latest English Housing Survey found that 25 per cent of privately rented homes are 'non-decent.' Some 14 per cent of all privately rented homes are below the 'minimum standard,' meaning that a dwelling poses a Category 1 hazard under the Housing Health and Safety Rating System (HHSRS).[19] That is, a hazard that can cause death, or that otherwise poses a serious and immediate risk to human health and safety.

Rented homes are also smaller. Shelter found that renters typically live in dwellings with approximately 30 sq. m. less floor space than owner-occupiers, a space equivalent in size to a master bedroom and a kitchen.[20] In addition, landlords are able to evict tenants at will (*see Chapter 1*), making renting very insecure. Shelter warns that 'renting families move so often they're nearly nomadic.'[21]

3. Rents are too high

Rents are very high compared with incomes. Analysis from the BBC revealed that 'a private tenant in the UK typically spends more than 30 per cent of their income on rent.' When you factor in income tax and national insurance contributions, this figure gets closer to 40 per cent of the average renter's take-home pay. In London, 60 per cent of the average renter's earnings seeps into investors' property portfolios. Compare this with 1980, when, according to the BBC, UK private renters spent an average of 10 per cent of their income on rent. In London, it was 14 per cent.[22]

For the very poorest renters, housing benefit and universal credit often fail to cover the cost of privately renting.[23] This lack of affordable housing for low-income families is fuelling a homelessness crisis across the country. In 2015-16, local authorities in England spent £1.1 billion in total on homelessness support services. Of this, £845 million went on temporary accommodation.[24] In 2018-19, councils spent £1.1 billion on temporary accommodation alone.[25] Not only is the cost of homelessness to the public sector increasing; a huge portion of the money is going on short-term fixes that do nothing to address the underlying problems.

Over a lifetime, the average renter will pay a million pounds more in rent than they would have spent on a mortgage.[26]

On the flipside, longer-term homeowners have done very well out of house price inflation, and may consider their gains to be just reward for their foresight and prudent purchasing decisions. But the system is not working well for society as a whole. It has made our economy inefficient, mis-allocating investment and draining economically-valuable disposable income. More personally, it has deprived millions of people of a home that they can call their own, or even just a home that doesn't make them ill.

Attempts to solve the housing crisis have ended in failure time and again. The market has failed. The state has failed. The banks have failed. Politics has failed. How did we get here? (and here's a clue: it's not because we don't build enough homes).

3. A short history of British homes

Fundamentally, all land in England and Wales belongs to the Crown.[1] The land in England was seized by right of conquest by William the Conqueror in 1066 at the Battle of Hastings, and a couple of centuries later Edward I used similarly violent means to add Wales to the Crown's holdings.

Following these conquests, large estates were doled out to barons and other noblemen (the original landlords). Many of these titles – and the acres that come with them – remain intact today. In an obituary for Gerald Cavendish Grosvenor, the Duke of Westminster, *The Financial Times* fondly recalled that he had once been asked what advice he would give to budding 'entrepreneurs' keen to 'emulate his success.' He replied: 'Make sure they had an ancestor who was a very close friend of William the Conqueror.'[2]

Even though the feudal system was largely dismantled in 1660 by the Tenures Abolition Act, hereditary peers have continued to sit in the House of Lords. In 1909, the Chancellor of the Exchequer, David Lloyd George, sought to tax wealth locked in the land to fund social welfare programmes. It triggered a constitutional meltdown. The House of Lords, comprised predominantly of landowners, vetoed a Finance Bill for the first time in 200 years.

Ancient feudal power was entrenched. At the start of the 20th century, 90 per cent of the population rented privately,[3] and landlords were unregulated. But that changed during World War One. The strain the war placed on the private rental market caused rents to soar, as did evictions for those who couldn't afford the hikes. In Glasgow, the backlash from tenants culminated in a rent strike in 1915 by more than 25,000 tenants. The government was forced to put in 'temporary' measures to defend tenants whose labour was so crucial to the war effort. Rents were controlled nationwide and tenant protections were enhanced.[4]

In the ensuing decades, private landlordism fell out of favour. Rent control played its part in this, because it made tenanted homes much harder to sell. But that's not the whole story. Many landlords were actually in favour of keeping the regulations from World War One, because rent-controlled properties were eligible for lower rates of mortgage interest. A far greater problem was the reputational damage landlords had inflicted on themselves. By making life harder for the munitions workers, and by attempting to evict the penniless wives of soldiers who were fighting in the trenches, private landlords were seen as unpatriotic leeches. They were frequently referred to in the press and public life as 'bloodsuckers, profiteers and despots.'[5] This tended to deter people from becoming landlords.

Renters also became more active politically. In 1918, when (some) women won the right to vote for the first time, the requirement to own property was finally lifted for male voters. Suddenly, millions of citizens with no interest in preserving the privileges of the landed classes had a political voice. This voice grew louder in 1928, when voting rights were extended to all women over 21 on the same terms as men. At the same time, the socialist ideologies of the Russian Revolution were sweeping across Europe, threatening to seduce the propertyless, newly-enfranchised masses into organising their own socialist revolution in the UK.

In the years between 1919 and the outbreak of World War Two in 1939, the proportion of British dwellings owner-occupied rose to 33 per cent,[6] spurred on by widening access to mortgage finance and a housebuilding boom in the 1930s.[7] World War Two intensified demands for more and better housing. German bombs had destroyed two million of the UK's homes and people of all backgrounds, professions, social classes and political persuasions demanded new homes.

The democratic power base of private renters, who still made up around half of voters, meant there could be no weakening of rent controls to encourage the private sector to provide more rented homes. Instead, the state would have to do it. Enter the council estate.

The Post-war 'Golden Age'

While council housing had been around in various forms prior to 1945, no government housing initiative before or since has matched the scale and ambition of the post-war housebuilding effort. At a time when ex-servicemen from World War Two were squatting in empty houses in protest at the housing shortage, the government found it politically acceptable to requisition empty properties and exercise compulsory purchase orders. Between 1939 and 1953, 1.3 million council homes were built. By 1961, another one million homes had been added to the nation's stock of social housing.[8]

This new age of housing would be exciting and democratic. Homes would be high quality and house a unified nation. The Labour politician Aneurin Bevan envisioned that publicly-funded housing would be a place where 'the working man, the doctor and the clergyman will live in close proximity to each other.' Alan Murie, a social housing expert, explained:

'Most public sector housing was purpose-built family housing, equipped with modern amenities and built to high standards. It was better housing than available to most private tenants and many homeowners. It housed affluent employed households and, until the 1970s, was often beyond the reach of the poorest households.'[9]

The future looked bright for municipal property. In Sheffield, Steve Mitchell, a mortgage adviser and landlord, told me:

'In the 1950s people like my mum got the opportunity to move from slum houses to a brand new council house. Take Lowedges council estate in Sheffield, where I grew up. Our family moved there in 1957 when I was two. You had a cooker, a fridge, carpets, lino, all that. It was like [council tenants] had got their own castles. It was fantastic.'

On the right there was also a sense that, while state-supplied housing was contrary to Conservative values, council housing could be a strategic compromise to fend off the spectre of soviet-style socialism that had haunted the ruling classes in the West since the 1920s. A nation of trapped and disgruntled tenants forced to live in squalor would become fertile ground for political extremism. So, even when Labour's time in office came to an end in 1951, council house building continued under the Conservatives. In fact, it peaked under the subsequent Conservative government, led by Winston Churchill, at just under 200,000 publicly-owned new homes per year.[10]

The mass building of council homes continued during the 1960s, throwing up many of the tower blocks that still dot city horizons. By 1971, homeowners owned half of British dwellings. Almost one in three homes were owned by local authorities. Only one in five remained in the private rented sector.

During these post-war decades, power and wealth was indeed seeping from private landlords, through a combination of iron-clad tenants' rights and a wildly successful social rented sector. But this state of affairs wasn't to last. By the end of the 1970s, the post-war consensus had begun to crumble. Now was the time for a new social order – where renting was seen to be inferior. Now was the time for an era of mass homeownership.

4. Selling off council homes

The notion that more people should own their homes was an important strand of 20th century thought. In 1923, a Conservative thinker, Noel Skelton, penned a series of articles for *The Spectator* on what he called 'Constructive Conservatism.' He warned his fellow Conservatives that, 'to make democracy stable,' the government should promote 'a property-owning democracy.'[1] The implication was that if most voters owned homes, they would resist taxes on property wealth, even if such taxes were funding better hospitals, schools, and other social goods and services. The masses would oppose laws that might make land and property vulnerable to state requisition or compulsory purchase, even if people and businesses were hoarding empty homes and developable land. The status quo would be maintained. Wealthy landowners would be protected. Slowly, Skelton's views gained ground. The right of council tenants to buy their own home was suggested several times before it was introduced.

Labour's 1959 manifesto proposed giving council tenants the 'chance to buy' their home, while in the 1960s the Conservatives argued that the 'huge municipal domains' that expanded 'state monopoly landlordism' ought to be broken up.[2] Arguably, the central question was not *whether* some form of Right to Buy policy would eventually materialise, but rather *who* would design it and put it into practice.

In the end, it was Margaret Thatcher, the free-marketeer who became prime minister in 1979, who finally gave full vent to Noel Skelton's idea of a property-owning democracy. In 1981, her Conservative government introduced Right to Buy, giving council tenants permission to buy their rented homes at a discount.

Council tenants who had been living in a property for at least three years could acquire it with 33 per cent off the market price. For every additional year the tenants had lived in the property, there was a further reduction of 1 per cent, up to a maximum of 50 per cent.[3] The discounts could double up as a deposit for a mortgage, so a lack of savings was not a barrier. The idea was that, for tenants, the transition would be imperceptible. Often, the mortgage repayments would be similar or even lower than their rent. No new sacrifices were required.

As such, if you could afford to do it, exercising your Right to Buy was a no-brainer. Many were delighted with their homes and looked after them well, repainting the front doors jollier colours, bringing splashes of pride to their once uniform neighbourhoods. However, while benefiting one generation of social housing tenants, the policy was designed to self-destruct. Rather than fund like-for-like replacement stock, councils were effectively forced to hand most of their Right to Buy capital receipts over to the Treasury.[4]

To counteract this, in 1982 local authorities were given control of housing benefit, which is paid to low-income tenants who would otherwise struggle to meet higher private rents.[5] Councils could set rates of housing benefit according to local market rents.

The hope was that by subsidising the demand for housing (rather than its supply), renters unable to take advantage of Right to Buy would be able to choose where they lived – a council or a privately-rented home. Gone would be the days of the 'you get what you're given' culture of local authority housing allocation. Market forces would foster competition, drive down costs, and deliver better-quality rented homes for all who wanted them, which would ideally be a tiny number, since most people were assumed to aspire to homeownership.

Sadly, housing proved to be a marketplace like no other, and by the early 1990s, a crisis was emerging. In a Commons debate in 1991, the Labour MP Clive Soley warned that rents in the housing association sector had gone up by 25 per cent in a year, adding: 'Is not it also true that council rents will go up dramatically in the next couple of weeks and that private sector rents are out of the reach of many people?' The response from the Conservative housing minister, Sir George Young, was revealing: 'If people cannot afford to pay that market rent, housing benefit will take the strain.'[6] The implication was that the government saw the housing benefit bill as a blank cheque. Cost wasn't the primary motivation for allowing public housing to gurgle down the plughole. Even if it cost more, the government preferred to give people money to rent privately, rather than municipal homes to rent cheaply.

As Right to Buy expert Alan Murie has pointed out, much of the current stock of council housing has been cost neutral for the Exchequer (some of it even produces surpluses).[7] Housing benefit, on the other hand, has shot up faster than any other welfare spending. In March 2019, for instance, it cost the government £22 billion a year – more than double its cost in the early 2000s, outstripping spending on police, overseas aid and many whole departments.[8] The Centre for Social Justice think-tank forecasts that, by 2050, housing benefit will more than treble to £70 billion.[9]

As well as this cost, the taxpayer has lost heavily on the sales of council homes themselves. Between the beginning of 2012 and the first quarter of 2019, the government raised £6.25 billion through Right to Buy receipts in England alone.[10] The homes were sold at an average discount of 45 per cent, putting the cost of the subsidy at roughly £5.11 billion.[11]

What's more, the stock of social housing has plunged year after year, depriving future generations of an affordable rented home. Between 1980 and 2019, 2.6 million council and social homes were sold under Right to Buy,[12] Now the majority of the best homes have been sold, never to be replaced.

The private rented sector swooped in to pick up the bargains. A study in 2017 found that over 40 per cent of former Right to Buy properties are now let by private landlords.[13] Councils have been in the absurd situation of paying billions in housing benefit to cover the 'market rents' demanded on homes they themselves used to own and rent out at a fraction of the cost. As we've already seen, in exchange for the increased rents, tenants in receipt of benefits now receive worse and less secure housing.

Right to Buy was a portal into homeownership which is now almost closed. Ultimately, it produced some winners and many more losers. The homes that released so many council tenants from the supposed burden of lifelong renting were only affordable temporarily. As soon as right-to-buyers sold their ex-council homes on the open market, the subsidy vanished, along with the fruits of decades of public investment in low-cost housing. Such was the concern that Right to Buy was scrapped in Scotland and Wales in 2016 and 2019 respectively, but, at the time of writing, it remains a government priority in more populous England.

While the stock of social housing was being squeezed over several decades by Right to Buy, those in private rented accommodation found it increasingly harder to exercise their own will to get on the property ladder. House prices have bounced up in waves for decade after decade, further and further away from tenant spending power. Surely the property market should behave just like any other, subject to the laws of supply and demand? Here we need to examine what happens to house prices when they come into contact with the magic ingredient of mortgage credit.

5. Boom! The impact of credit

Most people answer the question 'Why is there a housing crisis?' with one or both of these reasons:

a)   We aren't building enough houses
b)   There too many people in the UK

As a result, it is possible for the layman to deduce the culprits for the arrival of generation rent: overly strict planning laws, too many existing homeowners blocking planning applications, too much protection of 'green belt' land that could be used for housing, too much immigration, and stingy banks who won't lend to deserving borrowers.

However, the national conversation is missing something. As the *MoneyWeek* columnist Dominic Frisby points out, between 1997 and 2007, for every four new people added to the population, three new homes were built.[1] Yet during this time, UK house prices more than tripled.[2] While it's true that the population has been rising, and housebuilding has slowed compared with pre-2008 levels, these factors alone do not explain what's really going on.

That's because a third, obscure factor has been driving house prices to dizzying highs over the last 20 years: money creation. In a report in 2014, *Money Creation in the Modern Economy*, the Bank of England calmly explained how, contrary to what most people think, 'banks do not act simply as intermediaries, lending out deposits that savers place with them, and nor do they 'multiply up' central bank money to create new loans and deposits.' Instead, 'the majority of money in the modern economy is *created by commercial banks making loans*' (emphasis mine). High-street banks aren't just giant warehouses for the nation's wages and savings – they manufacture roughly 97 per cent of the sterling in circulation, with the remaining five per cent made up of notes and coins. In other words, around 97 per cent of British money circulating in the economy started life as a mortgage, a credit card transaction, a personal loan, a business loan or similar. It was conjured into existence at the push of a button by a bank.[3]

Why does this matter? When mortgages become cheaper and easier to access, homebuyers can afford to spend more on a home. In response, sellers start raising their asking prices. Seeing that house prices are rising, banks feel more confident in relaxing their mortgage lending criteria even further. So, borrowers take out bigger mortgages. Bigger mortgages mean more money is being manufactured to chase after the same limited number of homes. And so, prices rise even further, fuelled by an unchecked frenzy of money creation.

The cycle repeats until house prices have become so disconnected from real incomes that no new entrant can afford to buy even when there are 125 per cent mortgages, which lend the full value of the property plus an extra 25 per cent in cash. Northern

Rock offered this deal in its infamous Together Mortgage before 2008. Normally, at this point, the whole house of cards will collapse before the cycle starts afresh. That, essentially, is why the property market follows a pattern of 'boom and bust.'

Standard economic theory cannot describe this phenomenon. The textbook explanation of supply and demand is that rising consumer demand for, say, chocolate buttons will cause competing chocolate-makers to ramp up the supply of chocolate buttons until everyone who wants chocolate buttons can buy them at a fair price. In other words, the market reaches a point of equilibrium.

However, land – which is effectively what gives property its value – and bank credit are 'two phenomena quite unlike other commodities,' points out economist Josh Ryan-Collins. Land is scarce and fixed in quantity, while bank credit is 'essentially infinite.' When both land and bank credit are demanded by consumers, the end result is runaway house prices. Equilibrium only arrives in the form of a devastating economic shock that plunges the economy into recession. It is utterly dysfunctional.

To illustrate his point, Ryan-Collins pinpoints a strong correlation between the expansion of mortgage credit and house price inflation across all major developed economies. He writes: 'In the last 20 years, real house prices have increased by 50 per cent, while real average incomes have flatlined – but mortgage credit has increased exponentially.' Contrast this with the first 60 years of the 20th century when house prices remained flat '*despite* rising populations and incomes' (emphasis mine). The key difference between now and then is that between 1900 and 1960 mortgage credit was more difficult to access.[4]

Contrary to what some may argue, the 'boom and bust' cycle is far from natural or inevitable. It is a product of the man-made rules that govern the financial system.

Graham Hodges, a volunteer researcher for monetary reform think tank Positive Money, told me (in a personal capacity):

> Prior to the 1980s, virtually all mortgage lending was done by building societies. The odd bank loan was secured against a company director's house, but that was for the purposes of investing in a business. Building societies rationed their loans because they could only lend money that had been deposited by their savers.

That changed thanks to reforms begun by Margaret Thatcher in 1979. Big banks were unshackled from domestic deposits as a key source of funding, helping them to break into the residential mortgage market for the first time. The tax perks of building societies were removed, and the interest rate cartel they ran ended in 1983. Then, to level the playing field, the 1986 Building Societies Act gave building societies new powers to seek funding from wholesale 'money markets,' just like banks. Crucially, the link between savers' deposits and the availability of mortgage credit was broken. Mortgages could now be offered on demand.[5]

Graham Hodges points out that the previous rationing by building societies had 'kept the housing market in check... As soon as banks entered the mortgage market, house prices shot up.'

Along with the wildly successful Right to Buy policy, these reforms expanded homeownership in line with Thatcher's vision of a 'property-owning democracy.' They also paved the way for a spectacular boom in the housing market, which culminated in a crash in 1990 which left hundreds of thousands in 'negative equity,' owing more to the bank than their homes were worth.

Since then, property prices have zoomed up, then collapsed again, only to lurch back up again higher than they were before. All the while, the chances of people getting a foot on the ladder have been falling, partly because of another factor: the phoenix-like return of the private landlord.

6. Say hello to the landlord

Fresh from unleashing the sale of social housing to individuals, the Conservative government of Thatcher's successor, John Major, further relaxed financial regulation. Changes to legislation governing the private rented sector saw the introduction of the buy-to-let mortgage in 1996.

Money poured into the private rented sector and the number of renters exploded. During the 1980s and 1990s, private renters made up just 10 per cent of England's households.[1] By 2013, that proportion had doubled.[2]

Many of their homes were provided by a new army of buy-to-let landlords. Buy-to-let caught on in a big way in the early 2000s. One of its biggest cheerleaders was the Liverpool footballer Robbie Fowler, who sank so much of his sporting wealth into property that crowds at matches chanted: (to the tune of *Yellow Submarine*) 'We all live in a Robbie Fowler house.' He inspired many of his fans to follow suit, and to this day he still goes around the country giving seminars on how to build a successful property empire.

Fowler wasn't the only one. The former maths teachers Judith and Fergus Wilson worked out that they could buy new-build properties to rent out and remortgage them when the markets rose to fund further property purchases. They were dubbed 'the king and queen of buy-to-let,' eventually amassing an empire of over 900 properties.[3]

Their dazzling rags-to-riches tale lost some of its lustre in 2014 when Mr Wilson decided he no longer wanted to rent to families in receipt of housing benefit and started evicting 200-plus claimants living in his properties.[4] In the same year, he was found guilty of assaulting an estate agent,[5] and in 2017, a court found that his refusal to let to 'coloured people' on the grounds that 'they leave a curry smell behind' was illegal and racially discriminatory.[6]

In the pre-2008 property boom, the financial bar of entry into the buy-to-let market was so low that virtually anyone with a bit of housing equity could become a landlord if they wanted to. Industry veteran Julian Maurice, a property consultant, explained to me how the sums added up:

'Imagine you own a property right – you own your house and you're sitting in the house, and as you're sitting in it, it's going up in value. So, one minute it's worth, let's say £50,000, then a year later, it's worth £100,000. Suddenly you've got £50,000 worth of equity in your house. So what people would do, they would re-mortgage, pull the equity out of the house, and buy a buy-to-let property. This is what was happening. This is part of the reason why we had this property boom, because it was fuelling house prices.'

Around 1996 to 2007, he told me, 'prices were going up and up and up. And everyone was jumping on the bandwagon... It was a feeding frenzy.'

Did buy-to-let cause the housing crisis?

Concerned that younger people were being priced out of home-ownership by spiralling house prices, in 2006 the government set up a new quango called the National Housing and Planning Advice Unit.[7] Two years later, the NHPAU released a technical report that looked at whether or not buy-to-let had adversely affected young people's chances of getting on the property ladder. Its conclusion was, in essence, '*nothing to see here.*'

It conceded that 'BTL mortgage lending would appear to have increased house prices since its introduction in 1996' – which it estimated to be around seven per cent, or £13,000 on average. But it stressed that a variety of other factors were at play, adding: 'On the upside, it is important to acknowledge that there are significant economic and social benefits being delivered by the [BTL] sector.'

To this day, property and investment professionals say that it is renters, rather than landlords, who are driving the expansion of the private rented sector. In 2014, the Intermediary Mortgage Lenders Association reported:[8]

'Higher demand has been the main driver of growth in the private rented sector over the past two and a half decades. Rent deregulation in 1988 and the launch of buy-to-let mortgages in 1996 have *allowed individual landlords to respond to this demand*.' (Emphasis mine.)

Thus, we have an established order of events: tenants wanted it and landlords delivered it. Rising demand for rental properties was nothing more than a spontaneous force of nature, and landlords were only too happy to oblige the whims of the market.

Nowadays, there's a lot of emphasis on the idea that 'landlords provide a vital service that compliments social housing provided by local authorities,' to quote Susan Dyson of landlordvision.co.uk.[9] Dyson goes on to highlight that 'the private rental sector provides 1/5 of housing stock in the UK.'

In a similar vein, property developer Knight Frank passed on some optimistic news to investors: 'Younger workers especially are taking advantage of the increased flexibility of renting as a tenure,' though it acknowledged that affordability was becoming a major issue for generation rent.[10]

Among tenants, the narrative is wearing thin. Awareness is growing that their need to live somewhere has become someone else's investment opportunity. At a tenants' union meeting in Sheffield in 2018, a renter named Mike told me he had been asked pay the rent directly into a trust fund for his landlord's son. The slogan of Greater Manchester Housing Action Group is: 'Our homes are not your assets.'

Not only are renters angry that they can't afford to save for their own futures; they're angry that 40-50 per cent (or more) of their take-home pay is funding someone else's future – someone who is probably much more financially secure than they will ever be.

There is a stark disconnect between what landlords think they are doing (innocently investing their capital to meet a market need) and what tenants think they are doing (exploiting their need for shelter by taking half their earnings.)

When you factor in the reality that the average first-time-buyer now needs a deposit of between £16,000 (Wales) and £114,000 (London), *and* to be earning enough so that their mortgage isn't more than four-and-a-half times their salary, then it soon becomes clear that the many first-time buyers simply can't compete with the majority of buy-to-let investors, who typically already own their own homes and have equity to invest.

Access to finance – not the cost – is the issue

Buy-to-let borrowers today have a trump card they can play against first-time-buyers: access to interest-only mortgages. Early in my career at a firm of financial advisers, I was given the task of reviewing the compliance of case files for a new mortgage adviser. My pro-forma checklist indicated that, where the loan was made on an interest-only basis, the borrower needed a credible repayment strategy. I dutifully sent the cases back, highlighting that the buy-to-let borrower had neglected to detail exactly how the loan would be repaid at the end of the term. The adviser came back to me, incredulous. Didn't I know that this was the standard business model for virtually all buy-to-let loans? The landlord will typically mortgage the property on an interest-only basis to keep monthly servicing costs as low as possible. They will then pocket the difference between the rental income and expenses. When they want to sell the property, they can use the proceeds to repay the principal (i.e. the original amount borrowed).

Besides, I was assured, because buy-to-let mortgages were unregulated anyway: we didn't need to worry as much about the affordability of the loan as with an ordinary residential mortgage.

Although buy-to-let mortgages can be obtained on an interest-only basis, the interest rates are higher, loan-to-value ratios are typically stricter meaning heftier deposits are needed (75 per cent of the property value is the standard loan amount) and the fees are steeper. But costs alone aren't the full story. If you're already a homeowner with home equity, then you can cover the deposit by releasing equity from your property.

By contrast, interest-only mortgages for ordinary house buyers have now all but disappeared, under post Mortgage Market Review regulations, which came into force in 2014. In addition, many interest-only products taken out in the boom years are now coming back to haunt lenders. *The Times* reported in December 2019 that interest-only mortgages could be the 'next big mis-selling scandal,' as claims management companies seek new revenue now that the deadline for lodging complaints about payment protection insurance has passed.

The upshot of all this is that, nowadays, if an ordinary first-time buyer asked a bank for an interest-only mortgage, they would probably be laughed off the premises. In fact, restricting interest-only lending to ordinary consumers is sensible and necessary. But the fact that a home-owning landlord on a modest incomes can readily access the finance needed to buy a property on terms unavailable to a first-time-buyer earning the same amount puts people renting at a significant competitive disadvantage.

Are first-time buyers really in direct competition with investors?
A white paper by the investment firm Invesco in 2016 revealed that 82.4 per cent of all housing stock owned by private landlords was built before the 1990s, of which just under half was built before 1945.[11] Even the 9.4 per cent of housing stock in the private rented sector built after 2003 is unlikely to have been purpose-built for renters.

In other words, most landlords don't 'provide' housing – they snap up stock that was by and large intended for owner-occupiers or social housing tenants. Since the introduction of buy-to-let, landlords have converted to privately rented homes large swathes of the lower end of the market (especially small, low-cost terraced houses, once the perennial first-time buyer favourite).

Browse Rightmove.co.uk and you'll find adverts for small flats and houses often say: 'Attention investors/first-time buyers!' Estate agents know that there's considerable overlap between the two markets, and pitch their properties accordingly. Some have even stopped targeting first-time-buyers.

Tom Entwistle, residential and commercial landlord and editor of LandlordZONE, unwittingly highlights this reality when he makes the case for why landlords should be thanked, not 'targeted,' by the government for their role in the housing market.

In an article for *Landlord Investor* magazine, he argued:

'The private rented market has grown through the diligence and hard work of many thousands of small-scale landlords *investing their money into [the] sector*'[12] (emphasis mine).

In taking the credit on behalf of landlords everywhere for triggering the exponential growth of the private rented sector via 'diligent' capital investment, he exposes an inconvenient truth: not only does buy-to-let investment meet tenant demand, it creates it. The reason? Landlords have easier access to finance than tenants and people living with their parents.

Most of the millennials stuck living in rental and parental properties alike simply aren't in a position to buy. Either they don't have a big enough deposit, or they don't earn enough to meet the lenders' requirements. Why are they so strict?

7. Caught in the mortgage trap

Unlike property-owners, renters are not required to pay a large chunk of their earnings into a mortgage year after year to live in their home. They are required to pay a large chunk of their earnings in rent year after year for *temporary permission* to live in someone else's home. Worse, they are paying *more than a mortgage* to secure this inferior status. What is more galling, perhaps, is that paying large sums year after year does not persuade banks that they can afford a mortgage *with smaller monthly payments*.

In 2018, the Santander bank found that renting a home anywhere in the UK was more expensive than owning one.[1] London had the biggest gap, with rent typically costing £3,468 a year more than a first-time mortgage. But the problem is nationwide. On average, renters in Northern Ireland, Scotland, the North West and Yorkshire and the Humber were shelling out between £1,200 and £2,200 a year more than they would have done for a mortgage.

One young nurse told me that she worked 'full time to afford rent' and did overtime to 'afford luxuries like a peak railcard.' She resented the fact that if she were 'born a generation earlier,' she would 'be able to afford a house comfortably on a nurse's wage.' So far, so familiar. But then she revealed she had saved a substantial sum for a deposit but still couldn't get a mortgage, because the banks deemed that she earned too little. She earned more than the national average. She explained: 'Landlords are happy to take £1,300 off me a month, but a mortgage provider doesn't think I am a good investment for an £800-a-month mortgage.'

She isn't alone. Others shared similar stories, like the young woman who worked full-time and spent £850 a month on rent, but couldn't get the bank to give her a mortgage that would cost £400 a month because 'apparently [she] can't afford it.' Understandably, she was exasperated by the situation, because 'clearly I could [afford it] if I'm currently spending £850 on rent!' The seemingly nonsensical reasoning behind the decision makes it seem like there's some kind of institutionalised prejudice at work: 'It's like they don't believe a millennial is good at budgeting.'

Why are renters are being denied mortgages despite ostensibly being able to afford one? Much of the blame lies with the affordability restrictions imposed after the 2008 financial crash. First came the Mortgage Market Review led by the newly-created Financial Conduct Authority.[2] This demanded stricter affordability tests, in-depth assessments of spending habits and a crackdown on interest-only lending. Many lenders began implementing the review's recommendations before they became mandatory in 2014.

In 2015, parliament granted further powers to the Bank of England's Financial Policy Committee on mortgage regulation, which introduced two measures to reduce risk in the mortgage market. Firstly, lenders would have to cap the number of mortgages made at more than 4.5 times the borrower's annual income. Specifically, no more than 15 per cent of new mortgages could exceed a 'debt-to-income' ratio of 4.5. Secondly, lenders must ensure borrowers could cope with a three percentage-point rise in interest rates at any point in the first five years of the mortgage.[3] For many renters, the effect of this 'stress test' is dire.

The average 'starter home' costs roughly £207,500.[4] Let's assume the buyers have a 10 per cent deposit and take out a 35-year mortgage, which has a two-year fixed initial rate of 2.46 per cent.[5] After two years, they will revert to the lender's Standard Variable Rate (SVR) of 4.90 per cent.[6] This means that the monthly repayments[7] will be £664 for the first two years, and £931 thereafter.

Once initial period is up, it's common for borrowers to remortgage to secure another temporary fix at a low rate. So in practice, the buyers think that their eligibility for a mortgage rests on their ability to afford £664 a month in repayments. If they are currently paying £800 a month in rent, the average for a two-bed home in England,[8] the buyer thinks they can afford the mortgage.

The Bank of England's Financial Policy Committee, however, disagrees. Cheap introductory deals are barred from the stress test. Instead, the Financial Policy Committee asks, what if the borrowers can't remortgage in two years' time, and the lender's SVR goes up three percentage points to 7.90 per cent? This would take their repayments to over £1,300 a month. Unbeknown to the buyers, this is the figure used to determine the affordability of the mortgage.

You might think: why bother testing at such a high rate? Isn't it a bit extreme? Perhaps. Mortgage rates have flat-lined since the global financial crisis. However, the purpose of the stress test is to prepare for the possibility that interest rates return to their historical average. Mortgages with a low introductory fixed rate are common at the moment. For first-time buyers they're usually the only deal worth considering. But these deals are only viable because the Bank of England's 'base rate' is so low. (The base rate or, as it's officially known, Bank Rate, determines how much interest commercial banks earn on money they hold with the Bank of England.) Put simply, a low base rate makes cheap mortgages and other loans possible. It's also responsible for the dismal rates offered on high-street savings accounts.

When the banks stopped lending post-2008, the Bank of England slashed its base rate from five per cent in April 2008 to 0.5 per cent in March 2009,[9] as an 'emergency' measure to jump-start the economy. The original plan was that rates would drift back to normal as the economy recovered. For most of the last decade, however, the base rate has hovered between 0.25 per cent and 0.75 per cent.

Such low rates are a historical freak. According to Bank of England data, the historical average base rate since 1694 is just under six per cent.[10] Since 1975, the average figure sits at 9.5 per cent – scores more times than the current base rate of 0.1 per cent. At its peak in 1979, the base rate hit 17 per cent.[11]

As a report in 2010 from the now-defunct Financial Services Authority highlights, low interest rates mask 'the true extent of the vulnerability of many consumers to upward interest rate movement.'[12] Despite widespread talk of an economic recovery, the Bank of England believes the true health of the UK's finances should be determined by its ability to cope with pre-crisis interest rates, i.e. those hovering around the five per cent mark. On that measure, the economy is still very fragile.

And so, the central bank has painted itself into a corner. Its fear is that loosening lending criteria would generate another dangerous credit bubble. And this time, when it bursts, there will be no get out of jail card available, as it won't be possible to slash interest rates further. If borrowers can't afford to repay their debts in the lowest interest rate environment in history, then mass repossessions and debt defaults will ensue. The Bank of England wants to avoid this at all costs.

But it is coming under increasing pressure from the mortgage industry, which argues that the Financial Policy Committee's 'anachronistic' policies are barring young people from getting on the property ladder.[13] If the Bank of England caves to industry pressure and slackens its lending criteria, it will be to blame if the result is an apocalyptic financial collapse. But so long as it continues to resist calls to soften the rules, it will be blamed for the plight of young people locked out of the property market.

The problem stems from the Bank's response to 2008. Had nature had its way, the property market after 2008 would have gone into freefall. At first, that's exactly what happened: in 2008, UK house prices dropped by 16 per cent – the biggest annual fall on record.[14] Millions of homeowners risked being plunged into negative equity and losing billions in housing wealth.

However, the Bank of England's response to the crisis was sharp and swift. Not only did it cut rates to historic lows, it also embarked upon a programme of quantitative easing. Under quantitative easing, a central bank buys assets such as government bonds from financial institutions with newly-created money, injecting cash directly into the financial system and restoring confidence. The asset-rich, including property owners, benefit most from quantitative easing. This is because increasing the amount of cash in an economy without correspondingly increasing the amount of goods to buy pushes up asset prices.

Following £375 billion of quantitative easing,[15] house prices rebounded, and by 2015, the house price to earnings ratio for England and Wales had surpassed its 2007 peak of 7.1, and in 2018 it hit a record high of 7.8.[16] Crisis... averted?

'Should we bring back 100 per cent mortgages?'

The disappearance of 100 per cent mortgages after the 2008 crash unsurprisingly made it harder for young people to get on the property ladder. Recently, trade bodies like the Building Societies Association have been pushing for 'true' 100 per cent mortgages to be unleashed once more.[17] Currently, first-time buyer 100 per cent mortgages come with strings attached. Strictly speaking, you don't need the deposit, but you do need 'collateral,' either a parent or relative's mortgage-free house to 'secure' the mortgage against, or a deposit-sized lump sum from a well-wisher, in case you default on your mortgage.

But there's a big problem here which goes back to the credit bubble. House prices are able to stay where they are because enough people – mostly investors and existing homeowners, rather than first-time buyers – have the capital to pay the asking prices of those selling property today.

If 100 per cent mortgages arrived on the scene once more, demand for housing would rocket. And since one cannot take out a mortgage on a home that hasn't been built yet, this new demand would flow into existing property. So more relaxed mortgage criteria would almost certainly send high house prices further into the stratosphere. A few early adopters would benefit, while the majority of generation rent would remain priced out.

SECTION II. HELP FOR BUYERS

8. The Bank of Mum and Dad

Parents have become a major source of help to young people wanting a place of their own, as Lily knows. In 2017, aged 22, Lily had just graduated with a degree in Spanish and French from Oxford university. She was disgusted by the state and cost of the UK private rented sector. None of her friends seemed to mind it, but she didn't want the hand-to-mouth existence of a graduate in today's rental market, especially in London and the South East, where most of her Oxonian peers were looking to work. She explained:

'A large proportion of my friends who went to Oxford – from very good backgrounds, people with lots of money; sons and daughters of politicians and newsreaders – they're earning £1,500 a month before tax in London, but they're paying £700-£800 for a room in a crap area. I also have friends who are earning £2,000 a month before tax, and yet they're spending nearly their entire salary on rent, just for a place that's a bit more upmarket.'

Rather than attempt to eke out an existence in the capital, Lily decided to join 'the brain drain out of the UK' and start a new life as a freelance writer and translator in Spain. She knew from spending a year abroad as part of her degree that she could enjoy a much better quality of life in Barcelona: 'Here, doing the work I enjoy, I earn between €1,500 and €2,000 a month, but my rent is €300 a month for a nice room in a very expensive area. I can do things like volunteer because I can afford it, whereas I feel like the grind in London is just never-ending, because of the rent situation.'

She volunteers at the Barcelona Laboratory for Environmental Justice and Sustainability: 'This is what I'm talking about — because I can afford to work four days, I've got time to spare for work I'm really interested in.'

When Lily first got in touch with me via private message on Twitter, she expressed a mixture of relief and a kind of conspiratorial solidarity. She wrote: 'It's so good to see someone being angry about this and speaking up, because I find that a lot of my friends just don't seem to be worried.'

At first, this struck me as odd, since the housing crisis and abysmal conditions for private renters often make headlines. But as we talked, I realised what she meant. Studying at such an elite university, Lily was rubbing shoulders with some of the most privileged young people in the country. The children of the wealthy appeared to be dealing with the housing crisis with flat-out denial.

'I keep waiting for it to click...' she said. 'I keep waiting for my friends to have a moment where they're like, "Oh, I can't stay here, I can never buy a house, I can't rent here long term...". The quality of life in London has been so low for so long that it's become normalised – I think this is the crux of the issue. People who are traditionally privileged don't feel like they can live a good life without being a banker or a management consultant. And if that's not what they want to do then they just accept [low living standards], to the point where my friends don't even question it.'

To this I asked: Could this just be down to the free-spiritedness of early twenty-somethings? Sharing a hovel in a big city with your friends while you're companionably broke might be fun at 23, but maybe that lifestyle starts to pall when you hit your thirties?

Lily felt that a much more important factor was at play:

'They know their parents are well-off, and will be able to buy them a house or give them a deposit when they're ready. They know that the value of their parents' property is a big part of their family's wealth, so while they might want house prices to fall for their own benefit, they know how badly this would affect their parents, grandparents, etcetera. So they don't protest. It's creating this entrenched social privilege, where people with family wealth get ahead, and the people without ultimately have to leave the city.'

Not long after I spoke to Lily, I overheard a conversation on a train to London. Until this point, I had assumed that the impact of the 'Bank of Mum and Dad' on house prices was mainly the result of gifted deposits for first-time buyers. The exchange made me reconsider.

'Where does your daughter work, sorry?' a young woman asked.

'Canary Wharf,' said the woman sitting opposite, 'She's on an

HR graduate scheme... But she wouldn't be able to work where she does if we didn't pay her rent.'

There was an awkward pause. Then a man, also in his twenties, chimed in – he, too, was in receipt of rent money from his parents, because he was setting up his own business.

The younger woman commiserated, saying: 'It's so expensive in London. I have friends who literally spend half their salaries on rent, and they're earning good salaries.'

At this the older woman, whose large designer handbag and immaculate appearance suggested she was comfortably off, voiced the concern that her daughter might never get on the property ladder, even though she was 'saving everything she can into an ISA' while her parents paid the rent.

While I knew that almost everyone under 35 is struggling with Britain's out of control property market, what fascinated me was that these people spoke as if funding a child's lifestyle well into their twenties had become an inevitable fact of modern life. What's more, an unspoken truth seemed to linger in the air between them. In London, wealth and social privilege – which were once merely advantages to getting ahead in the corporate world – are becoming prerequisites.

Over the course of the conversation, the sentiment that 'parents shouldn't have to do this for their adult kids' never quite evolved into the recognition that 'not all parents *are able* to do this for their adult kids.' Perhaps the thought was too uncomfortable.

Lily told me she wasn't aware that parents paid the rent for any of her London-based peers, though it's probably not something young people would shout about. Statistics on this are unsurprisingly hard to come by, but research from the insurer Legal &

General found that one in nine renters received family help towards the cost of renting in 2017.[1]

Now colloquially known as the Bank of Mum and Dad (BOMAD), parents have long given their progeny emergency bailouts, paid their phone bills and car insurance, and provided interest-free loans that don't blemish a credit file. What has changed is that, increasingly and significantly for the country's house prices, they are handing over large lump sum gifts that can be put down as a deposit on a home that would be otherwise unaffordable.

Legal & General has estimated that if BOMAD were a real bank it would be the 11th biggest mortgage lender in the UK. The nation's parents are estimated to have supplied £6.3bn in home-buying assistance for their offspring in 2018, and the average parental loan or outright gift stood at £24,100 – £6,000 more than the previous year. You might think London is having an outsized effect on the figures here, but even in my own region – Yorkshire and the Humber, where houses are generally thought to be more affordable – parents are forking out £17,200 on average to help their children to buy a home.[2]

Millennials who already own homes are more likely than not to need financial assistance when moving and significant numbers of homeowners in their thirties and forties are also seeking help from parents and other family members. In effect, BOMAD is supporting property purchases on almost every rung of the property ladder.[3]

Parents frequently hurl ideals about social justice out the window for their child's wellbeing, but when the issue of personal responsibility crops up in the great housing debate, such as when airing the avocado toast theory, these distortions are seldom acknowledged.

Laurie Macfarlane, an author and economist who we'll hear more from later, tweeted: 'It seems there is now a whole branch of journalism aimed at trolling millennials.'[4] Below it he linked to a *Guardian* article which implied that all you had to do to save up a housing deposit was cancel your £120 a month gym membership. The young woman featured in the article just happened to be earning £60,000 a year, more than double the median full-time salary in the UK.

A journalist, Louise Ridley, tweeted a similar story from the *Daily Mail*. The headline suggested that the young person featured had accumulated her deposit through a lifestyle of extreme frugality. The article itself revealed that she'd also been able to work full-time while living at home with her mum rent-free. Ridley wrote: 'Stop. Telling. Stories. About. 'Frugal.' Young. Savers. When. Really. They. Got. Money. From. Their. Parents.' The tweet received 1,000 likes.[5]

Being able to live at home rent-free is a form of privilege that can mask the struggles faced by those on a low income. Becky, a 27-year-old healthcare assistant in a dementia care home in Sheffield, managed to scrape together a deposit of almost £10,000 over six years. That was enough to secure a 95 per cent mortgage on an ex-council house in Sheffield for £107,000, the low price reflecting the property's location on the edge of an estate that Tesco refuses to deliver to on the grounds of 'staff safety.' Becky's achievement took sacrifice, toil and grit. Still, she said: 'If I couldn't have lived at home for all that time, there's no way I could have done it. As soon as I moved out to live with my partner, rent and bills took up all of our money.'

What was once socially embarrassing, living at home beyond the age of 25, has become a sensible lifestyle choice. Not only does this trend disadvantage those without access to their own

BOMAD, it prevents the wider market from adjusting to the economic fundamentals.

The stark inequalities created by BOMAD leg-ups are further compounded by the accelerated wealth accumulation that can spring from homeownership. Mortgage repayments tend to detach from the true value of a property over time, as the local economy grows and house prices rise but the debt owing remains static. Rents, on the other hand, are acutely sensitive to the gentrifying forces that turn dilapidated high streets into parades of artisan bakeries and bicycle repair shops.

Long-time homeowners in London in particular are reaping the capital rewards. In January 2019, the *Daily Mail* featured the story of Geraldine Rudge, a 67-year-old writer whose London home had earned more than she had over the last couple of decades. 'I bought my current home for £301,000 16 years ago — and it is now worth £900,000,' she wrote. 'My house has earned an average of £37,438 a year; the most I've earned in any one year is £30,000.'[6]

As an article in *The Economist* points out[7], you don't have to be a landlord to collect rent. Owner-occupied homes also generate a kind of rental income, by virtue of the fact that rising rents and house prices make property ownership more lucrative. Many homeowners would probably balk at this idea, as it's an 'income' that doesn't take the form of a monthly cash payment. But if an owner-occupier is paying less than the equivalent market rent in mortgage costs, then the savings they make are a 'benefit in kind'. In other words, they are getting discounted access to housing in an area where demand is rising.

Since main residences are not liable for capital gains tax, and 'passing on the family home' is treated favourably by the inheritance tax regime, owning a home is probably the lowest-tax form of investment in the UK. This was not always the case. Until 1964, it was recognised that owner- occupied homes generate a notional income – termed 'imputed rent' – and homeowners were liable to pay income tax on it. The aim of this was to dampen the privileged status homeowners were afforded over renters, by taxing some of the hidden 'earnings' that owner-occupied homes bestow. In his book, *Radical Solutions to the Housing Supply Crisis*, Duncan Bowie recommends that we bring back income taxes on imputed rents for this reason.[8] After all, is it fair that, over the course of a career, someone can pay tens of thousands in tax on their hard-earned income, but not a penny on the property wealth they didn't lift a finger to amass? Currently, property ownership is incentivised more than hard work.[9]

The homeowning public may not welcome the return of a tax on imputed rents, because the wealth accumulation that comes with owning a home is a consolation for the taxes we must pay on other aspects of our financial lives. But if a tax on imputed rents could be offset with a cut to income taxes or VAT, the political conversation might shift.

On a macroscopic scale, the Bank of Mum and Dad is making property more expensive. Parents who subsidise their children's rent in a place like London are doing what is best for their children, but their behaviour is skewing the relationship between earned incomes and rents for everyone.

Employers will think they can get away with paying graduate trainees £25,000 a year in central London, unaware that they're disproportionately attracting candidates who have access to family money. Parental subsidy also skews the investment appeal of the local rental market. This carries on until we arrive at the situation we have in London currently, where rental yields are stalling because the incomes of even working people with parental subsidy cannot meet investors' expectations. Prices are now high because the location is popular with speculators, not because the properties being bought can generate an attractive return on investment.

All of this suggests that what we really need, to use the investment-speak euphemism, is a 'price correction.' We need house prices to come right down, so that they're back in line with the incomes and lifestyle choices of independent individuals. Or, as the financial journalist John Stepek argues, house prices need to stay nominally flat for a prolonged period while incomes and inflation catch up.[10] Thus, in real terms, house prices would gently fall, but no over-50s would need to fear seeing their net worth suddenly plummet. However, as we've seen, recent governments have not wanted to deflate the property balloon. Instead, they have come up with various schemes to help buyers and pump in more air. Let's see what impact they have had.

9. Official Help to Buy

While helping aspiring homeowners has been on Westminster's radar since the 1980s, the Conservative-Liberal Democrat coalition quickly took action when it came to power in 2010. It introduced a flurry of schemes and funds with the aim of getting more 'affordable' homes built and more people on the property ladder. Between 2013 and 2020, there were four main schemes. This is how they helped first-time buyers and affected wider property market:

1. The Help to Buy Mortgage Guarantee

As we have seen, after the 2008 crash banks became more cautious in their lending. In 2012, most demanded a minimum upfront deposit of 10 per cent on all first-time buyer mortgages. So the government guaranteed the first five per cent of a borrower's loan, making banks feel safer lending at loan-to-value ratios of 95 per cent. If the borrower defaulted, the taxpayer would cushion the blow. Because the money wasn't going into the production of new homes but being funnelled into the existing market, the International Monetary Fund issued a warning about the scheme's inflationary potential.[1] By the time the Help to Buy Mortgage

Guarantee was wound up in 2016, it had helped about 100,000 buyers. The Council for Mortgage Lenders declared that it had worked 'exceptionally well.' The Bank of England said it was 'no longer needed' because many banks and building societies were again offering 95 per cent mortgages.[2] Analysis by *The Independent* in 2015 showed that the area where the scheme was most used, the East of England, saw the biggest rise in house prices.[3]

2. The Help to Buy Equity Loan Scheme

At the time of writing, the Help to Buy Equity Loan Scheme, launched in 2013, is still available to homebuyers. Under it, a borrower with a five per cent deposit can receive a government loan covering further equity: 20 per cent outside London, and 40 per cent in London. An ordinary bank lends the remaining money. Buyers have five years' grace before 'loan fees' on the government's portion of the debt become payable. These fees increase in line with RPI inflation plus one per cent each year.

The crucial thing to remember is that the loan gives the government a percentage stake in the property. Therefore, if the house falls in value, the buyer owes less, and if it goes up in value, the buyer owes more.

Another feature is that buyers must purchase a new-build home. Ploughing public funds into new-builds was thought to lower the risk of house price inflation, because, while it fed more money into the market, it also increased the number of homes. Therefore, the demand created by the extra money in buyers' pockets would be met with a corresponding boost to supply. Unfortunately, the inflation happened anyway (we'll explore why later in this chapter).

3. The Help to Buy ISA

The Help to Buy Individual Savings Account ran between 2015 and 2019. The pitch was that first time buyers could put up to £12,000 in a special account and the government would top it up by another 25 per cent, up to a maximum of £3,000, when they came to buy.

Only, it didn't actually work like this. At the crucial moment of purchasing their first homes, thousands of Help to Buy ISA savers discovered that the government bonus would not be credited to their account until *after* they had put down a deposit and exchanged contracts. Buyers had to make frantic last-minute arrangements to borrow from family members, take out bridging loans, or even abandon their property purchases.

4. The Lifetime ISA

Keen to redeem himself, the Coalition's Chancellor of the Exchequer, George Osborne, came up with the Lifetime ISA, or LISA, which is still available. The LISA came with a strange twist: the savings can be used to buy a house, and/or to fund your retirement. The personal finance blog *Monevator* dubbed it 'a Help to Buy ISA with a personality disorder.'[4]

You can save up to £4,000 per year in a LISA, and the government will top that up by 25 per cent. There are some strings. To open an account you have to be under 40, and you can only contribute up to age 50. If you want to withdraw money for an unauthorised purpose (which, if you are under 60, means anything other than buying a first home), you will be hit with a 25 per cent penalty. Because of the way the maths works, this is not just the money the government gave you. It is the government's money and an extra 6.25 per cent.

Did these schemes work?

Now, it's true that individual success stories abound from people who have been helped into property by almost all of these schemes. After the following Conservative government announced an extension of the Equity Loan scheme in 2018, the *Daily Mail* featured a picture of a fresh-faced millennial couple beaming at the camera with the caption: 'It gives us hope for the future.' However, the National Audit Office has estimated that three fifths of those using the Help to Buy scheme could have afforded a home anyway.[5] While individuals may have benefited from them, these interventions have not reversed the long-term trends of the past two decades that halved homeownership among middle-earning 25-34s, from 65 per cent in 1996 to 27 per cent in 2016.[6]

A hint at who is being helped comes from the limits imposed on home-buyers using a government scheme. The Lifetime ISA scheme can be used to buy a first home worth up to £450,000. At the time of writing, the UK average property price is approximately £230,000, and that's across the whole spectrum of the market from John o' Groats to Lands' End. A house costing nearly half a million pounds in North East England, where the average property costs £131,000,[7] is still eligible for purchase using a LISA. For Help to Buy ISA savers outside London, the cap is a more modest £250,000, but this still exceeds the average house price in much of the country.

For buyers taking advantage of the government's Help To Buy Equity Loan scheme, the net is cast even wider: the government leg-up is available on new-build homes that cost up to £600,000 anywhere in England[8] (though the rules differ in the rest of the UK). Applicants don't even have to be first-time-buyers. So long as they aren't planning on letting the property or using it as a second home, existing homeowners can benefit too. Unsurprisingly, the rules are set to be tightened after March 2021.

Perhaps without Help to Buy, homeownership levels would have declined even more dramatically than they have done. We can't know. But even if the scheme has managed to delay the collapse of homeownership, it hasn't done anything to tackle the crisis in affordability.

Olivia, the software developer from Hertfordshire from the opening chapter, told me she saw the Help to Buy Equity Loan scheme as 'a joke.' 'Help to Buy properties round here start at around £400,000 for a place with two bedrooms, apparently that counts as 'affordable,'' she said. Her and her partner were already stretching themselves as far as they could to save for a home around the £300,000 mark. The thought of getting into a possible £380,000 of debt with the government's 'help' seemed too ridiculous to contemplate. Olivia said: 'I don't know who buys them. Rich people maybe. But then, why do they need help?'

Indeed, the evidence suggests that the benefits of Help to Buy have disproportionately accrued to the 'already well-off.' The ISAs geared towards first-time buyers proved genuinely 'helpful' for those with the means and inclination to save, as they shortened the time it took to amass the colossal deposit needed, and allowed the saver to maintain a degree of choice over the home they bought.

But they were also not means-tested, and, as journalist Claer Barrett pointed out in a *Financial Times* article, those who could probably have afforded to fund a deposit anyway have been the biggest beneficiaries. Claer recalled how she'd recently met a man in his 50s who was loading £4,000 a year into his university student daughter's LISA, to help her buy a house as soon as possible after graduation. 'It goes against every socialist bone in my body,' the man admitted. 'But if the government is limiting what I can pay into my pension, then why shouldn't I?'[9]

Perhaps the most embarrassing blow, however, came when it was revealed that the greatest beneficiaries of Help to Buy have been the property developers themselves. In the five years since its introduction, housebuilders Bovis, Barratts, Bellway, Berkeley, Redrow and Taylor Wimpey saw their operating profits increase by between 100 per cent and 400 per cent. Redrow took the crown with a 571 per cent jump in profits. Executive pay across these companies also tripled, despite the fact that overall housing output only went up by around half.[10]

One of the most notorious examples of excessive pay came at Persimmon, a top-five housebuilder, despite it accumulating a staggering number of dissatisfied homeowners. Between 2012 and 2019, the company featured in two separate investigations by the BBC's *Watchdog* consumer show, and the Facebook group *Persimmon Homes Unhappy Customers* had 14,000 followers until – *The Times* reported in 2019 – Persimmon obtained the administration rights and shut it down, 'deleting years of customer posts sharing problems with their homes.'[11] Help to Buy recipients bought about half of Persimmon's new homes in 2017.[12] In 2018, the company, whose share price doubled after the introduction of Help to Buy, assembled a £500 million bonus package for 150 staff, including a £75 million bonus for its chief executive

Jeff Fairburn in recognition of his 'outstanding performance.' Following a media outcry, Persimmon asked Fairburn to leave his job, allowing him to keep all of his bonus. Persimmon dismissed the bonus row as 'a distraction'[13] and continued to trade successfully.

In 2019, analysis carried out by removals firm reallymoving found that recipients of the Help to Buy Equity Loan were paying 10 per cent more on average than buyers of similar homes outside the scheme. Yorkshire was the worst-hit region, with an average 'Help to Buy' price hike of 22 per cent.[14] Another red flag came from a 2020 *Which?* report, which revealed that one in seven Help to Buy homes had lost value despite rising local house prices.[15] This is especially worrying in light of news that Help to Buy mortgage arrears were 'running at six times the average for commercial [non-government backed] mortgages' in February 2020.[16]

In other words, the Equity Loan scheme looks to have stoked new-build house price inflation, just as the funding for the mortgage guarantee variant of Help to Buy was absorbed by a surge in existing house prices. It transpires that it's not only commercial banks' credit creation that feeds the land and housing sponge. Easy credit from the government has exactly the same effect.

Supporters of cash-based solutions to the housing crisis argue that financial leg-ups serve a dual purpose: they increase people's purchasing power and stimulate economic activity. But in the current housing market all cash injections really do is increase people's bidding power in an auction of finite resources. All forms of well-intentioned cash assistance inevitably end up in the pockets of housebuilders, landlords or in higher asking prices of homes for sale.

Recent figures from the Ministry of Housing, Communities and Local Government indicate that 40 per cent of all demand for new-build properties in the UK is now underpinned by Help to Buy.[17] What will happen to the resale value of these homes if the government pulls the plug on the scheme, and demand for new-builds collapses by 40 per cent?

As we've seen, nothing in the property market happens in isolation. Every trend and transaction has a knock-on effect. This goes some way towards explaining why the government keeps extending Help to Buy, in spite of overwhelming evidence that it is a dud.

And the worst part is, it doesn't end there. There's one more government scheme feeding the housing crisis I haven't yet touched upon: shared ownership.

10. Sharing a home

Shared ownership allows people to buy between 25 per cent and 75 per cent of a home and pay rent on the remaining share. *MoneyWeek* magazine called it 'Help to Buy's poor relation.' It's touted as a literal 'half-way house' solution for budding home-owners who can't afford to buy a whole property.

Shared ownership is run in conjunction with housing associations, which are not-for-profit organisations that build and run housing, mostly in the social rented sector. Shared ownership arrangements have been available via housing associations since the 1970s,[1] but the first official government programme came into force in 2009 under the banner of HomeBuy Direct. The aim of this was to 'make more new affordable homes available to eligible buyers priced out of the housing market.'[2] Given that the first incarnation of Help to Buy – FirstBuy – seemed to take its inspiration from HomeBuy Direct, you could go so far as to call shared ownership the original 'prototype' version of Help to Buy.

So, how does the scheme benefit today's 'priced out' homebuyers? Gabi, a 28-year-old science teacher and friend of mine, used shared ownership to move into a home with her husband Adam, a marketing manager of the same age. They like animals and have a dog, a cat and two rabbits, which most private landlords would be reluctant to accommodate. Gabi said:

> '[Shared ownership] made it possible for us to buy somewhere in an area we genuinely want to live. We were really lucky to get the place, as our housing association's criteria said that we needed to have a local connection, and Adam grew up near here. Most base it on housing need, and as we have decent salaries and no kids, we would have been unlikely to get accepted anywhere else. The demand was insane. The housing association told us they were getting hundreds of applicants per home.'

At first, Gabi was wary of shared ownership due to the number of 'horror stories' she came across online. However, after hours of painstaking research, she felt confident she'd picked the right housing association. Now, having lived there a few years, the couple are glad they bought when they did. Gabi explained: 'Obviously, it's completely crazy that two full-time working professionals can only afford to buy 40 per cent of a house on the outskirts of Birmingham. But we felt that renting and owning a bit of something was better than just renting and owning nothing.'

What made them go with shared ownership over other forms of 'affordable' housing schemes? 'It was the only option we could afford,' Gabi said. 'Going via Help to Buy wouldn't have been impossible... but it would have meant taking on a lot more debt for a much smaller house.'

The couple are free to decorate their own home as they please, and so long as they keep up with their mortgage, rent and service charges, they can feel secure in the knowledge that nobody can force them to leave at two months' notice. Gabi said:

'The only downside I'd say is that it's really hard to save up enough to buy the rest of the house. Originally, we were going to do this thing called 'staircasing,' where you gradually buy more and more equity in the property. But it's like the problem of saving for a deposit all over again. Even putting another £10,000 into the property wouldn't bring our rent down by very much. Also, if our share of the equity goes up in value, that means the Housing Association's share goes up too, so rising house prices don't make it any easier for us to buy.'

Despite this, Gabi told me that the difficulty of not obtaining full ownership was 'not a major worry' and that she and Adam still felt much better off using shared ownership than they were when they were renting.

I was glad to hear it had worked out for Gabi and Adam, but concerned that 'horror stories' were part of the shared ownership landscape. Keen to get the full picture, I went in search of somebody who'd had the kind of experience that Gabi and Adam had carefully sought to avoid.

What happens when housing associations abuse their power?
I came across Ryan on a tenants' forum on Facebook, responding to someone's query about whether or not shared ownership was a good idea. He'd replied: 'I'm with a shared ownership scheme through a housing association. When I 'bought' the place it was a local association and affordable. Two years in it was taken over by a larger housing association from another part of the country.

Since then the 'rent' has increased and the service has gotten worse... and my neighbours and I are not happy.'

It all began when Ryan decided to make a concerted effort to get off the private renting treadmill. 'Being a civil servant, I don't earn tons, but it's a pretty secure job with a decent salary,' he told me. 'The trouble with renting is that you feel like you've got nothing to show for your earnings.'

Ryan lives and works in Leeds, where most one-bed rental properties cost somewhere between 30-45 per cent of the local average salary each month.³ He was a tenant in the private rented sector several years ago when rents weren't quite as steep as they are now, but even then, breaking the cycle of hopping from one insecure rental property to the next was difficult.

'I've also got four brothers,' Ryan added, 'so the Bank of Mum and Dad didn't exist for me. Eventually, I bit the bullet and thought, right, I'm going to move into the really shoddy end of town where the rent is so cheap that I can start squirrelling money away for a deposit.'

He lived in 'grotty' house shares in a 'rough area' for almost a decade before he saved up a deposit. 'For a while it wasn't too bad,' Ryan said, 'there were lots of students, it was close to the city centre; I could walk everywhere. I saved money. One day though, the guy in the other bedsit had a full-on mental breakdown and had to be sectioned. It just made me think... it's time to get out. I wanted my own space. So, I started searching online, and this place came up.'

It all looked perfect. The apartment was in a 'quiet and sleepy' area where Ryan used to live, 'with lots of young professionals and families.' The property was close to shops, bus routes and a train station, and he could walk to work in five minutes. 'I just thought, I'm jumping on this,' Ryan said. 'When I spoke to a mortgage adviser, I remember them saying, you do realise it's only 50 per cent ownership, right? But for me and my budget it was either that or a houseboat. I just wanted to get a foot on the ladder.'

The whole process went smoothly. Ryan said: 'They were giving priority to people earning less than a certain amount. It made me think: "Wow: someone's giving me a chance." So, I guess that's another reason why I acted so quickly.'

For two years, the service was 'brilliant.' The housing association employed a local handyman, who did repairs and maintenance promptly and efficiently. He would also clear the road when the residents got snowed in and scrape away moss in the car park so that people wouldn't slip, even though those things weren't strictly in his job description. 'You really felt like you were getting the best of both worlds,' Ryan said. 'The independence of homeownership with the service of renting.'

One day, however, a glossy brochure came through the door to announce that the housing association had been bought out by a new, larger housing association we'll call Brumble Housing Group (BHG). 'There was no consultation or anything,' Ryan said. 'We just got told.' That's when the difficulties began.

'We got a letter one day saying the service charge was going up, due to last year's repair costs or something, and I remember thinking, well, I suppose costs are bound to go up due to inflation. But then, less than a year later, it happened again. It used to be something like £124 a month... now it's £206. That's in the space of less than two years.'

It wasn't just a hike in charges, either. The actual 'service' for which Ryan and his neighbours were being asked to pay a premium rapidly deteriorated. 'The cleaner spends more time getting his hoover out the car and into the building than he does actually hoovering,' Ryan told me. 'It's ridiculous – we timed him once. It took him about three minutes to hoover both floors.'

Then there was the farce with the tree. Ryan said:

'One day, BHG decided that this tree – which was integral to the fence round our front lawn area – was a 'hazard' and needed to be chopped down. We thought that was rubbish – they probably just didn't want the hassle of pruning it. But there was no consultation with us beforehand on whether we actually wanted this work doing. They just hired someone who hacked the tree to bits, which resulted in the fence falling down.

'Then they tried to bill us for the "work," because apparently it wasn't covered by our service charges. To add insult to injury, they never even mended the fence they broke. It's like going into a restaurant and getting served with a load of horrible, gone-off food you never ordered, then being forced to pay for it.'

Another sign something was seriously amiss came when Ryan discovered his professional gardening service was being carried out by 'young lads who obviously didn't have the first clue about gardening.' He explained that they had set the height of the lawnmower far too low, so it basically shredded the garden, and the lawn became a giant moss patch. 'I confronted them about it, and they were pretty hostile until I pointed out that we were all being screwed. I was paying over the odds for gardening services, while they were obviously being paid next to nothing. This got them onside, and they showed me their time sheet. They had 15 other 'gardening' jobs to do that day.'

Ryan has his suspicions about where these gardeners come from:

'I used to work with young offenders on parole. This is the kind of menial community service work they're made to do – all for minimum wage, obviously. It would explain why they don't give a shit – because why would they? It's just something they're being forced to do, with no training and ridiculous targets.'

After months of 'firing off angry emails' and seeing complaints disappear into the abyss, Ryan and his neighbours clubbed together and agreed to refuse to pay the higher charge, until the housing association agreed to make amends.

Straight away they hit a problem: 'The team that sets the rents and service charges is based in Leeds, where the old housing association offices used to be. The team that collects the rents and charges however is based over in Manchester, and the maintenance team is based over in Manchester, and the complaints team is based over in – you guessed it – Manchester.

'So, when the finance people send us scary letters, saying *'you owe us all this money,'* I ring them up and say, *'have you spoken to the Leeds team? Have you bothered to ask why a whole block of residents is refusing to pay the higher charges?'* and they just say... *'No. No-one's told us anything.'* This makes me feel like they know what they're doing. Why wouldn't you investigate an entire building protesting about service charge increases? To me that says they're playing the long game.'

But if that's the case, what 'game' is Ryan's housing association trying to play? Is there a long-term strategy to their relentless ineptitude and intimidation tactics when residents don't comply? 'You're going to think I'm a crazy conspiracy theorist...' Ryan hesitated, 'but I've got a hunch that they're trying to push us out. Property prices round here have soared, and this patch would probably make much more money for BHG if they could knock the place down and build one of these horrible Meccano-style student tower blocks. I don't have any concrete proof, obviously, but when you're putting up with all this crap for so long, it's hard not to suspect that there's a wider game plan...'

Even if there is no conspiracy at work, the fact remains that a property management service that was affordable and efficient a few years ago has deteriorated sharply, according to the residents.

We'll revisit housing associations later in this book and delve into the forces that might be driving them to cut corners and hike charges. But part of Ryan's predicament arises from the fact that shared ownership schemes provide a type of home 'ownership' that isn't really ownership at all. It's a form of tenure known as 'leasehold.'[4] Even when a shared ownership resident has fully 'staircased' and bought out the housing association's share of the property, they often remain a leaseholder, and thus liable for uncapped fees and service charges.[5]

The Leasehold Knowledge Partnership campaign group has attested to the prolific scale of leasehold abuses in social housing, both for homeowners who took advantage of Right to Buy and shared ownership residents. In the trade magazine *Inside Housing* in April 2019, LKP chief executive Sebastian O'Kelly wrote: 'There is a suspicion that some local authorities and housing associations regard their private leaseholders as a cash cow.'[6]

His group was receiving frantic calls from social housing sector leaseholders hit with huge bills 'out of the blue' so often that he no longer found them shocking. 'The only suspense is the amount,' O'Kelly remarked. 'Is this one £10,000, £20,000, £30,000 or even more?'

What, then, is leasehold, and why is it so vulnerable to abuse?

11. Mortgaged tenants

Most people who own homes in England and Wales are 'freeholders,' which means they indefinitely hold the land and all property that sits on top of it.[1] But there's a growing minority who own homes under the 'leasehold' tenure. Leaseholders only have the right to occupy the property for a set period of time, typically between 99 and 999 years. Once the lease is up, ownership of the property reverts to the owner of the freehold, often referred to as the 'landlord'.[2]

Leasehold is commonly found in blocks of flats, where owners of individual apartments pay 'ground rents' and 'service charges' to the freeholder for the upkeep of the buildings and shared spaces. In the last 25 years, the practice of selling new-build houses as leasehold has also taken off (which we'll discuss in more detail later).[3]

Leasehold law is an 11th-century hangover, but it has made a significant comeback in recent years. In 2018, around one in four properties sold in England and Wales was leasehold, but that figure rose to more than one in three for new builds. As previously mentioned, all shared ownership and many ex-Right to Buy properties come attached to a leasehold contract. All this has worrying implications for those looking to get a foothold on the housing ladder.[4]

The doubling ground rent scandal

The national conversation on leasehold began when the doubling ground rent scandal made the national news in 2016.[5] Sophie's story is typical. She was living in a flat bought by her partner in 2013, which the couple were trying to sell. They'd found a buyer, had put an offer in on another home, and the whole process was 'running smoothly'... until 'the buyer's mortgage company declined their application.' It transpired that the refusal was due to a clause in the lease the couple had no idea was there.

When he first bought the flat, Sophie's partner was advised by his solicitor to 'get a lease extension.' Otherwise, he was warned, the couple might 'struggle to sell later down the line.' Trusting this advice, he agreed to the idea, and the solicitor 'sorted it with the management company' working on behalf of the freeholder.

'What we were unaware of at the time,' Sophie said, 'is that in the process, the management company had added some new clauses to this lease, one of which is that the ground rent went from being £100 per annum to £250, and that it would now double every 10 years.'

This may not sound particularly onerous, but given the nonlinear rate of growth, the ground rent would become astronomical over the term of the lease. If Sophie's partner signed up to a 125-year lease, a ground rent starting at £250 and doubling every 10 years would become £1,024,000 per annum before the lease expires.

The timescales involved may seem vast to individuals, but they worry mortgage providers. All the appeal of offering long-term, low-cost credit to homebuyers goes out the window when the security for the mortgage is leaking value with each passing decade. This is what Sophie was horrified to discover: 'We cannot sell the flat, as it is 'worthless' in the eyes of a mortgage company.'

When the pair sought independent advice, they were told a professional negligence claim against the conveyancing solicitor would take years, and wouldn't necessarily be successful. The management company meanwhile quoted them, 'off record,' a fee of £70,000 to have the offending clause removed, an amount the couple do not have. Sophie concluded: 'We found our dream home, our first child is due in six weeks, everything had been going great and now due to the rich wanting to get richer we may be stuck here until we can find 70k. We are heartbroken, hurt and disgusted that companies are allowed to do this.'

The financialisation of customers

Government figures show that between April 2013 and June 2018, one in four properties sold under the Help to Buy Equity Loan scheme was leasehold.[6] As pointed out by the consumer group Which? in 2018, half of these leasehold Help-to-Buy properties were houses.[7] There is no practical justification for offering a leasehold house, because they do not have shared corridors to hoover, door-entry systems to maintain and communal gardens to mow. There is, however, a financial benefit to the freeholder.

Which? documented some of the rip-offs awaiting leaseholders, including a £252 fee for 'permission to have a pet,' a £2,500 fee for 'permission to build a conservatory,' and a £60 fee for 'permission to replace a doorbell.' There's even a '£50 to £108 flat fee to respond to a letter,' meaning that residents must pay to ask for permission to do something to their own properties, then they must pay once more for the permission itself.

Ignorance of the rules is no defence. One anonymous leaseholder had bought her property second-hand, i.e. not directly from the developer. As a result, she had no idea about the very existence of permission fees when she purchased the property. After getting planning permission from the local authority for an extension in 2012, she went ahead and built it, and thought nothing more of it until five years later, when she received a scary letter from the property management company working for the freeholder. It informed her she had breached the terms of her lease, meaning 'our client [has] the entitlement to terminate the lease and, subject to due process of law, take back possession of your property.'

Panicked, the leaseholder asked if she could retrospectively pay the permission fees. She was informed that, had she made the request before constructing the extension, the fee would have been £500. Since it was a retrospective request, it would be £1,600, which she could pay in nine monthly instalments.

After a public outcry and pressure from campaigners, MPs launched a select committee inquiry into the leasehold system in 2018. During one evidence session, the Labour MP Clive Betts asked Jennie Daly from housebuilder Taylor Wimpey: 'We still have not had an explanation of what you collect ground rent for. What do you give to the householder in return for this money you are taking from them?'

Mrs Daly replied: 'In respect of leasehold houses, that is a fair question. It is one of the reasons that, when these matters came to our attention in autumn 2016, we made a very quick decision to convert the homes that we sell to freehold.' Mr Betts reworded her response thus: 'You were embarrassed into abandoning them, then, because you could not justify them.'[8]

In April 2017, Taylor Wimpey set aside £130 million to compensate customers affected by onerous ground rent clauses. While keen to stress that everything it had done was 'entirely legal,' the company admitted its actions had not been 'consistent' with its 'high standards of customer service,' and it was 'sorry for the unintended financial consequence and concern that [the leasehold contracts] are causing.'[9]

Later that year, Sajid Javid, then Secretary of State for Housing, Communities and Local Government, announced a government ban on selling new-build houses as leasehold without good justification. However, this ban wouldn't come into force for three years, wouldn't apply to shared ownership properties, and wouldn't apply to homes built on leasehold land acquired before 17 December 2017. Nor would it do anything to help existing leaseholders like Sophie and her partner, trapped in homes with escalating ground rents.[10]

The Law Commission's forays into reform have focussed on measures that could make leasehold extensions easier, fairer and more affordable. However, an obstacle to change is the need to ensure that the 'human rights' of freeholder landlords are not violated.[11]

In addition, many freeholds are now in the hands of third-party investors. In a promotional video released by the National Leasehold Campaign, leaseholders reveal how they were promised by developers that they would be able to buy back their freehold for a reasonable price after two years. Then, before the two years were up, their freeholds were sold off to anonymous investors, who subsequently demanded vastly higher prices.[12]

Thousands of freeholds are now in unsuspecting workers' pension funds[13] or squirrelled away in offshore shell companies.[14] They have become an 'asset class' in their own right.[15] In 2017, the department store chain John Lewis was found to have pension scheme investments in doubling ground rent funds. The Leasehold Knowledge Partnership uncovered that the management of the freehold 'assets' had been outsourced to companies ultimately owned by the Tchenguiz Family Trust, a holding company based in the British Virgin Islands.

While John Lewis swiftly disposed of the funds, the episode highlighted how financialisation – whereby everyday goods and services are repackaged as financial products – can erode the rights and freedoms of ordinary people. It can turn a trapped leaseholder into a passive source of income for a retired shop worker, without either knowing or consenting. Indeed, the leasehold scandal shows how the very nature of a home has been twisted to become somebody else's revenue stream. In reality, leaseholders are legally just mortgaged tenants. This is especially galling for tenants who thought they were escaping a life of insecurity by buying a property, only to be ensnared in a financial trap far worse than a tenancy agreement.

12. The homeownership dream sours

The whole point of the homeownership agenda when it was advanced in the 1980s was to set people free. If you owned your home, you didn't have to rely on anyone else to fulfil your basic housing needs. Paternalism would be banished from housing. In its place would come a new private model rooted in self-determination and personal responsibility.

For all its collateral damage, the agenda did temporarily fulfil its brief. Owning property as a means of personal capital accumulation and therefore a path to self-sufficiency was previously restricted to wealthier sections of society. Once big banks were unleashed on the mortgage market and Right to Buy was unleashed on the social housing sector, more people were allowed in on the property bonanza. For a time, owning a home was a great social leveller.

Fast-forward to 2020, and that same 'homeownership dream,' even when fulfilled, no longer promises the same sort of freedom. Today's first-time buyers are often mortgaged up to the eyeballs. Any remaining equity is often owed to other entities, such as relatives, the government, or a housing association. And swathes of homeowners nowadays still have landlords, because the leasehold tenure has been increasingly adopted and exploited by property developers and housebuilders to create a new form of mortgaged tenant.

In a last-ditch bid to resuscitate the homeownership dream in 2015, David Cameron, then prime minister, averred that owning a home was not about assets and wealth, but 'about someone standing there with their keys in their hand thinking 'this place is mine.'"[1] And yet the sense of autonomy and personal pride that used to be attached to the keys to a first home now accompanies a more complex blend of emotions. Many of the renters I spoke to who expected to be helped into property by their parents would shift uncomfortably, then say something like: 'I'm only going be able to buy a house one day because I'm lucky enough to have parents who can afford to help me.'

This undercurrent of embarrassment is often paired with a sense of indignation that such support is necessary for a fully-grown adult on a decent salary. It's not: 'I'm OK, my parents can help me.' It's: 'The fact that I can't buy a home without my parents' help is ridiculous.'

In 2017, *The Guardian* delved into the hidden psychological debt issued by the Bank of Mum and Dad. Laura Morris, a 31-year-old hospital doctor, had managed to buy her first home in Liverpool with her boyfriend, a local newspaper journalist. Both sets of parents gave them £2,000 as a gift, while Laura's parents lent them a further £2,000.

Laura told the journalist Rhiannon Lucy Cosslett: 'It was very generous, but you don't feel you should be in that position. I'm very conscious that I'm in a job that pays well above the average, and there are lots of people who are in much harder situations.' She added: 'It doesn't feel like a comfortable situation at all.' Laura was not alone: other interviewees shared similar feelings of unease towards the gifts and loans they'd been given by parents. Jenny, a 28-year-old events organiser, reported that, while the £150,000 gift she'd received from her dad following his redundancy pay-out had helped her to buy her first flat in south London, the privileged status of becoming a homeowner had driven a wedge between her and her friends.

'We all live in London, and most of [my friends] are not in this position. Some are obviously pleased for me, but there are some whom I can't really talk to about it, who have made remarks: that I'm part of the problem, that I'm propping up the housing crisis, and how lucky I am and how I don't know how hard it is,' she said.[2]

The housing crisis is also redrawing the demographic makeup of the UK's most unaffordable areas. In June 2019, ONS data revealed that London was losing nearly 40,000 aged 30-39 annually.[3] Writing about the need for 'sustainable rural communities,' the academics Nick Gallent and Mark Scott highlighted how the exodus of young people from 'gentrified' English villages was a disaster for rural economies. It meant farms, tourism businesses and health and social care providers in those areas struggled to find staff.[4] As a result, high house prices risk choking off the very things that pushed prices up in the first place – local amenities, good schools, small independent businesses and tourist attractions.

Of the homeowners under 30 I spoke to, quite a few downplayed the significance of buying a home by pointing out the size of the burden they were taking on. They had new-found anxieties about having bought at the top of the market, about being tied into 35-year mortgages, about how they would afford to start a family and simultaneously pay an enormous mortgage.

David Cameron thought that Generation Y (another term for the millennial generation) was turning into 'Generation Why

Do We Bother?' because they were priced out of the property market.[5] But what if renters are more likely to be saving for a holiday than for a house[6] because the homeownership dream itself has become such a deeply unappealing, grinding commitment, extending for decades?

Perhaps we shouldn't be using the mantra: 'Young people can't get on the ladder.' A more accurate version might be: 'Young people can see that the ladder is irreparably broken, and are feeling less and less inclined to waste the supposed best years of their lives working themselves into the ground, just to get on the first rung'. It's not as snappy, but it's the picture I have found.

One thing that muddies the waters in this debate is when people discuss 'houses' in the same way as they talk about cars: as if they serve a single, basic purpose. It makes sense to talk about cars in this way, because, while cars vary in quality, for the most part, they have one core function: travelling from A to B.

Conversely, talking about 'housing' is much more like talking about 'food.' If you are malnourished, you need 'food.' But what counts as 'food'? Are you going to get the nourishment you need if I respond to your non-specific request for 'food' with a lifetime supply of sausage rolls and luxury patisserie? What, you're a vegetarian diabetic, and even if you weren't, eating only those things would do nothing to alleviate your malnourishment? Well in that case, you're a snowflake! You asked for food and I gave you food! Beggars can't be choosers!

This analogy may sound absurd, but it mirrors a debate over planning policy that has been raging since Tony Blair's Labour government asked economist Kate Barker to investigate the property market in 2003. The Barker Review came around the time the crisis for generation rent was beginning to hot up. One of Barker's main recommendations was that relaxing planning restrictions would increase the amount of housebuilding. Greater supply would then make housing more affordable to first-time-buyers.[7]

Ministers interpreted this recommendation broadly. Luxury flats springing up left, right and centre? No problem. The wealthy will occupy the canal-side penthouses, and the homes they would have occupied will be filled by middle-class families. In turn, these families will clear the path for those on the next rung down of the property ladder, until eventually, there's space on the bottom rung for a new generation of first-time buyers. It's a 'solution' that has been engraved in the minds of politicians and media commentators alike, almost to the point of dogma. The upshot now is we have a glut of glass towers full of identikit 'luxury apartments,' and still a shortage of genuinely affordable homes. It's almost as if luxury flats and affordable homes aren't part of the same market, like patisserie and bread. A surplus in one won't alleviate a shortfall in the other.

A home, like food, needs to serve an array of complex needs and find a balance between them. It's not just 'a roof over your head.' Of course, you can buy what looks like an ex-drug den in the hinterlands of South Yorkshire for £30,000. But a lack of willingness to go and buy this property is not a lack of willingness to 'make sacrifices.' It is a lack of willingness to do something counter-productive. There comes a point where renting is better than owning *any* home.

The issue is compounded by the fact that the gaps between the rungs on the property ladder are getting bigger. In an article for the *Mail on Sunday* in 2015, journalist Laura Shannon wrote about the rising tide of what she called 'next steppers' – people who 'were lucky enough to get onto the first rung of the property ladder' but faced 'doubling their mortgage' if they wanted to upsize.[8] Research from Lloyds Bank in 2017 revealed that one in three 'next steppers' were expecting to receive a further loan from the Bank of Mum and Dad averaging £21,200, despite having already typically received £21,500 to buy their first home.[9]

Of course, owning still beats renting in terms of your rights, financial prospects and general security and wellbeing. If you've got the means to make it onto the property ladder without bankrupting yourself, it still makes sense to go for it.

Take Rosie, for example, a 27-year-old senior communications officer in the third sector. She managed to get a 15 per cent housing deposit while renting in Bristol without help from family. How did she do it?

By leaving Bristol and heading 'back up north.' Rosie explained how she'd set her sights on Sheffield for its 'connections to other cities, culture, size, proximity to the peaks etc.' She was looking for a home in the region of £150,000, a budget that would probably secure her a three-bed terraced house in a modest area in the city. She would need double the money to buy a comparable home in Bristol.

As a Sheffield native however, I could see a flaw. Well-paying jobs in Sheffield – especially in the third sector and the creative industries, where someone with Rosie's skillset would be most at home – are in fierce demand. They exist, but they aren't abundant or lavishly remunerated. It's arguably the very reason why houses in Sheffield are cheaper than they are in Bristol. On average, people earn less. I asked Rosie whether she thought the local jobs market would be able to support her long-term income requirements.

It turned out that this wasn't a problem: 'I'm extremely lucky in that I work remotely now so it doesn't matter where I live,' she replied. She was earning a pre-tax income of around £30,000 a year, and once her partner had completed his PhD and landed a job, their combined income would look even healthier.

Having previously struggled with her career before moving south, Rosie acknowledged that good jobs in northern cities can be scarce. But thanks to a stint working in one of the UK's most expensive cities, the switch paid off. Rosie said: 'I love my job and will happily stay indefinitely.'

Securing a good job in the south before moving north to work remotely is certainly a clever hack to circumvent the insanity of today's house prices. But it's yet another example of a workaround that only functions effectively because most people can't or don't do it. If this tactic became the norm, house prices in the north would rise to reflect the flood of new money coming in from the south. Rosie intuitively understood this caveat, as she expressed the desire for Sheffield to remain a well-kept secret: 'Just don't go telling all those Londoners looking to escape!'

This is not to say that Rosie and her partner got into the position of being able to buy through relocating alone. Saving up £20,000 before the age of 30 in one of Britain's most expensive cities on a relatively average household income is a formidable achievement. The pair had spent a long time making steep sacrifices, which enabled them to put £400 a month into a Help to Buy ISA for several years.

But Rosie's personal solution to Britain's housing woes cannot easily be replicated by the majority of generation rent – even if a few people do take heed of her story and follow in her footsteps.

When you scratch the surface of other stories of triumph in the face of an impossible housing crisis, similar 'hard-to-replicate' circumstances apply. One ex-PhD student in a survey of homeowners I conducted declared that he '[doesn't] really know why people make it look so difficult,' since he'd been able to buy a home with no outside help in 2015 on a household income of less than £15,000 a year. He hadn't even used a Help to Buy ISA. His survey responses revealed that he had bought his first two-bed terraced home in Derby for £57,000 – a third of the cost of the average UK home in 2019. For most Londoners, this would not even be enough for a deposit.

The sad truth is that first-time buyers today can't buy homes without substantial help, or a significant competitive advantage over their peers, such as a vast salary or a secure job near one of Britain's few remaining affordable postcodes.

And since roughly two thirds of first-time buyers aged 24-35 receive a helping hand from family,[10] and around a third boost their savings with a Help to Buy ISA,[11] homeownership has largely ceased to be an empowering path to freedom and self-sufficiency.

If anything, the relentless push to keep the homeowning dream alive has made the current generation of first-time buyers even more dependent on government help, parental support and towering debt than their parents were. It's little wonder that so many renters have stopped dreaming about it altogether.

The fact is, members of generation rent don't need more housing overall. They need more of the right sort of housing. That is, homes in the right locations that the average twenty and thirty-something can afford without a small army of benefactors.

And it is precisely this category of housing that the private sector, even with lavish government support, has systematically failed to deliver. So now we must turn our attention to the housebuilding industry. Why is it so hard to build low-cost housing in the areas that need it?

SECTION III. HOW HOMES ARE BUILT

13. Why can't we just build more new homes?

Big developers take an average of 15 years from receiving planning approval to handing over the keys to buyers.[1] This is approximately the amount of time it took the Ancient Greeks to build the Parthenon.

The builders would have you believe that bureaucracy at the local planning authority is causing the hold-up. Paul Smith, managing director of the Strategic Land Group, points out that the planning process involves a number of stages, all of which can produce unforeseen delays. Usually even after planning permission is granted, a host of 'pre-commencement' conditions must be met. As the Home Builders' Federation says, a 'frequent frustration' for housebuilders is that 'extensive discussions and reporting' can take place prior to planning approval, only for the same arguments and objections to be reopened post-approval in the pre-commencement conditions. Not only that, but the conditions can often be nit-picky and sometimes downright daft. The Home Builders' Federation gives examples of an East Midlands local authority who demanded the builders secure approval of *all* materials prior to commencement of any building work, which would require 'approval of roof tiles before any roads, sewers, [or] foundations can be built.' An authority in the South West made building commencement conditional on the builders carrying out 'works to a sports pitch' that had nothing to do with the existing development nor the future application. Another local authority in the South East stipulated 'approval of batboxes' for a 'contaminated brownfield site with zero ecology issues.'[2]

The entire 'post-planning stage' – during which time 'pre-commencement conditions are discharged, working drawings are prepared, contractors are appointed and infrastructure works are carried out' – takes an average of *12 whole months*. Looking at the development process, Paul Smith estimates that the overall process from empty field to suburban paradise can take 'somewhere between three to four years.'[3]

There's just one problem with this argument. If planning authority hoops are jumped through in three to four years, how come the likes of Taylor Wimpey, Persimmon, Barratts, Berkeley, and Bellway take 15 years or more to build a house?

In 2018, the Conservative MP Sir Oliver Letwin revealed the outcome of a review commissioned by the government – the sixth independent review in 14 years – into why new homes are being built so slowly. Like the five different independent parties to come before him, Sir Oliver found no evidence that 'land banking' was taking place on purpose. But he did find that on very large sites building companies were moving more slowly than they could. This, he concluded, was primarily down to two driving factors: the 'homogeneity of the types and tenures of homes on offer,' and the 'rate at which local markets will absorb such homogenous products.'

In other words, builders are churning out too many standard houses for sale, and not enough build-to-rent, social rented, affordable rented and shared ownership flats, terraces, bungalows and maisonettes. As a result, the properties that do get built must be drip-fed onto the market, otherwise the 'scarcity premium' they command will go out the window, and builders' profits will fall.

Sir Oliver called for a better (and frankly, more attractive) range of housing to cater to a wider range of needs, beyond the endless sea of tan-coloured cubes and characterless tower blocks that reputedly represent the best efforts of architects today. However, the *reason* he called for this seemed to have less to do with meeting local market needs and more to do with tackling the 'absorption' problem. Sir Oliver strongly believed that 'it would not be sensible to attempt to solve the problem of market absorption rates by forcing the major housebuilders to reduce the prices at which they sell their current, relatively homogenous products.' He warned that this would 'create very serious problems' – first for 'the major house builders,' then, potentially, for 'prices and financing in the housing market,' and then, quite possibly, for 'the economy as a whole.'[4]

The worry is that if, say, 1,500 new identikit homes all appear on a local market at the same time, and prices come down to reflect this sudden abundance of supply, then this will signal to buyers in the area that prices are falling. Buyers will then be able to pressure sellers into reducing their asking prices.

Sellers who can afford to wait might respond by simply holding tight, but there will always be a minority of sellers who will take a low offer to secure a sale. Thus, a deflationary cycle is established. And the dynamic could conceivably start a chain re-action that hits the wider economy.

Critics accuse housebuilders of refusing to sell cheaper homes with tighter margins. But what if 'selling cheaper homes' poses, not just the threat of lower profits, but an existential threat to the entire industry? This is not to absolve housebuilders of all the criticisms that have been levelled at them. But it's worth highlighting that housebuilding is especially sensitive to the cyclical nature of property, and hedging against ruin is just as important as maximising profits. If priced-out millennials and homeless people lose out as a result, then that is simply not the concern of housebuilders.

In general, private companies will not put people before profits. Expecting them to start prioritising the social good over shareholder value is a bit like expecting a lion to become a vegetarian. The government ought to have known this before it began pouring billions of pounds of taxpayers' money into the private property sector.

In short, building homes cheaply poses an enormous risk for the wider housing market, and it's a risk the construction industry isn't willing to take. Nobody, from government to housing executives, dares disrupt the status quo for existing homeowners. Sky-high prices must be protected, lest armageddon ensues. To add further insult, despite the premium price tag, many new-build homes today are appallingly poor quality. In 2017, Shelter reported that over half of the people buying new builds reported experiencing 'major problems,' spanning 'poorly constructed or unfinished fixtures/fittings/doors, problems with the exterior of the building,' and 'faults with utilities.'[5] That same year, the housebuilder Bovis reportedly had to set aside a £7 million fund to address the catalogue of faults and hazards that were flagged up in vast numbers of its newly-built homes thanks to poor workmanship.[6]

The industry is in dire need of a shakeup. So I spoke to somebody who is planning to do just that.

14. Shipping containers: cheaper homes

Shipping containers are one of the answers to Britain's housing crisis, according to some innovators. Among them is Jon Johnson, a former police officer turned housing pioneer in Sheffield. I first came across his bold vision for the future in an article in *City Metric* in 2018 headlined: *Meet the Sheffield social enterprise using shipping containers to tackle the housing crisis.*[1] Johnson was hoping to convert the metal boxes into one, two and three-bedroom homes for £35,000, £65,000 and £90,000 respectively. Forget the government's idea of 'affordable' housing: here was a serious plan to slash the cost of a home.

Made of corrugated steel, shipping containers are typically 20ft long, 8.5ft high and 8ft wide.[2] In their first life, they are loaded with freight and hoisted aboard large ships. Instead of letting them join the scrapheap when they are decommissioned, however, people are putting them to new uses. Not least because they have a Lego-like versatility. They are stackable, hard-wearing, relatively spacious, and can be reincarnated into a low-cost afterlife: as temporary accommodation for the homeless, trendy offices, hipster cafés, and luxury custom-built homes that would earn praise from TV design shows.

Johnson wanted to achieve cost savings on standard new-builds, but not by compromising on design and quality. Not only would his homes be genuinely affordable and tastefully designed, they would also be green, too. They would use 'Passivhaus' principles to regulate temperature and optimise energy efficiency. I decided to interview Johnson at his prototype show home, at Heeley City Farm, a community hub and working farm less than a mile from Sheffield city centre.

As thunderstorms raged outside, I arrived at the building, which doubles as Johnson's home. The container itself was business-like and unassuming. And yet, the giant blue steel shutters and roof-mounted solar panels somehow made the ordinary-looking front door seem quirky and whimsical. The place seemed to stick two fingers up at the drab, aesthetically unchallenging homes that make up most new builds. A large information stand had been erected outside the entrance for the benefit of passers-by, and a flurry of pot plants and flower boxes were dotted about the decking area. Despite the personal touches, the space still had the feel of an exhibit, a public spectacle rather than a home.

As a result I was wholly unprepared for the strikingly characterful interior. Despite being less than a year old, the place felt 'established,' with hardwood floors, an attractive kitchen area and modern décor that didn't stray over into that clinical feel so many show homes fall victim to. I don't know what I'd been expecting, but I was struck by how much it felt like a normal home. Johnson had been able to achieve the effect through his skills in making and restoring furniture. He gestured around the room as he handed me a cup of tea: 'Old bits of table, old bits of floorboard... all the wood in here is recycled, and it's all the kind of stuff we do at Strip The Willow.'

Strip the Willow is the name of a social enterprise Johnson founded, primarily dedicated to making and restoring furniture. Health issues had prompted him to take early retirement from South Yorkshire Police, and, stuck for something practical to do while recovering, he developed his passion for woodworking and joinery into a side business. He never intended Strip the Willow to be a social enterprise, but local people kept wanting to volunteer. Before long, the space was being used for book groups, craft groups, gigs... 'we've done all sorts down there really.' This paved the way for a more radical step.

Despite having been a homeowner for many years, Johnson moved out of the family home after his marriage ended, and the divorce settlement wasn't enough to buy a new house. As a small business owner with a modest pension, the thought of taking out another mortgage did not appeal. So, inspired by an episode of the *Channel 4* show *Grand Designs*, he decided to marshal his resources and community of volunteers. He aimed to:

1. Use the power of social enterprise to tackle the UK housing crisis; and
2. Design and build an affordable home from shipping containers, and prove the concept by moving in himself.

Thus, Reach Homes was born. It cost around £20,000 to convert the first container into a working prototype. But is something like this really possible to achieve on a bigger scale? Johnson was waiting for the council to decide on whether or not they would offer him a piece of land to construct nine affordable homes. A green light would unlock the funding to create an 'offsite factory', which would speed the process and lower costs.

'Modular' housing that can be manufactured offsite and assembled onsite is becoming more common. In 2019, trade magazine *PBC Today* estimated that the adoption of 'Modern Methods of Construction' (MMC for short) could lead to an extra 265,000 homes being built in the next ten years.[3] The industry is picking up the pace. The same year, a Japanese modular housebuilding company, Ilke Homes, struck a £100 million deal with the housing association giant Places for People. Dave Sheridan, Ilke's executive chairman, described the move as an 'Uber moment for construction,'[4] referencing the disruptive ride-hailing app.

For all the buzz within the construction sector, Johnson doesn't trust the big-name industry players to pass these savings onto customers. Thanks to traditional housebuilding practices, he says, 'about 100 million tonnes of building waste goes in landfills every year at the moment, most of which is just over-ordered, gets damaged onsite because it's just little chips, or it gets wet, you know on a day like this... Or it goes in the boot of somebody's car.'

While housebuilding companies will no doubt see MMC as a chance to reduce waste, Johnson suspects their focus is more on profits than contributing to the good of society and the environment. He noted how lobbyists for the industry 'got the Code for Sustainable Homes scrapped'[5] a few years ago 'because it was taking a little bit out of their bottom line.' Conversely, his vision is to use '60 per cent recycled' materials in his container homes.

Won't finance be a problem? Surely traditional mortgage lenders aren't going to allow people to borrow against homes made from shipping containers? Johnson was working on offering a 10-year guarantee, but his ultimate aim was to secure a longer one because they would last '80-90 years no problem.' In future, he expected Reach Homes to offer affordable long-term finance options for prospective buyers.

For Johnson, it was clear that the social goals were more important than large profits, although he was also upfront about the need for the business to make enough money to be sustainable. 'I want to make sure anybody that wants to buy a house can get access to one, and also I want to work with councils and housing associations to make sure that we can do them for affordable rent.'

But what did he mean by the word 'affordable'? He acknowledged that the term had been warped, and emphasised that he intended to make his homes available to 'care leavers and people on the lowest levels of housing benefit.' I wondered if this could turn out to be a drawback.

The journalist and housing activist Vicky Spratt wrote a stark exposé of the way in which a local authority in London was using low-quality shipping container homes as a sticking plaster for the shortage of social housing.[6] One shipping container resident called Sharna, a young single mother, revealed how unsafe she felt. The security gate to the housing complex had long been broken, and one of her neighbours had 'taken to banging on her window throughout the night.' Individuals with complex issues were being housed alongside her, and nobody was getting the right support. If shipping containers are simply used as a hack to reduce spending on hostels and other temporary accommodation, they might even forestall a longer-term solution to the housing crisis.

What Johnson is trying to achieve, however, isn't just about housing, to put roofs over people's heads. As we talked, it became clear that he wanted to create communities that make their own decisions. Reach Homes is a Community Interest Company, which uses an 'asset lock' to ensure its assets are used for the benefit of the community in perpetuity.[7] 'I was in the police for nearly 30 years,' he told me, 'and I've seen so many of the social problems caused by the fact that people don't feel they have any sort of shared stake in society, they're not listened to, they're just kind of... afterthoughts.'

He wants future residents to be able to access training and DIY workshops, and have a meaningful say in how the homes should look and feel. Those on a waiting list could plan small 'villages' of container homes. In the centre, he envisioned an all-purpose container complex that could serve as a pop-up GP, a community centre, a space for socialising or other events or services: whatever the community decided it wanted.

Johnson also wants to bar private landlords from buying or renting the homes. Instead, any rent or part-rent would be recycled back into the Community Interest Company. In this way, people can become their own landlords, taking care of shared areas and maintenance issues without needing help from an authority figure.

Housing co-operatives already operate along similar lines. Members share responsibility for the upkeep and management of the household in exchange for a secure tenancy at sub-market rent. Usually, they don't own a financial stake in the property, which is owned by the co-operative itself. This allows tenants the flexibility to leave without the need for the remaining tenants to buy out their share. A departing tenant simply needs to find a replacement, which is often easy given the appeal of housing co-ops.[8] In fact, the main problem with co-ops is that the cheaper rent, freedom from landlords, and their community spirit means that once people are in, they tend to stay put.

Another possibility for Johnson is to use a Community Land Trust, which owns and manages land and other assets so that they continue to serve the local community for generations to come. They can prevent homes from morphing into speculative assets by indexing their rents and sale prices to local earnings. They're 'not-for-private-profit,' meaning that they can make profits, so long as these are invested or spent for the benefit of local people. Community Land Trusts are gaining traction as a possible way out for those struggling in the private rented sector.[9]

But the problem, as ever, is land. Johnson is hoping that Sheffield City Council will gift or sell him a parcel at low cost, but he has had no success so far. No amount of enthusiasm can alter the nigh-on impossibility of acquiring land cheap enough to allow genuinely affordable housebuilding. While the government is making moves to help smaller builders access public land,[10] the process continues to favour the highest bidder. This is despite evidence that this approach has led to a massive under-delivery of affordable homes.

Research from the New Economics Foundation (NEF) estimates that, between 2011 and 2020, fewer than a quarter of homes built on sold-off public land will meet 'any definition' of affordable housing. Further, just six per cent will be 'genuinely affordable' socially rented homes. By comparison, the National Housing Federation estimates that 42 per cent of all new housing needs to be affordable if we are to tackle the housing crisis. The NEF concludes that, while the so-called 'fire sale' of public land might have benefited builders of 'luxury housing developments,' it has done little to alleviate the national affordable housing shortage.

As we'll see later, the process of buying land privately and securing planning permission is also biased in favour of those with the deepest pockets.[11] Johnson is acutely aware of this. He has set up the National Federation for Affordable Building, with the aim of building a network of like-minded organisations and unifying the voice of the nascent affordable housebuilding sector.

It's still early days, but over time Johnson hopes that the NFAB will give builders who are currently locked out of the market more political clout to challenge a status quo, which very much favours existing big landowners, as we will see.

15. Selling planning permission

Land is the ultimate collector's item. Unlike ordinary commodities, it is not interchangeable or 'fungible.' One gold bar, barrel of oil or sack of coal could be substituted for another, and nobody would know or care. Land is different. Its supply is fixed and no two pieces are identical. Hence why American writer Mark Twain quipped: 'Buy land, they're not making it any more.'

Another peculiarity of the land market is that when a developer bids for a plot, they are not usually bidding for it in its present state. Typically, they are bidding on the basis of what the land might become, such as housing. Therefore, what the developer is willing to pay directly reflects their plans for the site.

Naturally, when it comes to a sale, a landowner wants to secure the highest price possible. So, to acquire the site, a developer must go in with a price high enough to beat the competition, but not so high that it becomes impossible to make a profit. Now, you might think that this strategy carries a risk that ought to render it unviable: the danger of paying a vast sum for a piece of land, only to be refused planning permission. This is where we encounter something known to few people outside the housebuilding and land businesses: option agreements.

Option agreements sound complex at first, but they are actually based on a very simple concept.[1] They turn the land acquisition process into a 'no win, no (enormous) fee' transaction, by giving developers the legal framework within which to borrow the land, attempt to secure planning permission on it, and then have the option to buy it if the local authority gives the go-ahead.

Say a developer wants to acquire an acre of land for a new block of flats. The land is currently worth about £8,000 as an agricultural field,[2] but the seller knows it could go for several orders of magnitude more if it came with residential planning permission, possibly upwards of £1 million. Knowing that the landowner will refuse to part with the site for a measly £8,000, the developer approaches the landowner with an offer: 'I believe I can secure planning permission on your land. If you grant me the option to purchase it, I will agree to buy it from you after the planning application has been approved – so long as I can take a cut of the profits.'

The developer's cut might be, say, 15 per cent of the final market value plus costs. While the landowner could keep all of the gains if they were prepared to go it alone, they don't know how to navigate the planning system, and frankly can't be bothered to learn. The landowner is also reluctant to spend tens of thousands of pounds seeking planning permission that may never materialise. So, they accept the developer's offer.

An option contract is drawn up between the two parties, for which the developer pays £10,000.[3] This contract gives the developer control of the land for a fixed period of time, with an 'option' to buy the land during that period at the pre-agreed discount. The developer then does all of the work necessary to turn the site into developable land. If a planning application is unsuccessful, the developer can simply let the option expire, having sustained losses in the tens of thousands, rather than in the hundreds of thousands, or millions.

Let's say it's good news. The council says, 'Yes, yet another hybrid development of luxury flats and social housing is exactly what we need.' Everyone shakes hands, and the land is suddenly worth £1 million.

The developer can now acquire this land for £800,000, which factors in both the 15 per cent discount and £50,000 worth of costs. As a result, the developer's land acquisition costs won't take an enormous chunk out of its profit, since the costs of its legwork in the run-up to writing a successful planning application (and the costs of its other, unsuccessful applications) can be offset. At least, theoretically.

Unfortunately, due to the way in which the planning system encourages land speculation, legal instruments like option agreements have spawned an entire side-industry dedicated to gaming the system. Here, we need to introduce a new character to the scene: the land promoter.

Land promoters act as intermediaries between developers and landowners.[4] Now, in fairness, the land registry is patchy and incomplete, so identifying eligible sites *and people who are willing to sell them*, is useful. And once an appropriate site to develop has been sourced, applying for planning permission is a long, drawn-out process. Thus, it's easy to see why some developers are happy to skip the hassle and buy 'shovel ready' land from a promoter.

However, there's a new motive in the mix with the addition of this third party. Because they're not the ones who will be doing any building work, land promoters have no incentive to ensure that the developer pays a reasonable price for the site. On the contrary, since the promoter's profits are directly linked to the ultimate resale value of the land, they're strongly incentivised to secure the maximum planning gain possible.

What impact does this have on the building industry's ability to deliver affordable homes?

The Ambrosia Land University

While researching this book, Facebook's algorithms quite reasonably concluded that I was a budding property speculator. It flooded my newsfeed with sponsored content from 'property gurus' selling 'secrets' and 'insider strategies' that promised to help me escape the rat race – even if I lacked the time, money or talent.

Not so long ago, one caught my attention: an advert for the Ambrosia Land University [not its real name]. It was an invitation to join to a free webinar titled along the lines of: *Unlock the TRUTH about making money in the land market*. This was accompanied by a pitch that promised: 'Learn how use Option Agreements to maximise your gains – no experience needed!'[5] Sensing this could yield some useful insights, I signed up.

The webinar began with an introduction from the founder of the business, who we'll call Bill Pounds, giving a brief run-down of his career. Bill knew from an early age he wanted to do well for himself, and he couldn't help but notice that there seemed to be a lot of money to be made in property development.

This marked the beginning of his trek down a blind alley. Mistakenly thinking that the real money lay in *building* properties, he trained as a builder, then worked hard to progress through the ranks to become a site manager. To his dismay, this career path failed to deliver enough success. Not only was building 'the riskiest part' of the development process, it was also the least profitable. On the plus side, the experience taught him a valuable lesson: 'All the best people in development are the land people.' He busily set about retraining. After a brief detour into property surveying, he arrived at his current niche.

At this point, Pounds stressed that the 'visible' side of the land market – for example, where land is sold with planning permission on websites like RightMove – was for 'nutters' who don't really know what they're doing. 'Nutters,' it turns out, are the people you want to ultimately sell to (after all, 'it only takes one nutter to sell a site').

Another pitfall to watch out for is the 'pretend off-market deal' an estate agent might try to pitch to you. These 'deals' will be portrayed as 'exclusive,' but in reality about 300 bidders will be chasing after them. Pounds reiterated his point about nutters: 'If you're bidding against nutters, and you're the highest bidder, what does that make you?'

Then, finally, we came to the 'real' land market, which he described as an 'underground network of land agents and site finders.' In this market, net returns in excess of 1000 per cent were achievable. In one case study, Pounds demonstrated how to pocket a planning gain of £548,000, having incurred costs of roughly £45,000. By contrast, the developer only made around £375,000, despite shelling out nearly £1 million for the site, actually building the homes, and shouldering most of the risk.

Such outsized gains for land promoters and 'site finders' help to explain why developable land is so hard to acquire, especially for a price that makes affordable housebuilding possible. Most of the value created by a new housing development can be extracted by speculators before a single home is built.

Can't the builders employ their own land promoters?

The larger ones do, which goes some way towards explaining why small-to-medium developers have struggled to regain the market share they had pre-2008.[6] Not only are big companies like Gladman and the Strategic Land Group devoting all their time to helping landowners 'promote' their land, other firms are going around amassing portfolios of 'strategic' land – i.e. land that may be awarded planning permission at some point in the future, usually secured by an option or promotion agreement.[7] Given the relatively low cost of placing the 'bet' on a piece of land, coupled with the enormous windfalls when one pays out, it makes sense for strategic land investors to hoover up as much potentially developable land as they can afford. Legal & General, the insurer, for instance, has amassed 'a strategic land portfolio of 3,550 acres stretching from Luton to Cardiff.'[8] Others benefiting from 'strategic land' holdings include the Church of England (making 13.8 per cent returns on this part of its portfolio in May 2017[9]) and the Grosvenor Estate[10] – the bulk of which, worth £8.3 billion, was passed down tax-free to 26-year-old Hugh Grosvenor in 2017, after the Duke of Westminster passed away.[11] Given the sheer volume of people trying to 'bagsy' land for speculative purposes, developable land is in short supply, despite the fact that only around 6 per cent of UK land mass is built on.[12]

Remember Paul Smith, defender of housebuilders against charges of 'land banking' I quoted earlier? He happens to be the managing director of the Strategic Land Group. Could his confidence that housebuilders *aren't* engaged in land banking derive from an awareness that, by the time a lot of housebuilders buy land, promoters and other speculators have already mopped up most of the gains? In any case, it's clear the law on landownership has allowed what is arguably our most vital national resource to become little more than a speculator's casino. And unless the law is changed, the government is currently powerless to do anything about it.

What about compulsory purchase orders?

Compulsory purchase orders allow public bodies to buy land without the landowners' consent.[13] This is often necessary to clear space for big infrastructure projects, such as new railway lines, roads, and tunnels. Conceivably, compulsory purchase could be used to allow councils to acquire land for affordable housebuilding. So why hasn't the government done so? The answer dates back to when landowners successfully managed to overturn moves to democratise land use after World War II.

Prior to the 1947 Town and Country Planning Act, landowners had been free to develop their land however they saw fit. Clement Attlee's Labour government, however, wanted landowners to seek permission from the local authority before any new development or change of use could take place. Its aim was to ensure 'all the land of the country is used in the best interests of the whole people' during the post-war reconstruction effort.[14] Inevitably land with planning permission would be more valuable than land without. Labour realised that this disparity would allow landowners to pocket huge windfall gains at the stroke of the planning officer's pen, so it came up with a solution: a 100 per cent development tax.

The idea was to allow builders to buy land at its 'existing use value' (usually agricultural), let them build the homes needed, then, upon sale, 100 per cent of the development uplift, or 'betterment,' generated by the grant of planning permission would be paid to a brand new Central Land Board. In this way, builders would only be able to profit from building things, and not from land speculation.[15]

Unsurprisingly, this did not go down well with landowners, as it eliminated their ability to profit from selling land. Even worse, the Central Land Board and other government bodies had the power to compulsorily purchase land from recalcitrant landowners at 'existing use value,' depriving the owners of the opportunity to wait for the law to change and their right to profit from holding land to be reinstated.

In the years that followed, housebuilding flourished.

The landed classes, however, let out howls of anguish about the betterment tax until it was scrapped by the new Conservative government in 1953. Its abolition created a 'two-tier' land market. Landowners selling a plot privately could demand a price that reflected its speculative market value, while a landowner issued with a compulsory purchase order was still obliged to accept a price that reflected the land's 'existing use value.' Landowners argued that this gross injustice breached their human rights. Finally, after intense lobbying against the 'raw deal' they were getting in *The Times*,[16] the landowners triumphed: the Town and Country Planning Act was amended in 1959.

Local authorities wishing to acquire land for public benefit from an uncooperative landowner now had to pay site's full residential market value. Then, thanks to the 1961 Land Compensation Act, the development corporations set up after the war to build new towns were all but stopped in their tracks. The Act decreed that landowners would have to be paid the market value of their land plus its speculative 'hope value' – based on what it might have become had the land not been subject to compulsory purchase. Unsurprisingly, land prices surged on the back of this rule change.[17] In the 12 years between 1963 and 1975, land acquisition costs for the average council home went from less than £4,000 to almost £18,000 (in 2016 money). It took a few years for the changes to filter through the housebuilding pipeline, but by the 1970s, new social housing output was in steady decline – setting in motion a trend that would continue to the present day.[18]

But to come back to the original question, yes, the authorities can use compulsory purchase orders to buy land for housing. But if they do, they must pay a price that is essentially worked out according to the following formula:

1. What would a site be worth if it were covered in high-density luxury flats?
2. What's left after subtracting the cost of building those flats?

Once the government has paid an absurd sum based on what the land would go for if it were developed into a lucrative investment opportunity, it would no longer be able to afford *not* to build a lucrative investment opportunity. Affordable housing wouldn't get a look in. This is the case regardless of whether anyone else is bidding for the land. The law effectively forces government to be, as Bill Pounds would put it, 'the biggest nutter' in the auction house. The figures don't add up, so the government doesn't do it.

16. Letting the local economy

The fact that land is fixed in supply doesn't fully explain what makes one piece of land more expensive than another. In many ways, land containing residential property should be a liability. Homes, like cars, fall to bits over time. Mould, damp, subsidence, leaks, faults, pests, wear and tear... some or all of these things will get at even the most robustly built property.

So why don't homes, like cars, depreciate in value? Also, why is it that £800,000 will buy you a seven-bedroomed mansion in Worksop, Nottinghamshire, but only a tiny studio flat with a windowless bedroom in central London?

In 2018, Direct Line Premier Insurance released a study showing that around 40 per cent of the value of the average three-bedroomed property in the UK – £114,000 – comes, not from the 'bricks and mortar,' but from the 'quality of local amenities, transport links and schools.' The research also uncovered that homeowners tend to drastically overestimate the cost of having a home rebuilt if it burns to the ground, by an average of 38 per cent.

'Location, location, location' is the oldest adage in the property world. But it's not often we stop to think just *how much* of the value of a place to live is derived from where it is located. In London, the 'location premium' is a whopping 216 per cent more than the cost of the building on its own.

In other words, while it would cost approximately £205,000 to rebuild a three-bed semi-detached home from scratch in the capital, *buying* such a property would cost £647,571. That's an additional £442,571 in abstract 'locational value' – almost double the price of the average house in the UK.

London is obviously an extreme case, but Brighton, Bristol and Edinburgh all had 'location premiums' in excess of 60 per cent of rebuild values. House prices in every other city analysed (with the exception of Newcastle) were at least 25 per cent higher than rebuild costs.[1]

Why does any of this matter?

Landlords and homeowners don't create 'locations,' and yet they are able to reap immense profits from them. To illustrate this point, in her book *Doughnut Economics*, the economist Kate Raworth dug out a piece of 'political performance art' from the early 20th century.[2] In Rockford, Illinois in 1914, a billboard appeared in front of a scrap of undeveloped land bearing the words:

> 'Everybody works but the vacant lot'
> I paid $3,600 for this lot and will hold till I get $6,000. The profit is unearned increment made possible by the presence of this community and the enterprise of its people. I take the profit without earning it. For the remedy read 'HENRY GEORGE'
> Yours truly, Fay Lewis

Henry George's 'remedy' is explained later in this book. In

essence, Lewis' point was that property owners can cream off the economic value generated by the wider community just by sitting on land.

This has profound importance. Since it's not possible to create new land, the power to grant or deny access to a given economy resides with existing landowners. In other words, if you want to live, work or start a business in London, and benefit from the job opportunities, business connections, political networks and talent pools within, you have to pay the 'entrance fee' set by existing landowners.

In London, this 'entrance fee' mysteriously equates to almost all of the financial benefits to be derived from living in the capital. In a report in 2016, the Resolution Foundation think tank found that, despite earning less, Scottish workers kept more of their take-home pay than their London counterparts and thus had higher disposable income.[3]

In his former role as head of housing development at Shelter, Toby Lloyd, co-author of *Rethinking the Economics of Land and Housing*, made the same observation in a blog post entitled *Where's all the money gone?*. He pointed out that, between 1995 and 2017, the net worth of the UK tripled. So why is it that today's under-35s earn less and have fewer assets than their 1990s counterparts? It turns out that, during that same period, the value of land held by UK households grew by nearly six and a half times.[4] Wealth really does 'trickle down' – into the ground.

Hence, as a city or locality becomes more prosperous, rents rise to mop up the gains – and the communities and businesses who contributed the most to producing those gains lose out (if they are tenants).

Remember Olivia's words from chapter one? *'There isn't really a range of prices on offer'* – now we know why: it's because the majority of the value of the property in the area doesn't come from the fact that the windows don't leak and the décor is tasteful; nor does it come from having an extra bedroom. The lion's share of the profits made by landlords and homeowners in South East England is the result of their property's proximity to London, the engine room of the UK economy.

Even in Silicon Valley, venture capitalists are starting to grumble that too much of the money they invest in promising tech start-ups is lining the pockets of landlords, because rents in the region are astronomical. And yet, the only reason landlords can insist on such high rents in the first place is because Silicon Valley was the birthplace of the dot.com revolution, which no-one ever has chalked up to the productive endeavours of landlords.[5]

While the function of land as a kind of wealth vacuum may seem like a very modern phenomenon, it has, in various guises, been observed since the birth of economic thought. It was described at length by the French Physiocrats in the 18th century, then further explored by the likes of Adam Smith, David Ricardo, John Stuart Mill, Henry George; and a long list of others.

Perhaps the most impassioned speech ever made on the topic came from Winston Churchill when President of the Board of Trade in 1909:

Roads are made, streets are made, services are improved, electric light turns night into day, water is brought from reservoirs a hundred miles off in the mountains – and all the while the landlord sits still. Every one of those improvements is effected by the labour and cost of other people and the taxpayers. To not one of those improvements does the land monopolist, as a land monopolist, contribute, and yet by every one of them the value of his land is enhanced. He renders no service to the community, he contributes nothing to the general welfare, he contributes nothing to the process from which his own enrichment is derived.[6]

As Churchill pointed out at the end of his speech, the purpose of these observations isn't to suggest that landlords deserve to be 'punished' for doing something wrong.

The problem is that the legal system allows land to become a giant sponge that soaks up all the surplus wealth in the economy, while making it look like an inevitable force of nature. Owning land in strategic places not only lets you bask in the glow of a thriving local economy. It allows you to bottle it, pass it off as your own creation, and sell it on at a profit, while the real creators lose out.

SECTION IV. A NATION OF RENTERS

17. Helping out the landlords

In the 1970s, thanks to the post-war success of council housing and political consensus on the heavy regulation of the private rented sector, 'the private landlord' was on course to be 'as extinct as a dinosaur... within a generation.' In 1974, the Conservative Political Centre made the prediction, adding that there was 'nothing that could be done about it.'[1]

The economy, however, was stuttering. Unemployment was rising, inflation was heading towards 25 per cent, and industrial action was putting pressure on energy supplies. Traditional trades and industries, especially coal mining, started to decline as Britain struggled to keep up with global competitors, yet unions were demanding increased wages to cover the soaring cost of living. The largest-scale labour strikes in Britain in 50 years took place over the 1978/79 Winter of Discontent. In short, huge numbers of people were poor, cold and miserable – and housing supply was about to be squeezed.

Thanks to the post-war baby boom, demand for housing and public services continued to rise, but the economic slowdown hindered both the government's and the market's ability to provide them.

At this point, the Overton Window of political ideas was thrown wide open. The Overton Window refers to the range of ideas a politician can promote in public without being considered a lunatic. Often in times of crisis, the window opens up to let in ideas that might once have been considered ridiculous or even dangerous.[2] Any political strategist worth their salt knows that the number one priority of a revolutionary is to pour everything into being in the right place at the right time when this happens.

Enter: Neoliberalism. The intellectual groundwork for the neoliberal dream was laid in the late 1940s by Fredrich Hayek and Milton Friedman's Mont Pelerin Society, a group of disgruntled academics and businessmen whose overriding belief was that Big Government was the root of all evil. What they envisioned was essentially a society in which as many government functions as possible were replaced by free enterprise.[3] Margaret Thatcher's 1980s government, elected after the unrest of the 1970s, put these ideas into practice.

Council housing had no place in this Brave New World. As property of the state that provided a service outside the free market, it would have to go, and it did go with Right to Buy. But Right to Buy wasn't the full answer. Some people were so intractably poor and helpless that they couldn't even afford to buy the grimmest tower block apartment, even with maximum discounts reaching a staggering 70 per cent for those who had been living in a council flat for 15 years or more.[4] How could the state go about washing its hands of these people? Thatcher had a plan.

Her government did not share the pessimism of the previous Conservative administration towards that now seriously endangered breed of capitalist: the private landlord. It embarked upon a conservation campaign to protect and nurture this neglected creature, and in return, the private landlord would dutifully go around with a bucket and mop up all the non-homeowners, nomadic job-hoppers and dole recipients on social housing waiting lists. Private landlords would also provide low-cost homes for young strivers to bide their time in while they saved up for a deposit on a house. Problem solved. The day where the last miserable, dilapidated council house would be sold off was, finally, on the horizon.

However, there was a problem. Landlords didn't want to do it. Or rather, people with money didn't want to become landlords, and people without money couldn't access the finance to become landlords. Private landlordism has a long tradition[5] of being associated, as Victorian housebuilder Thomas Cubitt said in 1840, with the 'little shop-keeping class of persons,' adding that 'persons of great capital have very little to do with [private renting] at all.' Even now, in 2020, Capital with a big 'C' is only tentatively grappling with rented housing (and as we'll see later, its focus is mainly on the wealthiest tenants). In the 80s, very few ordinary people had the funds to buy additional homes without mortgages. Therefore, if the small 'c' capitalists were going to step in, they were going to need financial assistance.

Despite the government spending the best part of a decade ripping off layer upon layer of financial red tape, the banks didn't want to help. Their reluctance to lend money to humble shopkeepers, and thereby enable them to dabble in private landlordism, was compounded by the 1977 Rent Act. This Act lavished untold benefits on private renters, including that ultimate perk: *security of tenure*. Not only were you not allowed to kick your tenants out if they hadn't done anything to violate their tenancy agreement, but removing problem tenants was incredibly difficult.

Officers at the Valuation Office Agency set 'fair rents,' which were invariably lower than 'market rents.'[6] Such rent controls stifled short-term profits. To make matters even worse for landlords, the 1977 Rent Act allowed tenants to pass on their tenancies to the next generation.[7] So having a rental property often meant providing a long-term home for a family, which was a burden for the landlord. It was therefore imperative for the government to do away with these tenant benefits. As Mrs Thatcher remarked herself: 'We have done much to help the deserving tenant but comparatively little to help the deserving landlord.'[8]

The first helping hand the government gave to landlords was the Assured Tenancy. Introduced by the 1988 Housing Act, Assured Tenancies more or less ended rent controls. Rents could be increased periodically, either by a valid rent review clause in the initial tenancy agreement or by issuing a notice under Section 13. The eviction process for troublesome tenants was strengthened and clarified under Section 8 of the 1988 Act. Assured Tenancies were made the default tenure.[9]

But that's not all. The Act also contained an optional upgrade. For landlords who wanted more flexibility and control, there was the facility to offer another new breed of tenancy: the Assured Shorthold Tenancy, containing a revolutionary bit of legislative ammunition: the power to serve a no-fault eviction notice under its Section 21.

So, did the banks immediately jump on board with a landlord lending free-for-all? Curiously, no. The buy-to-let mortgage did not hit the high street until 1996. Why?

The epic housing market crash of 1990 was one reason. Hundreds of thousands of people, mostly younger, more likely heavily mortgaged people, found themselves in negative equity, shackled to mortgage repayments with interest rates running into double digits. Banks were too preoccupied with repossessing and selling properties of defaulting borrowers to worry about extending exotic new forms of credit to a new set of landlords.

However, that's not the whole picture. In 1996, under an amendment to the Housing Act, the Assured Shorthold Tenancy superseded the Assured Tenancy to become the *default* set of rules governing all new tenancy agreements. In other words, the Assured Shorthold Tenancy became something you had to opt out of, rather than opt into.[10]

Why was this so important for mortgage lenders? The Assured Shorthold Tenancy (with its all-important Section 21 rights) protected the banks from amateur landlords. Banks did not have to worry so much about whether a landlord had correctly issued the right sort of tenancy agreement. By default, *no tenant would enjoy security of tenure.*

The creditworthiness of the buy-to-let borrower became less important. If the landlord was suddenly forced to sell their rental property, they could serve a Section 21 eviction notice, shoo the tenants out the door, and put the property on the market. More to the point, Section 21 made it possible for banks to repossess rented homes without the risk that they would inherit the menial obligations that come with being a private landlord (it's hard to imagine a NatWest bank manager showing up to fix the toilet). Repossessed homes would be more likely to fetch full market value upon resale, too, as they would not come with sitting tenants who couldn't be evicted.

In short, Section 21 was a gift to banks and property investors and its importance cannot be overstated. A blog post published on the Residential Landlords Association's website in 2018 paid misty-eyed homage to the 1988 amendment to the Housing Act, calling it a 'game changer' and 'a vintage year' for landlords.[11]

Section 21 lowered the bar of entry to the private rental market and filled empty properties with benefit claimants and young professionals alike. It helped to 'take the strain' of the social housing shortages created by Right to Buy. It helped the state roll back its obligations towards society's most vulnerable. And it set the scene for today's skewed letting market, where almost all the power lies with the landlord.

18. The house of landlords

In January 2016, a proposed change to the Housing and Planning Act would have made it a legal requirement for all landlords to make their properties 'fit for human habitation.' When the amendment was voted down in parliament, the media and the public were baffled. Nobody could believe that serving MPs (309 Conservative, one UKIP, two from the Ulster Unionist Party) could be so indifferent to the idea of people being protected from inhumane living conditions. It meant that, in some ways, a human tenant was less entitled to a habitable home than their dog.[1]

The move was a gift to the left-wing press. Since David Cameron went on his PR drive to shake the Conservatives' reputation as the 'nasty party,' openly disregarding the interests of the poor and vulnerable went against the party line. And yet here was what looked to be a blithe acceptance that people should be allowed to live in squalid and dangerous living conditions.

Beneath a story reporting the defeat in *The Independent*, one commentator highlighted how bizarre it all looked to an outsider: 'I mean no offence or disrespect, but as a foreigner I wasn't aware that the UK didn't have such a piece of legislation. Housing standards in the UK are by far the lowest I have seen so far anywhere in Western Europe.'[2]

Overall, privately rented homes in England contain more mould, damp, insulation problems, fire hazards and generally old and decrepit interiors and facilities than any other type of housing, including social housing. By contrast, socially rented homes (housing association and council housing) are the best-maintained of all types of housing stock on average.[3]

Some 72 of the MPs who voted down the motion were themselves registered landlords. The law change had been proposed by a Labour MP, Karen Buck, partly because of the high prevalence of poor quality rented accommodation in her north London constituency. The legislation for a tenant's right to a habitable home actually already existed. But as it had not been amended since 1957, it only applied to tenants paying up to £80 a year in London, and £52 elsewhere – i.e. no-one.[4]

Traditionally, the Conservative Party has protected the interests of property owners. Its solution to generation rent has not been to make renting better, but to encourage more renters to buy homes. David Cameron made clear his government's priorities in his speech to his party conference in 2012:

'Look – it's OK for my generation. Many of us have got on the ladder. But you know the average age that someone buys their first home today, without any help from their parents? 33 years old. We are the party of home ownership – we cannot let this carry on. [...] There are young people who work hard year after year but are still living at home. They sit in their childhood bedroom, looking out of the window dreaming of a place of their own. I want us to say to them – you are our people, we are on your side, we will help you reach your dreams.'[5]

There was no mention of the private rented sector. According to Cameron, the most noteworthy consequence of the extraordinary cost of 'getting on the ladder' was that some young people were having to live with their parents. And yet, this was at a time when the difficulties of generation rent were already well known.

At the 2015 Conservative Party Conference, the 'adult children stuck in the family home' narrative was wheeled out once more, and the only mention of private renters was in the concluding remark: 'Let's turn generation rent into generation buy.' This speech was accompanied by the pledge to abolish the planning rules that forced developers to build a certain amount of 'affordable' rented housing as part of new developments. Cameron went on to explain: 'For years politicians have been talking about building what they call affordable homes, but the phrase was deceptive. It basically meant ones that were only available for rent. What people want are homes they can actually own.'[6]

Dan Wilson Craw, head of campaign group Generation Rent, told me that this argument in favour of promoting ownership over renting was circular. 'If you ask people what they prefer, they always pick homeownership. But the option of a decent rental sector doesn't really exist. If we reformed security of tenure, we could get to a point where renting provides all the security and autonomy of homeownership. It could be a genuine alternative.'

Instead, David Cameron chose to scupper further provision of new affordable rented homes to make way for his vision for 200,000 'starter homes' available for purchase at a 20 per cent discount on their 'market value.' In November 2019, the BBC presenter Andrew Neil challenged MP Liz Truss on how many of these 'starter homes' had been built. 'There haven't been as many starter homes as we would have liked,' she began, before saying she couldn't provide him with the 'exact numbers.' The exact number was zero.[7]

At no point, it seems, did Cameron seek to find out why private renters weren't piling onto the property ladder despite layer upon layer of government incentives (See *Chapter 9. Official Help to Buy*). Nor did he stop to consider why his fanatical mission to 'cut red tape' for property developers – a drive the *Architect's Journal* called 'a bonfire of regulations'[8] – hadn't dented the size and growth of the privately renting population.

In fact, by the mid-2010s, it was becoming painfully clear that everything David Cameron and George Osborne had put in place to keep the homeownership dream alive had either failed to have an effect, or made things worse. Evidence was mounting that Help to Buy and cuts to stamp duty had fuelled property price rises, and the continuation of Right to Buy had sent the housing benefit bill soaring to new heights.

Nick Clegg, the erstwhile Deputy Prime Minister, later reported that, during the coalition years, 'either David Cameron or George Osborne, I honestly can't remember whom' told him: 'I don't understand why you keep going on about the need for more social housing – it just creates Labour voters.'[9]

This statement reveals that the Conservatives didn't just want to solve the housing crisis, they wanted to solve it in a way that fitted with their ideology. The solution had to lie somewhere in the 'free market,' or else a solution did not exist.

Rejoicing at 'lost sheep who have been found'

In 2018, the Homes (Fitness for Human Habitation) Bill was debated and voted on again as a private members' bill, and the tone of the debate could not have been more different. A Labour MP, Andy Slaughter, even took the opportunity to congratulate the seven Conservative MPs present at the second reading who had reversed their stance since 2016. 'I would hate ever to be churlish in the Chamber,' he said, rejoicing at 'lost sheep who have been found.'

Not one negative voice could be heard throughout the debate, with MPs from all corners of the House expressing their delight at the 'cross-party support' the bill had garnered.[10] What did it take to change the conversation in such a short space of time?

The vote to leave European Union on the 23 June 2016, which brought both Cameron and Osborne's time in office to an end, may have had an impact. However, the most dramatic shift in political opinion on housing standards came almost a year later, when tragedy struck at a tower block in North Kensington, London. The fire at Grenfell tower reduced the 24-storey building to a blackened shell in a matter of hours. It was the worst fire in London since World War Two. It claimed the lives of 72 people and displaced 209 households.

It later emerged that the landlord of the building – Kensington and Chelsea Tenant Management Organisation, which was run at 'arm's length' by the local council – had signed off on unsafe refurbishments a year earlier that had effectively turned the building into a giant tinderbox.[11] What's more, residents had been raising concerns over the safety of the tower block for several years, but these had been repeatedly ignored and dismissed. In November 2016, seven months before the fire broke out, the Grenfell Action Group wrote on its blog that it had come to a 'terrifying' conclusion: that 'only a catastrophic event will expose [the management organisation's] 'ineptitude and incompetence.'[12] After Grenfell, the issue of poor housing standards for all tenants was brought 'starkly under the microscope,' as Conservative MP Rebecca Pow put it, while pledging her support for the Fitness for Human Habitation amendment in January 2018.[13] Pow, a private landlady, had voted against the amendment two years earlier.

A week after the fire, Sajid Javid – also a private landlord who voted against Karen Buck's original Bill – and then Secretary of State for Communities and Local Government, told the House of Commons: 'It is clear that any changes in the wake of this tragedy should not just be technical or legislative ones. What happened at Grenfell also showed us all that we need a change in attitude.'[14]

The Homes (Fitness for Human Habitation) Act 2018 became law on the 20 March 2019. Tenants who started a new tenancy after this date have the power to sue their landlords if their homes are deemed 'unfit for human habitation,' so long as they can afford the legal costs or qualify for legal aid. Existing tenants were covered from March 2020.

And yet, despite the political rallying cries of summer 2017, the public inquiry into the Grenfell tragedy is ongoing. The aluminium composite material cladding, which had been attached to the exterior of the building as part of the £10 million refurbishment works that took place in 2015-2016, is thought to have been key to the rapid spread of the fire. Since the incident, 435 high-rise buildings in England – both public and private; most residential – have been found to have the same cladding as Grenfell Tower. As of September 2019, the cladding has been removed from 114 buildings. Some 321 buildings are 'yet to be remediated.'[15]

19. Get out of my house

In April 2018, Karen Wilkinson (not her real name) posted the following question on a tenants' support group on Facebook: 'Can you sue a landlord for emotional distress?'

She went on to share how she'd been made homeless after nearly ten years in the same property. The landlord told her he was moving back to the UK from Australia, and needed his home back. Karen and her family were given two months to leave. Further down in the comments section, Karen revealed: 'I asked for 1 extra month so my kids could have Christmas but the selfish git said no!'

When we spoke on the phone, Karen told me how her kids had been wrenched from their schools and friends, and she was worried her daughter wouldn't find a secondary school place in time for September. Despite the fact that Karen did eventually manage to find a new rental property, the whole family had been left shaken by a stint in a grotty hostel while they searched for somewhere to live.

After several years of being blissfully unaware of the precariousness of their situation, the reality of what it means to be a tenant in 21st century England and Wales had hit home. Never again would Karen and her family feel confident enough to call a house their 'home', knowing how readily and unexpectedly it could be snatched away.

Karen's Facebook post concluded: 'My life is ruined now, I've had to move out of Bristol and I'm in lots of debt because of it! This sort of thing needs to stop! It's not over for me yet! My life was turned upside down, he shouldn't be let off for this! It's bang out of order.' In a further blow, Karen later discovered from her ex-neighbour that the landlord hadn't 'needed' his property back for personal use after all. He'd simply wanted to refurbish and re-let the property at a higher rent. A decade spent as a reliable tenant meant nothing. To the landlord, Karen and her family were an inconvenience to be brushed aside.

Everything Karen's landlord did is completely legal. By default, if you rent a residential property in England and Wales, then (as mentioned previously) you're bound by the rules of an Assured Shorthold Tenancy. This starts with a minimum six-month term, after which you'll be automatically switched onto a rolling or 'periodic' tenancy. Neither party can terminate the contract within that initial fixed-term period. If the landlord is feeling generous, they might offer an initial fix of twelve months or longer, though this is discretionary, and isn't always desirable. Once into the rolling contract, you are free to leave so long as you give one month's notice. The catch is that your landlord has the right to evict you with two months' notice, whatever the reason.[1] Provided certain basic regulatory requirements are met, the tenant has no legal comeback.

In Northern Ireland, the minimum notice period for a no fault eviction can be as short as four weeks, depending on the length of the tenancy.[2] Scotland outlawed evictions without valid grounds in 2017, but Scottish tenants can still be asked to leave with just under three months' notice if their landlord wants to renovate the property.[3]

Even if your kids go to the local primary school; your job is 10 minutes down the road; no other properties within a 15-mile radius are affordable: you must go. This may seem fair on both sides, but the UK is one of the few remaining places in Western Europe where law-abiding private renters can be denied the right to a secure home.[4]

20. Revenge evictions

The government has taken action against rogue landlords, to try to improve the lot of tenants. But only up to a point, as we will see.

In 2015, Parliament passed the Deregulation Act, which was supposed to put rogue landlords out of business. Not only does it make Section 21 evictions illegal for six months if the property is in serious disrepair, it contains booby-traps for lackadaisical landlords.

To retain their Section 21 eviction rights, landlords have to issue three documents before move-in day: an Energy Performance Certificate, which shows tenants the energy efficiency of their homes; the latest edition of the government's *How to Rent* guide, which contains useful information on tenants' legal rights and responsibilities; and a valid gas safety certificate. Omit to tick any one of these boxes, and the landlord cannot evict well-behaved, rent-paying, contractually-compliant tenants.[1] In theory.

The experiences of Laura and her husband Mike (not their real names) in a privately rented house in a town in western England show how, in practice, the system often fails tenants. Laura and Mike are both aged 29 and work in health/social care and hospitality. They have two young children. They were paying their rent on time in full and taking good care of their rented home. However, there were a lot of issues with the property – penetrating damp caused by neglected gutters, mouldy floorboards, dodgy wiring, leaking pipes in the bathroom, poor insulation and warped doors that let in icy draughts in winter.

Every time Laura asked for maintenance work, the landlady would drag her feet, make reluctant promises, and then not follow through. Ultimately, in 2017, the landlady served the couple with a Section 21 'no fault' eviction notice.

'It was basically the day after I stood up and told her my rights.' Laura explained. 'I knew that if we went, she'd just let it out to someone else with all the same issues left unaddressed. So, I wanted to push for her to do the work. We'd even got the council involved, because it was becoming an environmental health issue.'

This was Laura's first brush with the regulations put in place by the Deregulation Act in 2015 to protect tenants from revenge or 'retaliatory' evictions – eviction notices delivered as punishment for requesting repairs to the property.

According to Laura, the law is 'a load of rubbish.' 'It doesn't work. Even if you can prove it's a retaliatory eviction, which is hard in itself, the landlord is still within their rights to evict you after six months. All it really does is buy you a little bit more time to find somewhere else.'

And yet, the eviction notices Laura's landlady served 'were all invalid,' because 'she'd not done any of the things she was supposed to do.' Laura was confident that the landlady's case was legally shaky. In spite of this, Laura was desperate to avoid a court case at all costs. 'We couldn't afford for it to not go in our favour,' she told me. 'So we just wanted out as quickly as possible.'

Laura struggled to find a new place within commuting distance of their jobs, which would accommodate a small child and several pets.

'It's dogs most landlords seem to have a problem with – never mind that I'm a certified animal behaviour expert and the dogs are highly trained. They just flat-out refuse. Also, not all rentals are child-friendly. We got to the point where we, a working couple with no problems paying the rent, were on the verge of homelessness. We were thinking that my husband was going to have to live in a tent with the dog while I went into temporary accommodation with my daughter. It was that ridiculous.'

Eventually, Laura came across a property that seemed to suit their requirements, advertised by an online-only letting agent.

She recalled: 'What actually first caught our attention about the property was the price. It struck us as being a fair bit lower than the other ones we'd seen of a similar standard in the area.' However, upon making an enquiry, the reason for the modest price became clear: 'It turned out the advertised rent was just a starting price. It was put to us that, if we wanted to secure the property, we would have to bid.'

Estate agents are famed for pulling dirty tricks to play prospective house-buyers off against one another. As anyone who has ever been 'gazumped' when a new mystery bidder turns up will know, being asked to compete with an anonymous third party who may not even exist can be dismaying. However, using similar tactics to extract the maximum amount of rent from tenants on the verge of homelessness takes the practice to a whole new level.

The company might defend itself by suggesting that, if prospective tenants are unhappy with its methods, they are at liberty to go elsewhere. But, as Laura pointed out: 'When you're desperate, there's no such thing as choice.'

Not wanting to take any chances, the family went in with a bid that was at the limit of what they could afford. It was accepted immediately. Yet, even after managing to 'win' the property, the costs continued to mount.

Despite earning more than the minimum demanded by the agency, the couple were made to pay to arrange someone to guarantee their rent because they were on zero-hours employment contracts. Laura said:

'We ended up using a family member, but it was completely pointless. Zero-hours contracts are just the done thing in the industries we work in. I've never struggled for work, and nor has my husband – and we've got the bank statements and pay slips going back years to back it up. They could clearly see we weren't having any difficulty paying the rent at our last place. You're just made to feel like a little child, like you can't be trusted.'

Laura's family has several pets: two dogs, two cats, and a rabbit. Under the 2015 Consumer Rights Act, a landlord may only refuse permission to keep pets based on reasonable evidence, such as the animal's size and potential to cause damage.[2] In practice, it appears the law is rarely followed. Research from rental listings website SpareRoom.co.uk found that 69 per cent of UK landlords refused to let to pet-owners as a general rule.[3] In Germany, a famously tenant-friendly nation, pets are 'generally allowed'[4], which suggests the bias is more cultural than practical.

Would Laura's situation be transformed if she rid herself of her beloved animals? I'm not so sure. 'Our pets are all that keep us going,' she told me. 'We have no trouble affording them, they're our main joy in life – some people eat in fancy restaurants or go on foreign holidays; we've got our animals.'

Laura's unwillingness to cater to pet-averse landlords is also influenced by the fact that her family's chances of becoming homeowners are vanishingly slim. There's no homeownership salvation; no reason to hold off in pursuit of some idealised future they might one day have. It's now or never.

Sadly, the new property has serious faults, too, and the new landlord is similarly disinclined towards making repairs. Laura ended up paying for a safety check of the electrics, as a leak had gone on for so long that the internal walls had become 'squidgy' to touch. The couple were told that their shower, which had been faulty for some months, might electrocute them. The landlord maintains that an electrician he sent round to the property declared the shower to be safe. On and on the arguments go; a permanent adjunct to Laura's daily life.

What struck me in the course of our conversation was how humble Laura's expectations were. She talked of having enough for food and essentials as something to aspire to. When I suggested it was okay to want to enjoy yourself from time to time, she said: 'I don't want a flash car or the latest telly. I really don't give a shit about that sort of thing. I just want my family to be comfortable. We bring home £30,000 a year, as a household. That should be enough. But somehow it's not.'

21. The reality of renting

In summer 2018, Generation Rent, the charity organisation, invited people to share their renting horror stories on Twitter via the hashtag #ventyourrent. The anecdotes flooded in, each documenting a weirdly similar set of complaints.

One tenant called Amy Wilson tweeted a picture of the 'stunning' bedroom in her '£1,650pm Clapham flat' which showed a large patch of black mould spattered up the wall like a Jackson Pollock painting. She went on to say how complaining about this apparent health hazard had led to a threat of eviction, which she reported to Lambeth council, who 'did absolutely nothing.'[1]

Daniel Sparrow, another renter, made what he thought was a reasonable request for something to be done about the lack of heating or hot water in his home in December. The response he got was not only intimidating but completely bizarre: 'You think you have a hard life? I'll show you a hard life if you're not careful.'[2] Can you imagine Sainsbury's responding with that line to a customer who complained about their shopping?

A lot of the complaints aired under the #ventyourrent hashtag were about landlords who expected to receive full market rent for their properties but were reluctant to provide even basic standards of service. Rachel Collinson, a writer, tweeted that, 'because

London rent is so high, I've never lived alone with my partner since we met 6 years ago. £2,250pcm for a shared flat with regular plumbing and internet access problems. 40 and still renting.'[3]

There were also numerous stories of tenancy deposit theft. Deposits are only supposed to serve as a security for landlords whose tenants fall into arrears or damage the property. Ciara McKibbin, a customer service manager in London, concluded: 'Landlords see your deposit as extra income only to be returned if you know your rights!' This was based on her experience of successive landlords trying to deduct '£1,000+' at the end of her tenancies, only to 'back down' when she challenged them with 'evidence/tenancy law.'[4]

The many angry stories seem to arise from a common source: landlords who hold the belief that 'It's my property, I can do what I want with it, if you don't like it you can leave' – despite the fact that their tenants are paying more in rent than they are for any other service they receive.

As a Twitter user calling himself Erroneous Monk put it: 'Normally, if you spend £1000s pa on something, you're a valued customer with the status and power that goes with that.' If you're a tenant however, you're 'a serf.'[5]

The comparison between feudalism and modern-day private renting is pertinent when you consider the curtailed rights inherent in the landlord-tenant relationship. Tenants can be made to seek permission before they are allowed to hang pictures, carry out minor repairs – or even switch energy supplier. A Uswitch report from 2015 found that landlords were adding £161 million per year to renters' energy bills by denying them the right to change provider.[6] In a Facebook support group for private tenants, one poster called Dom shared how he had returned home one day to find his thermostat covered in a sealed plastic case. The cost of heating was included in the rent, and the landlord had decided that Dom and his housemates couldn't be trusted to set the heating during the winter.[7]

Periodic 'inspections' are the norm for thousands of renters in the UK, because the landlord's right to peace of mind over the condition of their investment property trumps the tenant's right to privacy. An anonymous user on the London Assembly discussion forum shared how she is forced to undergo 'three-monthly property inspections,' highlighting that, '[the letting] agent's staff can walk into my home and invade my privacy in a way that even the police can't.'[8]

Another tenant, who'd been given the pseudonym Angela, wrote in to landlordlawblog.co.uk to ask whether she could do anything about the fact that her landlord's letting agent had 'spent over an hour' taking photographs of 'each room' of her home 'from every angle,' as part of a routine flat inspection. She was told that the photographs would be used in a report for the landlord. 'I hadn't been asked and felt powerless to stop them. I just felt like crying,' she wrote. 'It seemed to me that the majority of the photos taken were unnecessary.'[9]

By law, tenants do have the right to receive 24 hours' prior notice if the landlord or letting agent wants to enter the property, and they are even at liberty to refuse entry to their home – unless there's an emergency in need of urgent attention.[10] But ultimately the landlord holds the power. As Tessa Shepperson, the landlord and tenant lawyer who responded to Angela's enquiry, points out: 'If the landlord and agents feel that you are being uncooperative, there is no reason why they should not serve a section 21 notice on you and require you to vacate.'

Which is not to say that Shepperson didn't sympathise with Angela. On the contrary, she agreed that the agent's behaviour was appalling and most likely a breach of the common law covenant which gives tenants the right to 'quiet enjoyment' of their homes.[11] But since the cost of taking a landlord to court is beyond the means of most ordinary renters, Angela's best option was to write to the agents to ask them not to do it again. Even this option was risky, as the new 'retaliatory eviction' laws do not protect tenants who complain about breaches of their fundamental right to 'quiet enjoyment.' This prompts the question: are rights that are unenforceable in practice really rights at all?

Some would-be private tenants don't even get as far as having their privacy invaded: their social status or household composition effectively bars them outright from the majority of rental properties on the market. Writing in *The Guardian*, Rupert Jones wryly commented how the slogan 'No DSS, no pets, no children,'[12] so frequently seen on rental listings today, has become the modern-day version of the racist signs that used to hang in the windows of rooms for rent in the 1950s and 60s: 'No blacks, no Irish, no dogs.' The Department of Social Security no longer exists, but is still used as a blanket shorthand to say: 'No benefit claimants, including the disabled.'

The public sector offers no escape. Since 2012, socially rented homes (the catch-all term for what was once known as 'council housing') have been disappearing at an average of about 25,000 a year according to the Chartered Institute of Housing.[13] With more than a million people now languishing on social housing waiting lists – some waiting for more than a decade – there is a catastrophic log-jam in the UK housing sector.

Meanwhile, for all the hand-wringing in the media over how UK house prices have been 'stalling' in recent years, the cost of buying a home remains stubbornly high.

Rather than restore equilibrium, it seems the private rental market's 'invisible hand' has chosen to give struggling renters the middle finger. In the UK, average rents went up by 16 per cent between 2011 and 2018. At the same time, earnings failed to keep up – rising by just 10 per cent.[14] Despite this, Savills, the estate agents, predicted that between 2019 and 2023 rents will soar by 13.7 per cent across the UK, with London rents expected to spike by 15.9 per cent.[15] Unless we see a dramatic uptick in wages, it looks like rent rises will continue outstripping pay rises well into the next decade.

The *Huffington Post* reckons that, for those struggling with extortionate rents, there's a simple solution: move to a part of the country where the average rent is still affordable on local wages.[16] However, it's no co-incidence that many of the locations on the *Huffington Post*'s list of places with the most affordable private rental markets – for example, Sunderland, Hull, Salford, Stoke-on-Trent, Bradford – also appear on Adzuna's widely cited list of Worst Cities to Find a Job.[17]

That's not to brand these areas as unattractive places to live. As someone who grew up and currently lives in Sheffield, I know how frustrating it can be when the public perception of your city as a post-industrial wasteland is 40 years out of date. But the fact remains that rents tend to reflect the strength of the local economy in a given area. It makes no sense to suggest that the housing crisis can be solved by getting the majority of renters to move to the areas with the fewest job opportunities.

Moreover, if hordes of Southerners did descend on Durham (home to the UK's most affordable rented housing, according to the *Huffington Post*), to start businesses and rent homes, this surge in demand would push up prices and price out the locals. The problem would not be solved, just shifted.

In her 2017 book *Big Capital,* Anna Minton traced in sharp detail how this 'domino effect' in the housing market is already displacing families and communities in a chain reaction that runs from the very top to the very bottom of the economic food chain. London's multi-millionaires are being displaced by foreign billionaires from the hottest 'super prime' postcodes; multi-millionaires are in turn pushing millionaires out into the commuter belt; millionaires are pushing the affluent middle classes even further afield towards Oxford, Reading, Cambridge, Brighton and Bristol; and so on.[18]

As this tide of wealth sweeps from one postcode to the next, it is society's most vulnerable who pay the steepest price. Through Facebook I got chatting to a private renter called Ali, who told me how she was effectively priced out of Bristol, which had been her home for almost all her adult life, when her 'lovely, affordable house' was sold by her landlady of five years. 'I was lucky as my rent never went up, and it was in a nice street in a gentrifying area where the rents doubled within about three years,' she explained. 'When it was abruptly sold off and I only got two months it was a nightmare.' A few years ago, Ali fell ill with a chronic pain disorder that forced her to give up work. As a result, she now relies on benefits to survive. Ali's struggle to find somewhere else to live in Bristol was hampered, not only by the vanishing scarcity of affordable housing in the city, but by the fact that, 'if you get housing benefit, most landlords just say no, they don't care about your circumstances... and why should they? They aren't social housing providers.'

Ali ended up having to move to Wales, where she is now 'really isolated.' 'I've got no friends or family here,' she said, 'just one nice neighbour, and my cat!' To make matters worse, she has fallen into the clutches of a rogue landlord.

The landlord owns all five flats in Ali's building, and, according to Ali, his favourite pastime is to turn up unannounced, 'lurk around' outside for a bit, then knock on his tenants' doors to make incessant, pointless intrusions. He'll say: 'I just came to tell you I'll be back next week for...,' or 'I'm here to see another tenant and thought I'd pop round,' or even 'I'm just checking if my key works.' 'It's basically territorial pissing,' Ali said. '[It's as if he's trying to say] 'it's MY property, not yours... So you must not be allowed to feel comfortable at any time of the day or night!'He believes he is perfectly entitled to roam about the garden at 10.40pm, as he regards it as a 'shared space,' despite the fact that the garden was advertised as 'private' on the rental listing.

As affluent Londoners are priced out of the capital, they move to areas like Ali's old neighbourhood and start families, pushing up rents and house prices for longer-standing residents. It comes as no surprise to learn that the housing crisis is especially acute in Bristol. 'I have friends in their fifties still living in house shares,' Ali told me. Apparently, the sight of people sleeping in vans or cars parked up in the street is common. Bristol is among the least affordable areas by local authority in the country;[19] it is also among the top 50 local authorities for homelessness.[20]

Following a Freedom of Information request, *The Bristol Post* revealed in May 2018 that, as of the previous month, there were around 11,500 households on the social housing waiting list, while there were just 20 – yes, *twenty* – social rented properties available. The council's website reportedly warns prospective applicants: 'It's very unlikely that you'll be offered a council property because the waiting list is very long.'[21]

The result is that thousands of individuals and families are being forced to live in hotels and B&Bs for years at a time – or else sleep in a vehicle, or in sleeping bags on the street. Or, like Ali, they are forced to leave.

Interestingly, when I mentioned to Ali that I live in Sheffield, she said: 'I know quite a few people who have moved to Sheffield because they can't afford to live in Bristol any more. It's one of the places I've been considering myself, actually.' In 2018, the property listings website Zoopla revealed that, over the previous year, house prices in Sheffield had soared at a faster rate than any other city in the country.[22] According to totallymoney.com's 'Buy-to-Let Yield Map,' there are 25 postcodes in the UK where median rental yields are between seven and 10 per cent, and not one is in London. L1 (Liverpool) comes top, followed by FK3 (Falkirk) and G52 (Glasgow). Postcodes in Leicester, Leeds and Sheffield all make the top ten.

This is significantly more attractive than the 2-6 per cent yields London-based landlords are currently getting.[23] How long will it be before the mass exodus of young people from the South, coupled with the tantalising investment opportunities in the North, turn cities like Sheffield, Leeds, Manchester and Nottingham into the next Bristol?

It's time we do away with the narrative that the housing crisis is primarily a problem in London and the wider south east. Usually, when London is described as the 'worst hit' area in the housing crisis, it paints exploding rents and house prices as a meteor that careened into the UK sometime around the millennium, leaving a radioactive crater in the centre of London. The fallout from this impact then rippled outwards, generating difficulty (and vast capital gains) across the country, albeit lessening the farther you went from the impact zone.

Unfortunately, this is an oversimplification. London and the south east are not so much the 'worst hit' areas as the 'first hit' areas. Unless something drastic is done to tackle the root causes of the housing crisis, then conditions in the London private rented sector will only serve as a chilling preview of the future for all of generation rent.

This is why so many renters look to the future with rage and despair in equal measure. The worst thing about being stuck in the private rented sector is not just the current state of play – the mould, the stolen deposits, the eviction notices. It's the dawning realisation that housing affordability is still worsening and the housing crisis is just getting started.

22. Regulating the rental market

Regulation is supposed to stamp out bad practices until only good ones remain, but it can be crude. Humans are clever, and when their livelihoods are threatened by government edicts, they have a habit of finding ingenious ways to skirt those rules.

This is especially true of rules that apply to private lets, which are often set and then not enforced properly by struggling local authorities. A case in point: everyone thought the rogue landlords' register was a great idea until, six months after it was introduced, it was revealed that it did not contain a single name.[1]

I spoke to Jess, a friend from university, who'd seen my calls on Facebook for stories about life within the private rented sector. 'I've got a story for you,' she promised – and it did not disappoint. Her experience of renting in a fiercely competitive rental market helps to demonstrate why so many tenants feel that tougher regulations are the only way forward.

It all began when she moved to Leamington Spa, a small market town in the middle of England where there happens to be an acute shortage of rented housing. Why would a place like that be teaming with people clamouring for private rental properties? 'I don't know,' she said. 'It's quite a short train journey to London but... it's just absolutely mental and I didn't realise this. I'd set up a full day of viewing flats and by the time we'd actually got to Leamington Spa, half of them had already gone.'

This degree of ferocious competition did not bode well. On viewing the properties that *hadn't* been immediately snapped up, Jess realised she was right to be apprehensive. It started with a '£500 a month basement flat with this tiny slit window' that, in her dad's words, 'looked like a scene out of *Trainspotting*.' The whole 'flat' contained nothing but a 'rusted cooker in the corner,' which was 'more rust than cooker.' When the woman from the estate agency said: 'What do you think?,' Jess asked her, 'Are you going to replace that oven?,' and the woman replied: 'Oh no!'

Mercifully, the next flat was 'actually really nice.' It had 'a little lounge area, a kitchen, a bedroom and a little bathroom.' She thought nothing of the fact that, rather than a purpose-built apartment, it was a converted old Victorian house. She was just glad to have found somewhere she could picture herself living in. The relief didn't last long. She recalled: 'One of the first things that ticked me off was when I said I wanted the flat, they said, 'you're going to have to pay a £200 holding fee to make sure no one else can view it.' And this is on top of any admin fees they wanted.'

I asked if this was refundable. 'No. Completely non-refundable,' she said. 'It was literally £200 so that they would not then show the flat to anyone else.' By this point, Jess was 'desperate,' because her options were essentially the *Trainspotting* basement or this place. So, rather than protest, she 'paid the fee, moved in and was just relieved' to have finally secured a flat.

That's when the real trouble began. 'I think it was only two weeks that I'd been there and in the middle of the night I heard this gushing sound. I run into the kitchen and the sink was full of black sewage water. It was overflowing and the drain pipe burst off the bottom of the sink. Water was running everywhere, and it stank. This is at three in the morning and I'm frantically mopping it up.'

Horrifyingly, this 'sewage water' was bubbling up from the plughole of the sink Jess had been using to wash her dishes. Even worse, 'the next day it happened again,' she said, 'not quite as bad, but there was still this stuff in the sink.'

When Jess called the letting agent and asked for help, she was told: 'This is not our problem.' This is despite the fact that 'they were supposed to be a property management agent as well – it was their number that was on the contract to call if there was a problem.' Jess described the problem in detail, and the man on the end of the phone said, 'that sounds like external plumbing issues and so we're not liable for it.'

The agent's plumbing expertise seemed to be very detailed as to who was responsible for drainage, but very sparse as to how Jess might go about fixing a health hazard. She was instructed to contact the 'management company' responsible for the entire building for guidance. The agent told her: 'We have no idea who they are. Ask around.'

Jess set about knocking on doors and hoping her neighbours knew more about the building than she did. 'I eventually got hold of someone via a neighbour who was able to give me a number,' Jess went on, '...and it turns out the 'management company' was just a committee of residents who decided what kind of flowers they'd like in the carpark.'

Thankfully, Jess discovered that a handyman lived in the building, who 'very kindly managed to sort out' the exploding sink problem for free. She phoned the letting agent again to update them on the situation, and they were unrepentant – they 'insisted' that the sewage had 'clearly come from an external drainpipe and if it's outside the flat then it's not their problem.' They didn't waver even when Jess pointed out that her tenancy agreement contained 'a specific clause that says all drainage problems are the landlord's responsibility.'

This acute sanitation crisis wasn't the only thing that lingers in her memory from the flat. 'During the winter, it was so damp. There was mould growing on all of the walls – every single wall in the flat – and it wasn't just a bit of mould, it was coming off the wall in clumps. There were mushrooms growing. It was horrid. We had to clean it all the time.'

When she informed the agent that her home was turning into an exotic fungus sanctuary, Jess was told to 'keep the windows open.' This wasn't such an issue in the summer, but since the flat had only 'a couple of electric heaters' leaving the windows open in winter was not an option.

Jess recalled: 'About halfway through me living in this flat, my boyfriend moved in with me – which he probably regretted once he got there – and during the winter we would just live in the bedroom because it was the smallest room and we could just about keep that warm. Of an evening we would make dinner, then go to the bedroom with our dinner, shut the door, put the heating on and basically not leave. It felt like we were in some sort of Dickens novel.'

Jess felt able to joke about her experience, but her story has disturbing implications for the fundamental nature of the private rented sector. Rogue landlords tend to cluster at the bottom end of the market. But, as Jess' experience reveals, poverty is not necessary to drive you into the clutches of one.

All it takes is an abundance of tenants for landlords to choose from. Then, it doesn't matter if – like Jess – you have a good job, two degrees and a second language under your belt, the balance of power remains firmly in favour of the landlord. In short, when opportunities to exploit are plentiful, exploitation will flourish.

The power relationship is fundamentally skewed, to the point where landlords have to deliberately eschew the temptation to hike rents to the maximum and cut every corner going if they want to treat their tenants fairly.

Steve Mitchell, the Sheffield mortgage adviser and landlord who shared with me his experience of growing up in a council house, said something about being an 'ethical landlord' that stuck with me. Partly thanks to his upbringing, and partly thanks to his personal moral code, he told me that he refuses to exercise his right to evict a tenant at two months' notice, whatever the circumstances. 'I just think it's wrong – whatever the reason, one of my tenants is a single mum. It shouldn't be allowed,' he said. He also charges below local market rates, and never raises the rent for existing tenants – even for tenants who've been with him for several years. 'It's in their tenancy agreements that I technically can, but I'd rather keep the tenants happy.'

Granted, Steve is able to afford to do this because he owns both his rental properties outright; he does all the repairs himself rather than using an agent, and he doesn't desperately need the additional income his properties generate. He pointed out to me that quite often the demands made of tenants by risk-averse landlords are actually the stipulations of insurance companies or mortgage providers. These third parties often force landlords to charge minimum rents, or turn away certain tenants by threatening to void their mortgage or insurance contracts if they don't comply.

But the most telling pressure of all on landlords to fall into step with the rest of the market came when Steve reflected on how it made him feel to be letting out his properties £150 per month below local market rents. He said: 'I suppose I'm just a mug, really,' and laughed. He meant it in a jokey way, but I felt there was a twinge of resentment that his reward for trying to do the right thing was to make less money than all the landlords who provided a shoddy service to their tenants while squeezing them for every penny.

And here we get to the crux of the matter. Regardless of whether or not stricter regulation will solve or intensify the ills of private renting, the market in its 'natural state' is inherently biased towards rogue landlords.

Ethical landlords end up feeling done over, while negligent rogues reap the greatest rewards with apparent impunity. Thus, the 'freer' the market becomes (for landlords), the more loudly tenants end up calling for it to be regulated. If the current situation goes on for much longer, the clamour for politicians to take drastic action will be impossible to ignore.

What's more, as Dan Wilson Craw, head of campaign group Generation Rent, told me, there's an argument for controlling rents now even if it isn't a permanent fix. Building enough social and other low-cost homes to diffuse the housing crisis is likely to take several years, possibly decades. Rent controls can take some of the pressure off in the shorter term while more lasting solutions are being implemented.

Influential figures are starting to listen. The Mayor of London, Sadiq Khan, has called for the introduction of a London Living Rent, which would cap rents in the capital at one third of local average income.[2]

The Labour Party has also come out in favour of indefinite tenancies as standard, along with curbs to rent rises.[3]

Most importantly, in April 2019, the Secretary of State for Housing, Communities and Local Government at the time, James Brokenshire, announced the government's plans to take down the Goliath of the private rented sector: the Section 21 'no-fault' eviction.[4] This came after a campaign launched in 2018 by Generation Rent, ACORN, the New Economics Foundation and the London Renters' Union. Housing lawyer Giles Peaker announced the news on his popular housing blog Nearly Legal in stunned disbelief, writing 'I found out on Friday, under embargo, and am still taking a moment.'[5]

Renters are gearing up to go to war, and the government is finally taking note. And because there are now so many of them, landlords might not be able to carry out their threats of exiting the business in retaliation, because exiting the business might mean attempting to sell an entire property portfolio just as virtually every other landlord in the country is trying to do the same thing.

As we saw in Chapter 3. *A Short History of British Homes*, the rights of renters have waxed and waned. In the 19th century, the private rented sector was wholly unregulated, with the poorest families living in slums plagued by cholera outbreaks and high infant mortality rates. Following the introduction of universal suffrage in the early 20th century – where owning property was no longer a pre-requisite for being eligible to vote – the 90 per cent of the population living in the abysmal private rented sector began to make itself heard.

The 20th century then saw a series of progressive reforms that significantly improved life for the privately renting population. This culminated in the tightly-regulated protected tenancies that could be handed down to the next generation in 1977. Ironically, the popularity of social housing helped pave the way for these protections to be dismantled. Once private renters were outnumbered by home-owners and social renters, there was little they could do to stop Margaret Thatcher's government from re-writing the rulebook.

As we emerge from the liberalisation drive which began in the late 1980s, then, we are once again beginning to see a reversion to a 19th century-style free market, complete with slum conditions and meagre rights for long-term renting families. Now that the renting population is growing by the year, the pendulum swing back towards stricter regulation may be the natural next step.

Could a lightly-regulated private rental market work well?

Jess' experience in Leamington Spa wasn't the only story she shared with me. After several months of shivering and wheezing in a soggy flat, Jess got a new job in Exeter.

'It was really chalk and cheese, because the rental market in Exeter is OK,' she said. This is the point when Jess realised it's not normal to pay a 'securing fee' to make sure no one else views the property. In fact, when Jess asked the lettings agent if there'd be a fee to 'hold' the property, she was met with an expression of sheer bafflement, as if to say, 'No?! That would be weird!'

Being a fully-fledged city, I would have thought that Exeter would have worse problems for private tenants than somewhere like Leamington Spa. Why did she think the two markets were so diametrically opposed? 'Exeter's kind of unique because of where it is,' she said. 'Even though it's a big, lovely city, there's not a huge influx of young people looking for jobs.'

To see if the data backed up Jess's observations, I did a quick survey of the job openings available in each location respectively.

According to Indeed.co.uk, Exeter, with its population of 124,856, had 5,229 live job openings as of 24 February 2019. Comparatively, Leamington Spa, with its population of 57,812,[6] had 19,277 live job openings on the same day.[7] Despite having a population of roughly half the size, Leamington Spa boasts four times as many job opportunities as Exeter. It is a hive of economic activity, and thus it is buzzing with property investors.

By contrast, the scarcity of jobs in Exeter, which translates into a scarcity of tenants, seems to jolt the market's 'invisible hand' out of its slumber in the private rented sector. Not only was the place Jess and her partner rented in Exeter much nicer than their place in Leamington Spa for the same rent, but their new landlord was a shining example of professionalism and ethical conduct.

Jess said: 'They really left us to it. They did two inspections in the year and a half we were there, just to check we hadn't trashed the place, but they didn't bother us. There was nothing severely wrong with the house, I think the couple of times things were broken they replaced them straight away, no questions asked. So, they were a really good example of how to do it.'

This suggests that the private rented sector can regulate itself – so long as landlords are forced to compete for a limited number of tenants. As soon as renting becomes the dominant tenure in an unregulated market, then landlords and agents will exploit the fact that, in Jess's words, 'they're free to take the piss.'

Perhaps this is why, in the countries where renting is the norm, the private rented sectors are some of the most heavily regulated markets in the world.[8] Take the Netherlands, for instance, where 40 per cent of dwellings are rented, and three-quarters of rented homes are let by social housing associations.[9] In the social sector rents are set according to a points-based system that takes into account size, location, facilities, energy efficiency, and so on. Rents cannot be raised by more than a fixed percentage each year, and if the maximum rent for a particular dwelling falls below what the tenant is currently paying, the tenant can formally request a rent reduction.[10]

Even in the 'liberalised' private sector, getting thrown out of a Dutch rental property is a job of work. You'll have to spend time and energy racking up several police-documented noise complaints from neighbours, or trash your apartment, or neglect to pay the rent despite several written warnings. The landlord can theoretically evict a tenant if they urgently need the property for personal use, but this is rare because the landlord must then actually live in the property for at least a year following such an eviction.[11]

In early 2018, I caught up with my Dutch friend Anouk over Skype, who lives and works in Amsterdam with her boyfriend of ten years. We first met when I left a house share in Birmingham early and needed to find a replacement tenant. Anouk fitted the bill. She was a master's student at the University of Utrecht who was set to start a six-month work experience placement at a literary agency in Birmingham. I was keen to find out how renting in the UK compared with back home.

'It's definitely much fairer for tenants here,' she said. 'Me and my boyfriend don't qualify for the controlled rent housing because we earn too much. But it does give you piece of mind that there's a safety net there if you ever needed it. That safety net was obviously not there in the UK. In Birmingham there were so many more homeless people on the streets... I'm not used to seeing that in Dutch cities.'

The rental market is a lot more service-oriented too. 'Our rent payment is split into two elements,' she said. 'There's the rent itself, which goes to the landlord, and there's a service charge, which goes towards the maintenance costs of the flat. It's all very professional – if you have an issue, it gets fixed straight away.'

The whole system appears to be leaps and bounds ahead of the situation we have in the UK. I asked how it could be possible that the Dutch government had got it so right, when just a short hop over the North Sea, the British government had got it so wrong.

To this, Anouk she said something that surprised me: 'Don't romanticise the way it is here. We are still struggling to save anything because of the cost of renting. We want to buy a house, but it's going to take years for us to build up a deposit.' And just like that, I was back talking to a typical member of generation rent.

Doesn't the relatively secure private rented sector make renting more appealing as a lifestyle choice? She was clearly unenthused by the prospect. 'Maybe we could just carry on renting, but… I don't know if you can see well in this room–' she angled the camera so that the dim bedroom came into view '–but I didn't choose these decorations; these pictures hanging up are not my taste at all. It seems like a small thing but, when you rent… it's not really yours. Then there's also the cost. I don't know if we can afford to rent for the long-term and have children.'

I wanted to know what she thought was driving these high rents. 'One problem is that all the major cities are very close together,' she said, 'so there's not much opportunity to move to a cheap suburb. I could probably afford to buy a house where I grew up in the countryside, but then I'd struggle to find work, and it's not possible to commute that far. So as a result, the competition is so intense in the cities.' Again, a sense of *déjà vu* crept over me.

'Then you've got people who keep their property empty on purpose,' she added, 'just to make money from the prices going up. We call them...,' she paused for a moment, before saying 'we have a word for it in Dutch, but I don't know how to say it in English–'; and she mimed milking a cow.

I couldn't help but laugh. It was completely unexpected and painfully recognisable at the same time. According to a report by Dutch real estate investment company Bouwinvest, cities in The Netherlands have seen a huge influx of private investors in residential property since the global financial crisis, thanks in no small part to a decade of 'record-low interest rates.'

The situation is especially acute in Amsterdam, where housing is now 'out of reach for entire groups of people' – especially amongst those on middle incomes who earn too much to qualify for social housing.[12]

Anouk also told me how the Dutch housing shortage is further complicated by the influx of refugees to the country, who have a right to stay on humanitarian grounds, but for whom there simply aren't enough homes. 'It's one thing that is really horrible at the moment in this country,' Anouk told me, 'because it's giving very loud far right politicians an audience.'

This, in turn, provides a platform on which hardline free marketeers can argue for ending investment in social housing. All they need to do is conjure up the spectre of faceless migrants receiving houses while natives sit on waiting lists, and with enough repetition, they can start to change the national conversation, which is arguably exactly what has happened in Britain. And thus, the dearth of low-cost housing would worsen.

Private rented sector regulation: kill or cure?

In the private rental market, it's clear that regulation alone is not a panacea. Despite all of the legal protections afforded to tenants, people who don't qualify for social housing are still struggling to afford to build their own financial safety net in the Netherlands, because prices remain so high.

However, it's also clear that regulation does not 'kill' nor even dampen the private rented sector. If we compare Amsterdam with London, it's obvious that property prices can remain stubbornly high in major cities regardless of the number of rules landlords must follow.

Plus, the argument that rent controls lead to badly-maintained properties falls flat when considering that we already have a glut of dreadful-quality housing in the private rented sector. So long as people are clamouring to live in a particular location, shoring up tenants' legal rights doesn't make a dent in the viability of the market. It simply makes life a little easier for renters, which is welcome – even if it doesn't solve the deep-seated problems in the UK property market.

A report in 2015 by Civitas, a centre-right think tank, surprised everyone by essentially arriving at this very conclusion about the UK rental market. It argued that the government should embrace 'indefinite leases as the norm' and restrictions on 'in-tenancy rent increases to an index-linked ceiling,' alongside more characteristically right-wing measures like phasing out housing benefit and subsidising investment in new privately-rented housing stock.

Further, the report calls for 'a market that promotes supply rather than choking it off, and forces landlords to compete on price and quality rather than too often taking desperate tenants for granted.' It cites the example set by Germany, another country with a highly regulated rental market, where tenant satisfaction is substantially higher than it is in the UK.

This, the report suggests, is due in part to the autonomy and freedom afforded to German renters, saying that tenants generally tend 'to furnish properties themselves and take more of the responsibility for improvements, right down even to installing kitchens, which also reinforces their long-term commitment to a property.'[13]

There are problems in German cities with housing shortages and power imbalances created by corporate landlord monopolies.[14] But it's still in much better shape than the UK, where tenant groups are fighting for the basic rights enjoyed by their European counterparts.

23. With the community activists

On 21 February 2018, a grainy selfie of two young people clutching beers and looking slightly traumatised popped up on my Facebook newsfeed. They were both wearing bright red T-Shirts emblazoned with the word ACORN, and the post read:

'Recovering in the pub. Tonight 10 of us had to leave a council consultation on selective licensing early because a landlord physically threatened us when we gave testimony about our experiences of renting.'[1]

They turned out to be Jonny Butcher and Rohan Kon, community organisers for the ACORN renters' union. Community groups such as these fight for the rights of ordinary tenants.

Jonny and Rohan told of a roomful of landlords 'shouting and snarling,' with one calling Jonny 'a twat' and another telling them to 'shut the fuck up.' Appalled that an incident like this could be allowed to happen at a council-run event, I got in touch with ACORN to find out more.

'It was pretty incredible. I've never seen anything like it,' Jonny told me a few weeks later. We'd met in a pop-up café on the ground floor of Union St in Sheffield, a co-working space which hosts local freelancers, businesses and community interest groups, including ACORN's Sheffield branch. Jonny came across as both principled and diplomatic. It was hard to imagine him sending anyone flying into a blind rage, let alone being hounded by a group of strangers to 'step outside' for a fist-fight in the car park. Why, then, were emotions running so high?

The subject of the consultation was selective licensing. Selective licensing allows the council to select an area and require all private landlords in that area to get a license, regardless of the size of the property or number of tenants living there. The license costs £750 over five years, and the consequences for non-compliance are potentially severe. Landlords found to be in breach of the scheme can be issued with unlimited fines and have their licenses revoked – effectively banning them from trading in the selective licensing area.[2]

A council might decide to designate an area for selective licensing if it has acute problems with overcrowding, vermin, health and safety hazards or anti-social behaviour. But the council can't simply point to an area and demand that all its landlords obtain a licence. There must be solid evidence that additional local authority scrutiny is necessary, hence the consultation.

During a two-year investigation, Sheffield City Council's inspectors found many of the rented properties along three major roads, London, Abbeydale and Chesterfield, breached fire safety regulations because they didn't have adequate fire escapes, despite being directly above takeaways and restaurants.[3] The area is populated largely by students, professional sharers and young families, and is one of the most ethnically diverse in Sheffield.[4] Some 70 per cent of the properties investigated were found to contain 'serious health and safety hazards,' including fire risks, damp, mould and excessive cold.[5] Michelle Houston, who works for the council in Private Housing Standards, told the *Sheffield Star* that at the extreme end: 'We've found properties that don't have a toilet, it's just a bucket on a corridor.'[6]

You might think all of this amounts to pretty clear evidence that an intervention was warranted. Nonetheless, the reprisal from potentially affected landlords and letting agents was fierce. Knowing that all tenants in the designated area had been given a questionnaire to fill in, landlords and agents embarked upon a campaign. One landlord warned in the *Sheffield Star* that rents could be hiked by as much as £50 a month,[7] effectively four times the cost of the license itself. Despite the fact that, 'in public meetings landlords exclaimed that their properties were good and that [the council] should go and look at them,' the council wrote in its cabinet report that when it asked for 'contact details to follow them up, most either refused or gave false information.'

In the end, in an area with 1,040 properties earmarked for selective licensing, just 13 properties were put forward for a voluntary inspection and these were owned by four landlords and one property agent. Even among some of the properties proactively volunteered for inspection, which you'd expect to represent the best of the bunch, life-threatening fire hazards were found by council officers.[8]

'We ran a campaign to make sure as many tenants and residents as possible were participating in that consultation,' Jonny said, explaining that, without this proactive approach, there was a risk that individual tenants might be cowed by threats of rent hikes into opposing selective licensing.

Once it became apparent that ACORN was rallying local

tenants, a group of landlords hostile to the licensing scheme hit back. On the day of the final open discussion forum, Jonny and his fellow ACORN members got wind of 'a massive WhatsApp group' through a landlord ally, which was inviting landlords in the area to come down to the council meeting and cause trouble.

'They were definitely looking for a fight,' Jonny said. As a result, ACORN put out a last-minute call on Facebook for support:

'Hey everyone – really need your help on this tonight. Just found out Landlords are planning to mobilise en masse to oppose [the licensing scheme] at a council hosted drop-in session tonight from 6-9pm at Bramall Lane. We're going there to show them that renters in Sheffield support this and not let the landlords win. Can you join us? Drop us a message, or just turn up.'[9]

Despite this last-ditch call for assistance, when the ten ACORN members and tenants due to give testimony before the panel arrived, they were hopelessly outnumbered. 'There were at least 50 landlords, probably more like 60 or 70,' Jonny said. The council had anticipated, perhaps understandably, a relatively staid affair. They were wholly unprepared for what was about to happen.

The forum was held in the Platinum Suite function room at Bramall Lane Stadium, home of Sheffield United football club. A panel of council officers was due to put questions to the room. Both sides would then have an opportunity to air their views via a microphone that was being passed around.

'Straight away, it descended into chaos,' Jonny said. 'As far as I can remember, hardly a single question was asked. It was basically just landlords shouting and being abusive.' He was also amazed at the fury over the cost of the scheme: 'It was going to cost them about £3 a week. Judging by some of the cars parked up outside before the event, these guys weren't exactly on the breadline.'

That said, Jonny and his colleagues think they know why this measure was perceived by so many as an existential threat: 'To get a license, you need to pass a 'fit and proper person' test,' he told me. This means that if your properties aren't meeting certain basic criteria; if you've got any past criminal convictions, or it is deemed that you are not capable of carrying out your duties as a landlord for whatever reason, then you will be denied a license. 'This is what we think was driving them to be so aggressive,' said Jonny. 'They knew they wouldn't pass the test.'

The meeting had dragged on fruitlessly for over an hour, and the tenants were beginning to lose patience. According to ACORN, its members had barely had the chance to speak, and whenever they did manage to get a word in, they kept being cut off and shouted down before they could finish. In a bold move, when Jonny finally got hold of the microphone, he told the room: 'Please everyone, you're acting like school children here, I would like to ask a question and I've been waiting an hour and a half.'

This did not go down well. Several stood up and started heckling; the guy in front 'kicked off' and told Jonny to come 'outside, now.' The council lost control of the situation, and generally things started to get 'quite scary.' 'There was nothing we could do but leave as quickly as possible,' he said.

What is a tenants' union?
In the last few years, renters up and down the country have been joining unions. While several renters' groups exist in London,

most prominently the London Renters' Union, elsewhere in the UK ACORN is leading the charge to transform the lives of its members through the power of collective action. But what separates these unions from ordinary charities, lobbyists and campaign groups? And what separates them from old-fashioned trade unions?

Quite a lot, it turns out. ACORN is the gig economy's answer to the trade union. 'With precarious work undermining people power, we felt there was a need for a union outside the workplace,' Jonny explained. 'We exist to counteract negative forces like welfare cuts, poverty, the stresses and strains of being a single parent... whatever the people in the community need help with. It just so happened that, after listening to lots of people and finding out their concerns, housing issues came out top.'

Despite being only four years old in the UK, the original organisation was formed in 1970 the US, and the name stands for the less catchy 'Association of Community Organizations for Reform Now.' The movement was inspired by self-described 'radical' Saul Alinksy, who defined his seminal book 'Rules for Radicals' as Machiavelli's *The Prince* 'for the Have-Nots.'[10]

Alinsky's methods centre on bringing communities together to fight common struggles (and often, common adversaries). Barack Obama's younger years spent working as a community organiser in Chicago are thought to have been a defining phase of his political career,[11] and the Alinskyan idea of knocking on doors to form community action groups ended up becoming a cornerstone of David Cameron's 'Big Society' agenda.[12]

This is where ACORN's UK incarnation comes in. Nick Ballard, one of ACORN UK's founding members in Bristol, was trained as a community organiser by the government's flagship scheme.

Following this, he and his co-founders decided to 'start a union in the community.' It was around this time that Jonny got involved as a member and volunteer. 'We started off knocking doors in this one area in Bristol, and four years later we've expanded into five cities,' he explained.

'The way it works is that it's a membership organisation, so if you want to join you have to pay membership dues', Jonny told me. The dues are 'pay what you can,' but the organisation asks that you try to commit one hour's wage per month. 'We think that's the way it's got to be, because if you want an organisation that's democratically run and controlled by the people, then it's got to be funded by the people.' The funding pays for full-time organisers, who co-ordinate teams of volunteers that focus on four main areas: campaigns; member defence; communications and recruitment.

Member defence is the union's mainstay, where it serves literally as the last line of defence for tenants and their families facing revenge evictions, deposit theft, harassment and criminal negligence. One family was saved from an illegal eviction by ACORN members forming a human chain outside their home. Another tenant had an abusive landlord who was forced to back down after ACORN protesters staged a noisy demonstration outside his e-cigarette business. The union's policy of direct action arises from the fact that, often by the time tenants come to ACORN for help, the legal avenues have failed.

'It's been a really successful year this year – we grew our membership, and we opened two new branches,' Jonny said. 'There is a feeling of anger in this country that an increasingly narrow pool of people are controlling all the resources. It's our job to channel that anger.'

Of course, not all tenants are angry at their individual landlords. But the anger Jonny is talking about is more deep-rooted. 'Obviously, some tenants have great landlords,' he said, 'but whether or not you have a great landlord or a bad one, the balance of power is always in favour of the landlord. That's the issue we're trying to fight.'

I told him that, in my experience, landlords tend to believe the opposite to be true.

He said: 'When I get frustrated is when people say: "Well there are bad landlords and bad tenants." Fundamentally you can't compare the two. If you're a landlord, and you get a bad tenant, the worst thing that's going to happen to you is you'll lose money. If you're a tenant who gets a bad landlord, not only might you lose all your money, you might lose your home, you might end up on the street. At the extreme end, you might die. The point is, very few tenants choose to be a tenant, while every landlord makes an informed choice: it's a business risk. Being a tenant is not a business risk.'

It's a strong argument. Still, I wonder if 'people power' is sufficient to stand up to the lobbying power of landlord groups like the National Landlord's Association. The latter boasts a full-time research department, the money to commission studies from research groups and universities, and contacts in Westminster to request tweaks to legislation that goes against its interests.[13] Can a group of ordinary people set the agenda when they lack that financial clout?

For Jonny, it's all about playing the long game. 'We start with local campaigns to build power from the ground up,' he said. 'If you're trying to change the law, and you've only got ten mates to back you up, you might not get very far. But if there's 10,000 of you,

you've got a real chance.'

The union also draws strength from its democratic structure, ensuring that there are as many members as possible backing the campaigns they choose to pursue: 'The issues we fight are the issues our members decide. Rent control, better enforcement of standards, ending Section 21... I'm pretty sure they're on the horizon.' (Jonny and I spoke not long before the Section 21 campaign was launched.)

Like its member defence work, ACORN's campaign work is designed to have the maximum PR impact. For example, ACORN researchers found a clause in TSB's buy-to-let lending policy that banned landlords from letting their properties to benefit claimants. It also just so happened that ACORN's fourth birthday was approaching, which was due to coincide with the 10th anniversary of the global financial crisis. It was an opportunity too good to miss.

Activists stormed TSB branches across the country, waving placards and shouting into megaphones. Aware of the PR damage the stunt was likely to cause, TSB swiftly confirmed that it would be scrapping the benefits clause, which they claimed they had been reviewing 'for some time.'[14]

NatWest was next on the hitlist. NatWest's parent company RBS was handed £45.5 billion in state aid to save it from going under in 2008. Ten years on, it made headlines for telling one of its buy-to-let mortgage borrowers to evict a tenant on benefits or face a crippling penalty fee. To put pressure on the bank, ACORN protesters descended on city centre branches of NatWest waving flags and banners, chanting 'NatWest, say yes to DSS!' – to the tune of *Go West* by the Village People.[15] Several branches were forced to close. While the bank did not capitulate immediately, it promptly invited housing charity Shelter to help it conduct a review into its lending policies.[16] Then, in March 2019, the bank agreed to meet ACORN's demands.[17]

But what about that common refrain – that the end of Section 21 will lead to landlords leaving the sector, putting further pressure on the supply of rented housing? What if rent controls lead to landlords neglecting to invest in renovations and maintenance, as economists so often caution will happen when you interfere with the market? Jonny said:

> 'When people object to rent controls and other regulations, what they don't realise is that, we aren't interested in whether or not landlords sell their investments. This is exactly why we build a union. Say we just did a one-off campaign for rent control, but we didn't deal with the issue of shit quality housing… we probably wouldn't get that far. Rent control is something that would be an immediate help towards the cost of living, as it would put a cap on the amount rents can go up by… but if rent control then leads to other problems for tenants, we'll fight those too.'

Ultimately, whether you believe that direct action is the right way forward is irrelevant. Looked at through the lens of cold Machiavellian logic, ACORN's approach and that of similar organisations is often the most effective means of getting results.

The law isn't working. The market isn't working. Milder, more diplomatic forms of campaigning have yielded only incremental changes. If millions are facing the prospect of a lifetime of insecure and often unsafe housing, and they feel completely abandoned by the political and legal establishment, then it's no wonder they're starting to lose patience.

'I don't actually care about whether I own a home or rent a home,' Jonny told me, 'and most of our members probably don't care about that either. We just want three things: security, affordability and decent living conditions.'

'It's a war out there'

When Chartered Surveyor Stephen Hill was invited to begin his talk at the Manchester Friends Meeting House as part of a conference hosted by the Housing Futures collective,[18] he stepped out in front of the audience brandishing a large wooden sword.

'You may be wondering why I've brought this,' he said casually. 'Well...It plays a rather important role in the story I am going to tell.' He added: 'It's also a rather handy pointer,' gesturing towards the projector screen, and the audience laughed.

He recounted a visit he made a few years back to a 'not-terribly-salubrious part of south Boston' in the US, as part of his investigations into community housing projects. The US proved a particularly good case study for this type of inquiry, since its politicians didn't tend to get involved with 'affordable or state-provided housing.'

Instead, 'the market decides everything.' Hill wanted to see what people were doing to escape the chokehold of market forces in the absence of political support for non-market alternatives.

Upon arrival he was taken to what on first appearance seemed to be 'a big public meeting.' This, it transpired, was a kind of 'talk show' held for the benefit of people facing homelessness. The show – hosted by an organisation called Vida Urbana or City Life – provided a platform for people under threat of imminent eviction or foreclosure on their homes to tell their stories.

One by one, Stephen explained, 'members of the audience would come up and tell their story about what happened to them in their lives.' Afterwards they would be 'connected with advisors from Harvard Law School' to see what actions could be taken to buy them some time to find somewhere else to live. Mostly, this was just a case of ensuring the landlord or mortgage lender was following 'due process.' But occasionally, it could work to postpone the eviction or foreclosure itself.

An aspect of this whole spectacle that especially caught Hill's imagination occurred after the storytelling, but before the audience member was ushered offstage to speak to the legal advisers. The show's presenter would ask the storyteller: 'Will you fight to stay in your home?' to which they would respond, 'Yes.' The audience would then call out in unison: 'And we will fight with you!'

The important thing to bear in mind here, Hill stressed, was that the audience was made up of individuals who 'were just people like you.' He went on: 'They were black. They were white. They were middle-class. They were working class. They were young. They were old. People in their twenties, also past working age. All in situations where their lives were very precarious, who were being ruthlessly exploited by either their landlord or the mortgage companies.'

Hill has devoted the majority of his life to the housing sector. According to his bio on the Housing Forum, he has '40 years of public and private sector experience of housing, planning and delivering mixed-use development, urban extensions, new settlements, and community-led neighbourhood regeneration.'[19]

Forty years is almost the exact span of the unravelling of the British housing dream. Over the course of his career, Hill has seen the meteoric rise of housing as an investment expected to generate bigger returns than any other asset class. He has fought for improved access to decent-quality housing and stronger communities over the decades, even as the humble family home was being turned into a lucrative retirement strategy.

If anyone had a right to be weary, humourless and downright cynical, he did. Despite this, his message wasn't one of despair. It was one of resounding hope.

Ostensibly, he was championing Community Land Trusts as the answer – or the concept of 'Community-led housing' at large. He is the Chair of the UK Cohousing Network and a board member of the National Community Land Trust Network. But his message was more fundamental than that. 'Never let a good political slogan go to waste,' he said. Solving the housing crisis is, at heart, about 'taking back control.'

All of the various 'models' of community-led housing, Hill argued, share a common characteristic: 'It's that citizens are coming together to provide the housing for themselves and their communities, that neither the market, nor that state, is offering.' The particular 'model' in question is nothing more than one expression of this underlying principle.

This concept sits within a nuanced ideological space. The culture wars of our times pivot around the clash between capitalism and socialism, private and public, individual and state. But Hill's vision alludes to something else entirely. He dismisses the idea that politicians should be expected to provide solutions. But he also talks of the need for citizen and state to work together to empower individuals and communities to help themselves.

It recalls the work of Elinor Ostrom, who won the Nobel Prize in Economics in 2009 for disproving the theory of 'the tragedy of the commons.'[20] Since the early 19th century, it was widely accepted that all forms of collective ownership led to the decay and abuse of common resources. When everybody owns everything, the argument goes, nobody can be bothered to look after anything. Thus, private ownership of everything is justified and necessary for the responsible stewardship of the Earth's natural resources. Ostrom's ground-breaking research revealed, through extensive fieldwork, that communities can work together to share common assets without destroying or depleting them beyond redemption. She identified eight 'design principles' necessary for effective common resource management. Key among these is that the direct, regular users of the shared resources must be integral to the decision-making process.

The author and activist David Bollier, writing in *Forbes* not long after Ostrom's Nobel victory was announced in 2009, drew comparisons between her ideas and how communities self-regulate on the internet. He points to open-source software, Wikipedia and the Internet Archive as examples of self-moderating communities, where each one acts 'as a conscientious steward of its collective wealth.' Community-led housing is underpinned by similar principles.

Currently, property development is the preserve of those with the deepest pockets, and the planning system favours land speculation over genuinely affordable housebuilding. Until this changes, we're unlikely to see generation rent 'taking back control' of their housing prospects.

Which brings me back to the sword. 'The property market – it's a war out there. That's what they're saying in the States.' Hill told the audience. 'People say it isn't happening here,' he added, before dismantling this quaint notion with his many stories from the front-lines of housing war raging across the UK. There were too many to list all of them here, but one in particular stood out.

A leaseholder was facing a compulsory purchase order on his flat. The council wanted to sell the building in which the flat was situated to a private developer for a fancy 'urban regeneration' project. The problem was, the sum the leaseholder was being offered in compensation was nowhere near enough for him to purchase one of the flats in the new development. Despite the leaseholder's objections, the developer argued that it wasn't 'financially viable' for it to provide more than a token amount of 'affordable' housing.

Dissatisfied with this explanation, the leaseholder went to the information commissioner, and eventually to the high court, for a copy of the viability calculations on which this argument was based. This process revealed a startling truth: nobody in the public domain had this information. The developer had arm-wrestled the council into accepting its demands without providing a shred of evidence to back up its claims.

This in turn gave rise to a local public inquiry. Activists and planning officials alike pressed the developer on the amount of money it claimed it could put towards non-luxury accommodation. Based on the scant amount of technically 'affordable' housing it had offered to provide, the QC for the developer was reported to have said that 'we really have got nothing out of it.'

As this hearing was taking place, one of the campaigners anonymously received a PowerPoint presentation. This turned out to be the original pitch that had been made to city investors at the outset of the project. 'When you do your planning for a village, you calculate how much money you're going to make from selling one of your properties,' Hill explained. The figure investors had been given as an inducement to buy into the scheme was, 'rather unsurprisingly,' considerably higher than the figure submitted on the planning application.

'Can anyone guess by how much?' Hill asked.

'£50 million?' one audience member suggested.

'£300 million,' Hill replied.

The audience laughed again, only this time it was mixed with a sharp intake of breath.

When this discrepancy was highlighted, the QC reportedly 'jumped up' and shot back: 'Well of course [the two documents are] different, they were made for different purposes!'

What this, and countless other examples demonstrate, is that passivity or even modest resistance is liable to be steamrollered by wealthier, more powerful interests, whose access to expensive lawyers and political influence make them invulnerable to the pushback of lone individuals. What gets results is collective and sustained action.

When Hill clicked onto the last slide of his presentation, the words: 'WE ARE NOT YOUR ASSETS' were emblazoned in white across a bright red background.

Then he handed his sword to one of his fellow speakers. He asked: 'Are you willing to fight, to ensure that you don't become one of their assets?' The speaker obligingly raised the sword in triumph and shouted: 'Yes!'

And the audience boomed back: 'And we will fight with you!'

24. Could build-to-rent help?

A new business model in property development is promising to revolutionise the private rented sector: build-to-rent. Rather than selling off newly-built homes to investors, build-to-rent companies design high-quality apartment blocks specifically aimed at catering to the needs of generation rent. The idea is that the products on offer are not just places to live but come with a complete service package, comprising an on-site maintenance team, concierge, gym, pool, games room, study space and roof terrace, depending on the individual development.

From the outside, they're indistinguishable from office blocks: towering plate-glass monoliths that blend in seamlessly with multi-storey car parks, modern art museums and inner-city skyscrapers. The British Property Federation recently produced a map showing that these vertical communities are springing up the length and breadth of the UK. Nearly all are situated in busy urban areas, with the prominent hotspots outside London being Manchester, Liverpool, Leeds and Birmingham.[1]

Lots of people – and not just the developers themselves – are excitedly proclaiming build-to-rent to be the future of private renting, and even a solution to the housing crisis. Savills covered the subject in 2018 in a blog post entitled: *Things Can Only Get BTR*. Developers Knight Frank forecast market growth of 180 per cent between 2017 and 2023[2], and a British Property Foundation report published around the same time found widespread cross-party support for the idea, with 75 per cent of MPs of all colours signalling their approval. No other proposal to solve the housing crisis garnered anywhere near such widespread, multilateral endorsement from MPs.[3]

Not only that, the government has put its money where its mouth is. In 2014, it launched the £3.5 billion Private Rented Sector Housing Guarantee to lend money to developers for the construction and management of purpose-built rental units.[4] Some £65 million in funding was injected in August 2017. The government said: 'The deal will help to unlock over 7,600 new, high quality homes at the Wembley Park development in Brent, London, one of the largest strategic regeneration projects in the country. At least 6,800 of these homes will be for rent.'[5]

Does this mean that the die-hard proponents of the home-ownership dream are finally waving a white flag? Perhaps not quite. After all, Help to Buy and shared ownership schemes are alive and kicking. Nonetheless, the government's commitment to the build-to-rent sector doesn't end there. In 2017, the Homes and Communities Agency (now Homes England) bought a £25 million 10 per cent stake in the nation's first ever 'Private Rented Sector REIT' (Real Estate Investment Trust). The fund is run by Sigma Capital, a property developer turned investment manager. Promising to target an annual six per cent rental yield, rising to 10 per cent in total returns after capital appreciation is factored in, it's no wonder the investors piled in. The company met its £250 million investment target almost as soon as it launched in May 2017 and quickly became heavily oversubscribed.[6]

As a result of all this activity, the sector is gaining momentum. After years of tentative dabbling and outright disinterest in rented accommodation, big, so-called institutional investors – pension funds, insurance companies and the sovereign wealth funds of foreign governments – have finally started to get in on the action.

For example, the former Olympic Village flats in east London, which now comprise a smart build-to-rent complex, are jointly owned by developer Delancey and the Qatari government's sovereign wealth fund. Another BTR company, Essential Living, is funded by M3 Capital Partners, which is underpinned by American pension schemes. Other heavyweights to join the BTR party are M&G Investments, Legal & General, the Dutch pension fund APG, and the Australian asset manager Macquarie Capital.[7]

Safe to say that the investors are sold on the idea. But what about the tenants?

Who are these futuristic apartments really for?

Build-to-rent apparently exists to cater to the increasing numbers of young professionals, and even families, that are now starting to cluster in the big cities, reversing the trend towards suburbanisation that took place in the 20th century up until the 1990s. This was the finding of think-tank Centre for Cities, and, if it is correct, suburbia is about to become a whole lot sleepier.[8]

All of the problems with the old-school private rented sector are but a distant dream in the promotional literature of London-based Essential Living, which, having been founded way back in 2012, is one of the older companies in the build-to-rent sector. Pets aren't just tolerated, but welcomed; one to three year tenancy agreements are available as standard, and there's 24/7 access to the onsite 'residents' team,' at the ready to help you with 'any issue, whether big or small.'[9]

When the *Financial Times* interviewed 30-year-old Rebecca Stevenson, a private tenant in the East village (formerly the athletes' village at the 2012 Olympics) she said that, 'when my parents come and visit, they say, 'This is so cool. It's like a retirement village, but with young people''. She has friends aged between 20 and 60 on the complex. Prior to moving there, she had never in her life spoken to her neighbours. There are all manner of social events ranging from 'pounding house parties' to 'knit and natter groups.'[10]

These schemes are unabashedly for generation rent. Once a political catchphrase to highlight a growing social problem, 'generation rent' can now also refer to an aspirational class of millennials who have embraced renting as the new normal. *Generation rent and the end of 'forever furniture'* – ran a 2018 headline in the *Financial Times,* reporting on the nomadic lifestyles led by today's young professionals, who nonetheless, 'because of social media and Instagram' are 'definitely decorating'. Interior designers are apparently having to respond to this new, transient way of living among the younger generation, with suggestions like 'lean overlapping picture frames against the walls' to get around the common interdiction against picture hooks, Blu-Tack and other paint-damaging wall hangings tenants often have to contend with.[11]

The Times reported that the fashion industry had made a bid to extend the renting concept even further by targeting generation rent with 'pay-as-you-wear' clothing services.[12] Insurers are starting to impress on millennial renters the importance of income protection and critical illness cover – policies that pay the bills or pay out a lump sum if you become unable to work, formerly marketed exclusively at homeowners.

But does the generation rent being fawned over by property developers and retailers in general bear any resemblance to the generation rent undergoing a socio-political struggle for somewhere to sleep that doesn't cause respiratory infections?

Research conducted by American investment management company JLL found that, across London, build-to-rent complexes cost 11 per cent more on average than local market rents. Given that market rents in London are already deemed to be by far the least affordable in the country, rents that cost 11 per cent more than this can only be described as 'super-unaffordable.'[13]

In 2018, a *Guardian* article on the shortcomings of build-to-rent highlighted that renting a one-bedroom flat in the Get Living development at Elephant and Castle in south London costs £1,841 a month. Since the company stipulates that tenants need to earn a household income of 30 times the rent, this would necessitate an income of £60,000 a year for an individual tenant or a couple both earning £30,000 a year and willing to live in *very* cramped conditions. Even then, £900 a month on rent for someone on £30,000 a year still amounts to about half their take-home pay.[14]

The market demonstrably can provide top-quality rented homes accompanied by responsive and efficient customer service. It can provide long-term, secure tenancies. It can facilitate a range of lifestyle choices, including the desire to keep pets and start families, and it can foster a genuine sense of community spirit. It just can't do it for anyone earning a normal income.

SECTION V. SOCIAL HOUSING NOW

25. Living on a council estate

If private rented accommodation is too expensive or you get evicted, you can, in theory, turn to social housing. But now the system is under so much strain, social housing is no longer a credible option for many.

First, it is hard to get. The number of people far exceeds the properties available and some people have little chance of ever being offered one. Places are given according to a 'priority need' system, where the vulnerable and those with children are given priority over healthy adults with no dependants. In June 2018, 1.15 million people were on social housing waiting lists, while only 290,000 social homes became available in the previous year. Two-thirds wait for at least a year to be housed, half for at least two years, and over a quarter wait for more than five years.[1] If applicants can't afford to rent privately while they wait, they may have to live in a hostel, where conditions are often cramped and grim.

Where council housing is offered, it is often (though not always) unappealing, too. Right to Buy didn't just affect the quantity of public housing stock. It had a perverse effect on the quality, too. In the early 1980s, the most popular homes – three-

and four-bedroom family houses with good-sized gardens – went first. After this, the people choosing to buy were better off and more likely to be in a desirable neighbourhood.

By the early 1990s, few of the homes that remained were desirable. Flats in high-rise tower blocks[2] were hardest to shift, even at half price.[3] As a result, the council housing stock went through a process of reverse natural selection, or what might be crudely termed 'survival of the shittest.'

According to research by Criminology Professor Stephen Farrall and others, the 'priority need' system exacerbated the unusual social mix on council estates. Introduced in 1977, the system favoured families with children, pregnant women and vulnerable adults, and in 2002 was expanded to encompass 16-17 year olds, 18-20 year old care leavers, those fleeing violence or the threat of violence, and those vulnerable after leaving care, the armed forces or prison.[4] It's self-evidently right to give priority to those in the greatest need when allocating social housing. But given the dwindling number of homes remaining in the social rented sector, the system has changed the social composition of British council estates. Poverty, drug abuse, unemployment and crime have become concentrated disproportionately in them.[5]

This means the worst-hit estates can be deeply unappealing places to live, even to those in desperate need. A housing association officer (who wished to remain anonymous, so we'll call him Geoff), told me that even despite waiting lists bursting at the seams, one ex-council tower block contained a huge proportion of places where even many homeless people refused to live. How can an indoor home, however grotty, seem preferable to living on the streets, or in a hostel? Geoff explained:

> 'The other week we picked up some CCTV footage of someone coming out of one of the lifts with a huge knife. There are also some issues with squatting, and drug use. And the fact that, once you're there, and you've accepted a social home, your chances of ever leaving are practically nil. So, on the one hand you might think, well, beggars can't be choosers. But when you look at all the different factors, you understand why people would prefer to stay in temporary accommodation and hold out for something better.'

While the composition of estates started to change decisively from the class and wealth balance achieved in the post-war years, council tenants began to be disparaged in popular culture.

The term 'underclass' was first popularised by an American social policy researcher, Charles Murray, in 1989. Invited by *The Sunday Times* to find out whether the so-called 'plague' he had documented in the US was spreading to the UK, Murray found exactly that: a subsection of society who he considered to be products of their own degeneracy, trapped in a self-perpetuating state of fecklessness by government handouts.[6]

During the 1990s and early noughties, a stereotype of a council tenant emerged: 'the chav.' Gangs of teenagers in lurid tracksuits sporting chunky necklaces, hoop earrings and high ponytails became a source of fear and ridicule in equal measure. On TV, the likes of Vicky 'yer-but-no-but' Pollard and Lauren 'does my face look bovvered?' Cooper would provide the evening's family entertainment, followed by the customary *Newsnight* segment on gangs of hooded 'youths' terrorising neighbourhoods, violating Antisocial Behaviour Orders and generally hanging around on street corners looking intimidating. Before long, rumours began to swirl that the word 'chav' was an acronym for 'Council Housed And Violent.' The theory turned out to be bogus,[7] but the fact that it caught on is telling. Council estates weren't just places where troublesome characters ended up, they were deemed to be the birthplace of society's ills.

From *Principles of Social Housing Reform* by Stephen Greenhalgh and John Moss

A report by the Localis think-tank in 2009 – cited in a blog by John Boughton,[8] author of *Municipal Dreams* – intellectualised why this happened. Entitled *Principles for Social Housing Reform,* it was authored by Stephen Greenhalgh and John Moss, a London councillor and an estate regeneration specialist respectively. In it, the authors identify what they call a 'virtuous circle of dependency' *(see illustration).* The assumption is that 'bricks and mortar subsidy' is the first step on the slippery slope that culminates in 'poor health, crime and social poverty,' which then becomes 'ever-increasing cost to government.'

More recently, TV shows like *Benefits Street* and *Saints and Scroungers* have helped to bolster the idea that everyone living in publicly-funded housing is either a charity case or a workshy 'chav.' The message being sent to 'ordinary' people is loud and clear: don't live on a council estate if you can help it. Either you will be terrorised by gangs of hoodies, or your children will grow up to be idle idiots. Even the prepositions we use to describe where people live have subtle yet revealing implications. For example, you live 'in' a good neighbourhood, where you're woven into the fabric of society. Conversely, you live 'on' a council estate, where, no matter how close-knit your community, you sit on top of the social fabric like a deadweight.

So, what is living on a modern estate like?

A modern-day council estate

On a warm Wednesday evening in Spring 2018, a small group of us were standing outside a block of council flats near Sheffield city centre. It's one of the most socially deprived areas in the city, yet it's only a few minutes away from streets of grand stone-built

Victorian homes with bay windows and long leafy driveways. The building exterior has been spruced up with colourful panelling to mitigate the 1970s concrete jungle aesthetic.

I was volunteering with ACORN, the renters' union, to raise awareness of a new neighbourhood action group being set up by its Sheffield branch. Jonny, the branch leader, briefed us on the evening's plan, while another volunteer handed out biros and questionnaires on clipboards. Before my door-knocking partner and I set off, I remembered a tip I'd been given the previous week by a long-time community organiser: 'Make sure you go to the top floor and then to the end of the corridor and work back – just in case you get followed.'

Despite our initial misgivings, we quickly learned that our biggest obstacle was getting people to talk. At one point we spent five minutes negotiating with a small boy on the other side of a letterbox, which ended in him gleefully kicking a football at the foot door and telling us to 'go away.' After several flats, not much luck and a lot of refinement of our technique for pushing flimsy leaflets through junk-mail-proof letterboxes, someone finally opened the door and agreed to chat.

She was a long-term council tenant who we'll call Maureen. She told us how she'd always worked and had never been on benefits. Generally, she was pretty happy with her situation, remarking that, 'the council's always good if I ever need anything fixing.'

We were pleased to hear she'd found the council quick to deal with problems, but this didn't tally with the surroundings. The window in the door of a nearby flat was smashed, and there was evidence of fire damage. An old sofa lay in the middle of the walkway. I asked her if she considered vandalism and fly-tipping an issue, or if the abandoned sofa and burnt-out apartment were just one-offs.

'The thing is,' she leant in and lowered her voice, 'you can't stop people from doing things like that. The council can come and clean it up, but they can't force people to take pride in their own home. People used to be out on these corridors, sweeping up, keeping it nice. Now most people don't seem to care. At the end of the day it's people that make a mess. So what can you do?'

Reading between the lines, Maureen seemed to be wistful about the declining sense of community in the area, but felt powerless to do anything about it. 'We used to have a TARA [Tenants' and Residents' Association],' she told us, 'but someone was caught with their hand in the till, so I think that's all run by the council now.'

Despite our best efforts to pitch the neighbourhood action group as a chance to rebuild that sense of community, she politely declined our invitation to attend the first meeting. It seems that neighbourhood activism is easier to promote when people believe that the root cause of their problems is a bad landlord or a bad authority figure in general. It's much harder to engage someone who believes that the true issue is merely a 'bad neighbourhood.' If, like Maureen, you walk past drug dealers and emaciated addicts on the way to and from your front door each day, it's easy to understand why you'd see your fellow citizens, and not government policy, as the cause of the deterioration.

And yet, the fact remains that people like Maureen – employed full-time, devoid of 'complex needs' and not in receipt of benefits, are sent to the back of the queue on social housing waiting lists nowadays, virtually excluding them from social housing.

Maureen will be able to stay in her home for life. But as far as the government is concerned, social housing is no longer for the likes of her. It's for the downtrodden souls she encounters on her way to work, buying their latest fix in a darkened stairwell.

The upshot is, the ghettoisation of council estates is not, as Charles Murray would have us believe, due to the spontaneous emergence of an underclass – the product of a society with declining morals and an overly lavish welfare state. It is the product of social engineering on an industrial scale. Right to Buy shrinks the social housing stock in a selective manner and leaves behind the most undesirable homes. Then, the 'priority need' banding system drives society's most troubled and vulnerable individuals to reside alongside each other on social housing estates.

As a result of these insidious forces, everyone else who happens to live in a council or housing association property must endure the stigma of living in the social rented sector.

In short, the argument that 'bricks and mortar' subsidy creates 'poor health, crime and social poverty' is wrong. The reality is actually the reverse – the destruction of bricks and mortar subsidy has only served to accelerate the transformation of council estates into pools of social deprivation and criminal activity.

What was supposed to take the place of council housing, the housing association, has also started to fail to live up to expectations.

26. Housing associations under pressure

While housing associations have been around in one shape or another since the 19th century, they became central to Margaret Thatcher's reforms to housing policy in the 1980s. Much to her exasperation, housing associations were exempted from the Right to Buy policy after fierce lobbying in the House of Lords.[1] However, rather than force the issue, her government found alternative ways to put housing associations to good use.

Firstly, the Housing Acts of 1985 and 1988 encouraged councils to 'voluntarily' transfer their housing stock to housing associations, which were regulated at 'arm's length' by a quango called the Housing Corporation. This helped to weaken local authority control over the provision of low-cost housing, and paved the way for a more market-oriented social rented sector.[2] In 1988, the Treasury re-classified housing associations as 'independent' bodies, meaning their debts wouldn't show up on the government balance sheet. This gave them access to private finance – something that had long been denied to local authorities. As a result, they superseded local authorities as Westminster's affordable housing provider of choice, and received capital grants to fund new social housebuilding and homeownership promoting schemes alike.[3]

Geoff, a health and safety officer in a mid-sized housing association, also quoted in the preceding chapter, was willing to speak to me about the pressures in the sector today, provided I concealed his identity. He began: 'Our customer satisfaction surveys tend to come in at around 80 per cent, which I suppose isn't too bad... And all of our governance ratings and Social Housing Regulator gradings are always top of the range. But the cases I deal with on a day to day basis are things like *'I've fallen down the stairs because you didn't fix this light, even though I called hundreds of times to request for it to be fixed.'* You know, it's basic stuff. Maybe I just get a warped view, working in the health and safety side of things. But to be perfectly honest, I don't think we're as great as the satisfaction surveys suggest.'

This disconnect reminded me of what Ryan, the shared ownership leaseholder, told me about his housing association, Brumble Housing Group. He spoke of a stark contrast between the marketing messages and the day-to-day experiences of residents. 'The brochures Brumble send out read like they're from a commercial property developer,' he said, adding: 'They seem to think we actually care that they've got this huge portfolio of houses all over the country.'

I had a look at Brumble's customer-facing annual report, and was amazed to find it even goes so far as to show off about the multi-million-pound surplus they've managed to accumulate by 'driving efficiencies.' Could this be corporate code for the sharp drop-off in the quality of services Ryan and his neighbours have been receiving?

Buried in a different report on the group's Value for Money strategy, customer satisfaction with 'maintenance and repairs' among shared ownership residents is revealed to be 40 per cent – far below the 80-90 per cent satisfaction rates it received in other areas.[4]

Geoff wasn't surprised when I told him Ryan's story. 'It's the same with us,' he said. 'You look at how much the shared ownership residents are paying in rent and service charges, and you just think: *"What are they actually getting for their money?"* I don't know, it doesn't seem fair. If one of my kids told me they were considering buying a shared ownership property, I'd tell them not to touch it, because I don't think it's a very good deal.'

A recurring theme in the pages of trade publication *Inside Housing* is whether housing associations have lost touch with their charitable roots. The articles veer between cautionary criticism and rallying defences of the sector's continued sense of moral purpose. Social landlords are also in the midst of what's been called 'merger mania' in industry circles, as large housing associations gobble up smaller, less profitable ones. What's behind this lurch towards the commercialisation of third sector social landlords?

Geoff is pretty certain he knows the answer: 'The big thing to bear in mind is that the housing associations had their grants pretty much cut in half in 2010. Then there was the rent cut in 2015, which hit a lot of smaller housing associations really quite hard.[5] In practice it's meant that housing associations have had to commercialise in order to recoup the shortfall. That's why we're seeing all these mergers and acquisitions – the smaller ones are getting picked off by the ones who can afford to absorb the funding cuts. It's why everyone's trying to diversify too – 'market' rented housing, student housing... Some housing associations have even started doing Help to Buy now – which I suspect is just another money-spinner.'

This economy drive doesn't seem to have extended to the pay-packets of the top executives at housing associations. The highest-paid boss, David Cowans of Places for People, took home total remuneration of £591,256 in 2017/18[6] – more than double that of the highest earning civil servant.[7] Even the average earnings of a housing association chief executive come in at £173,274[8] – nearly three times the average salary of an NHS surgeon.[9] What's more, as of September 2018, executive pay across the sector rose 4.3 per cent on the previous year – nearly twice the rate of inflation.[10]

In other words, the sector is 'booming' if you look at the balance sheets, where vast operating surpluses[11] and generous executive salaries are par for the course. And yet, when you look at actual housing provision for social housing tenants (whom Geoff has been told to refer to as 'customers'), the total number of homes available at 'social rent' is in freefall.[12]

In light of this, Geoff finds the lavish pay packages especially bewildering. 'I know CEOs of massive companies earn a fortune,' he explained, 'but they have to take risks, look after the brand, keep growing sales and what have you... But housing associations have massive waiting lists of social housing tenants – sorry, 'customers' – lining up for somewhere to live. They're virtually guaranteed to make money... it's not as if their customers can take their business elsewhere.'

Another trend is the emergence of social housing providers backed by investment funds, as revealed by *The New Statesman* in a report in 2018 entitled: 'Investment funds have found a new cash cow: social housing.' These funds will buy the land and properties from cash-strapped local authorities and housing associations, and then lease them back to the social housing providers to generate an income. The funds are then floated on the stock market for investors to tap into the 'low-risk' reliable income derived from social housing.

Paul Bridge, chief executive of Civitas Social Housing PLC, told investors that they can expect 'modest' returns of around five per cent per annum, adding 'this is safe and ethical; [it] isn't a high-return vehicle; it's about longevity of income.'[13] He neglected to mention that a huge component of that income comes from the British taxpayer, whose housing benefit bill helps fund the rent payments now effectively ending up in the pockets of private investors.

In a derisory interest rate environment, where a cash account that pays more than three per cent makes headlines, a 'low-risk' investment that reliably returns five per cent is a solid selling point. But is it accurate to call an investment proposition that diverts cash away from a desperately underfunded social housing sector 'ethical'? How did the organisations inspired by the Ken Loach film *Cathy Come Home* in the 1960s end up having their assets packaged up and sold off on the stock market in the 21st century?

In 2018, Channel 4 aired an episode of *Dispatches* called *Getting Rich from the Housing Crisis*. It took aim at some of the worst practices among housing associations, presenting a bleak and ruthless corporate world, full of accountants and business managers more interested in the numbers on the bottom line than the people on the breadline.

And yet the programme divided opinion, and aspects of it were missing context. Social housing professionals led the backlash: they protested that the documentary made no mention of the funding cuts to housing associations in 2010, nor the rent cap imposed five years later. And it neglected to point out that operating surpluses aren't the same as profits, as surpluses in a non-profit housing association are reinvested into projects to build affordable housing.[14]

Time and again, those writing on behalf of the sector kept returning to the same defence: the blame for all of these things ultimately lies with the government. Politicians rewrote the rulebook – the housing associations have simply responded to dramatic changes imposed from above. 'Subsidised housing needs subsidy,' wrote David Montague, Chief executive of housing association L&Q, in *Inside Housing*, 'and that subsidy can come from government... or it can come from housing association surpluses.'[15]

The problem with this excuse is that people like Ryan never signed up to be a stand-in for the welfare state. He and his neighbours quite rightly expect to receive a decent service in exchange for the money they pay, and not to have their services stripped bare as part of a bid to 'drive efficiencies' for a housing association left reeling by government cutbacks.

In truth, the housing associations that win out in this giant game of hungry hippos are not really interested in becoming more 'commercial.' If they were, they would start treating the people who pay their salaries like real customers, and not just labelling them as such. Instead, they have chosen to recoup their losses by exploiting the massive power imbalances that arise in a desperate, lop-sided market – where payment is obligatory, but service is optional. The end result is a social rented sector that is forced to shrink to make way for the market-based alternatives needed to fund this 'cross-subsidy.' For those who turn to social housing when under threat of homelessness, the shortage of homes can have devastating consequences.

27. 'Intentionally homeless'

Mia's Story

To protect the identities of those involved, all names have been changed in this case study.

'How could you do this to me?!' she screamed. 'I'm going to be out on the street!'

Nobody knew what to say. Mia's heart was racing. Joe, her eldest son, watched in stunned silence. In March 2018, Mia had got home from work to find a 'for sale' board outside her house. Her landlady, Denise , came over that evening to explain. She gave Mia a big hug, said how sorry she was to have to do this, but explained that unexpected financial difficulties meant that she had to sell up.

Mia was 27, a single mum with two boys aged seven and four, and she worked part-time as an Early Years Practitioner in the Midlands. She also had a mobile beauty therapy business on the side. She had lived in her rented home for nearly six years; she'd even spent money on home improvements. Still, Denise assured her she had nothing to worry about. The house would be sold to a new landlord, and all Mia had to do was agree to some viewings.

However, during one of the viewings Mia noticed something was off. The prospective buyer was visualising where they might put their chest of drawers. Mia queried this with the estate agent, who said, without blinking: 'Oh, hasn't Denise told you? She wants a fast sale, so she's opening it up to offers from all buyers.'

Now aware she needed somewhere new to live – and fast – Mia went online. What she discovered made her heart sink. Prices had shot up in recent years. Her current rent was £525 a month, but similar properties within driving distance of work and her kids' school were on the market for over £750 per month, on top of which she'd be expected to put down around £900 as a deposit, plus agency fees. There was no way she could afford this, so she got in touch with the local council.

The council took a different stance. Rather than help Mia find a new place, it declared she hadn't been served with a legal eviction notice. And so, it told her to stay put. Mia was also warned that, if she did leave the house at the landlady's request, she would be classed as 'intentionally homeless' and ineligible for help.

Mia sent Denise a text to update her. Nothing could have prepared her for what came next. According to Mia, Denise stormed over to her house, and, in front of a small child and Mia's ex-partner, screamed: 'How could you do this to me?! I'm buying food on credit cards! I'm broke! I'm going to be out on the street!'

Just like that, six years' worth of amicable relations vanished in a fit of rage. The landlady served an 'official' Section 21 notice, proclaiming that, if Mia refused to budge, she'd take court action. Not long after, an unmarked envelope was pushed through the letterbox. Mia opened it to find a wad of regulatory documents: a gas safety certificate, an Energy Performance Certificate and the government's *How to Rent* guide.

All documents were dated from 2015, the date at which they

should have been delivered in order to serve a valid Section 21 notice. Because they had been delivered by hand, Mia had no way of proving she had not received them years earlier. Suddenly, her grounds to protest the eviction were weakened. Having hit a brick wall with the council, Mia had no choice but to wait for a court summons.

On her eldest son's eighth birthday, she received a text: 'Hello Mia, happy birthday to your son. Just to let you know I'll be start-ing court proceedings tomorrow, which will cost £350. You will be liable for the cost. Denise.' Mia went back to the council, sure that now she had proof she was about to be evicted, they'd be able to do something for her.

She was wrong. 'My banding was upped to 2b,' she told me after the meeting, 'but I'm basically 60th-70th in line for a basic crappy flat. I was asked lots of questions about whether I have any of these social issues. I got the impression if I'd been mentally ill or an al-coholic, I'd have been moved up the queue.' As Mia's only issue was that she faced losing her house, her problems weren't deemed serious enough to warrant help.

She went on: 'I'm trying to stay positive and keep going to work and doing school runs and dealing with the council, the landlady, kids, family bills, bidding on crappy council flats.' But the ordeal was taking its toll. Mia's son told her that 'all he wants for his birth-day is a new house for us, because it's making mummy sad packing.'

And that wasn't even the worst part. 'It's absolutely heartbreak-ing being forced out of our home,' she said, 'but it's not something that's unexpected. What's unexpected is the 'safety net' we're sup-posed to have when we're in a situation caused by an outsider has got HUGE holes in.'

The Homelessness Reduction Act

When Mia first shared her story with me, I was at a homelessness conference in Kings Cross run by housing association network Homes for Cathy. The Conservative MP Bob Blackman was there to talk about the Homelessness Reduction Act 2017, a new law he helped enact. Blackman had set out to tackle the very issue Mia faced: councils who 'fold their arms and say, it's nothing to do with me' when approached by a tenant clutching a Section 21.

Supported by housing charities such as Crisis, St. Mungo's and Shelter, Blackman had co-ordinated extensive research involving 'mystery shoppers' to find out how councils dealt with people facing eviction. He discovered that across the country people were being told to 'wait until you're homeless, then come back in.' He also found the lack of preventative action meant evicted families would 'arrive at the housing office, literally with their bags packed, and nowhere to go.' Due to social housing shortages, most would end up in temporary accommodation – often bed & breakfasts or hostels in appalling condition. Blackman said: 'If we can reduce the [temporary accommodation] bill by five per cent, the Act pays for itself.'

The legislation was certainly needed to counteract some perverse incentives for landlords. An anonymous council officer revealed to *Inside Housing*'s Kate Belgrave in January 2018 what was really going on in a typical local authority housing department. Pseudonymously named Alex, he cited an example in 2016 where a family had been evicted by their landlord, only for the council to send them straight back to the home they had just left, which was now registered as temporary accommodation.

'Imagine how pissed off they were,' Alex recalled, 'They'd been packing their stuff up for three weeks and put it in storage.' The only winner was the landlord, who was now in receipt of guaranteed rent from the council at 'more lucrative' rates on a nightly-let basis.

Alex also shared how successive rounds of cuts and 'underfunding' had fuelled the loss of many highly trained and experienced staff members. The dearth of expertise had prompted some truly appalling decisions: one woman was deemed 'intentionally homeless' after she'd left her home to escape a man who had raped her. The work culture was, in Belgrave's words, dogged by 'the ingrained belief that all benefit claimants and homelessness applicants lie about their circumstances as a matter of course.'[1]

Enacted on 3 April 2018, the Homelessness Reduction Act 2017 redefined the term 'threatened with homelessness' to include someone who is 'likely to become homeless' within the next 56 days, rather than the previous 28 days. It also requires councils to assist those facing homelessness regardless of priority need, that is, even if they are child-free, employed and mentally and physically healthy. Assistance should involve free, personalised advice on homelessness support services, service users' statutory rights and their options for next steps.

Was it actually working? Mia had first approached her local council for support three weeks after the law had passed. After the conference I emailed Blackman, explaining Mia's situation and asking whether he believed the council was in breach of the Act. He responded quickly. 'On the basis of your detailed information,' he wrote, 'it certainly appears that the council are in breach of their duty.' He also offered to assist Mia's MP in taking the local authority to task.

This new development had a noticeable impact on Mia. Until now, she'd put up with endless 'patronising' and belittling behaviour from her landlady, as well as condescending remarks on social media when she vented her frustrations. One commenter implored her to 'look at [her situation] from the landlord's side,' and another suggested she should be glad that the glut of student accommodation driving up rents in her local area was 'hugely adding to [the] economy!'

No-one in authority had ever told her that her situation was unacceptable. Now however, there was a strong chance she had the law on her side. And she had an email from the man who wrote the law itself to back her up. That night, she sent a long message to her local MP, a long-standing Labour politician, attaching Blackman's offer to help. Then she poured herself a glass of rosé to celebrate. 'I've had such a long day working, I was so ready for bed,' she said, 'and now I'm adrenaline pumped!'

Homelessness is a political choice

I want to say what happened next was that Mia's MP hauled the council over the coals for their non-compliance with the Homelessness Reduction Act, and Mia was swiftly rehomed in an affordable council property.

What actually happened was Mia spent four months in her sister's spare room with her children, 20 miles away from work, diligently bidding on council flats. One day, in what she described as a 'happy mistake,' she landed a 'brand new house' around the corner from the children's schools. Her personal ending was happy, but the broader story arc is not.

Mia never did hear back from her MP. There were vague promises of a phone call from his assistant, but the hoped-for cavalry never arrived. And, as it turned out, the council behaved correctly under the letter of the new law. As highlighted by the housing solicitor Giles Peaker,[2] the Homelessness Reduction Act does not stop councils from telling tenants who are facing eviction via Section 21 to wait until 'the bailiffs arrive.'

Instead, the government's Homelessness Code of Guidance accompanying the new law encourages authorities not to 'adopt a blanket policy or practice' on the issue. It states that they must 'not consider it reasonable' for tenants to wait until they are evicted by a court order. But it is just that: guidance. The law itself stays silent on the topic, despite the 'considerable friction' surrounding the issue during the passage of the bill.[3]

Crisis, the homelessness charity that was instrumental in drafting the bill, raised concerns over the guidance. It warned that it 'does not encourage the culture change in local authorities that will be needed to deliver on the ambition of the legislation.'[4] And it appears the main reason the Act had to be watered down before it could be implemented was, as ever, funding.

The government set aside £72 million over three years to help councils in England with the additional costs of the Homelessness Reduction Act. Split between 201 district councils, 55 unitary authorities, 36 metropolitan boroughs and 32 London boroughs, that translates into an average of just under £75,000 extra per year per council. By comparison, the Act's successful pilot scheme, run by Southwark council in London, was allocated £1 million over two years by central government. The council then topped this up with £750,000 from its own funds.

Of course, part of this disparity will be due to the relative size of Southwark council versus smaller authorities elsewhere. But a 2019 survey revealed that two thirds of councils believe they have insufficient funds to fulfil their obligations under the new law.[5] As Councillor Stephanie Cryan said in *The Guardian*, the Act risks being 'the sticking plaster on the severed artery.'[6]

Bob Blackman and others may have made the Homelessness Reduction Act a reality, which is a formidable achievement. But for it to function as intended, it seems that Blackman himself must step in to enforce it. Even in the few weeks since the law came into force, he revealed that he had personally had to intervene on four occasions to make his own local authority comply with its spirit.

To realise the original ambition of the Homelessness Reduction Act, an attitude shift is needed at the highest levels of government. Thanks to four decades of policies bent on keeping the homeownership dream alive at all costs, the prevailing view in government and in society at large is that homes are trophies for individual success, not basic prerequisites for a decent life. And as Mia's experience shows, to become a buy-to-let investor, all you need is enough cash to get started. You don't have to be deemed 'fit and proper,' earn any qualifications, or be financially secure enough to provide a long-term home for a family.

The temporary accommodation racket is just another spoke of the wheel. The government would rather pour good money after bad, wasting billions on housing benefit and temporary accommodation, than disrupt a booming investment sector. And, despite the soaring cost of private sector solutions to the housing crisis, the future of even the remaining social housing hangs in the balance.

28. Social housing: the end game

In May 2016, the fate of social housing in England looked to be sealed. David Cameron's government had just enacted what an aide to the former shadow housing secretary described to me as 'the worst piece of housing legislation ever written.' It had passed through parliament with a minimum of fuss, and it went by the unassuming title of The Housing and Planning Act 2016. Its unspoken purpose? To destroy social housing once and for all.

Several of the Act's measures were never actually implemented,[1] but they give a clear insight into that government's agenda. Chief among these was the doomed 'starter homes' initiative, which local planning departments were expected to prioritise above all other proposed developments, regardless of local housing need.[2] These would be newly-built homes for first-time buyers under 40, somehow offered at a 20 per cent discount on their 'market value.' The scheme was a literal non-starter; to this day not a single 'starter home' has been built.

The second measure that was apparently shelved due to low take-up was the extension of Right to Buy to housing associations. Until the 2016 Act, housing associations had lobbied strenuously – and successfully – to be exempted from the Right to Buy policy. In a bid to soften the sector's resistance, the government made provisions for the scheme to be offered by housing associations on a 'voluntary basis,' subsidised by local authorities. The 2016 Act proposed that local councils should be made to sell off their 'high value' social homes as soon as they became vacant. The government would then impose a levy on local authorities to collect the proceeds of these sales, but this would be payable regardless of whether any 'high value' council homes had actually been sold.[3]

The funds raised would then reimburse housing associations who had sold their stock at a discount via 'voluntary' Right to Buy. If implemented, the initiative would have led to the loss of yet more socially rented homes in the name of helping better-off social housing tenants get onto the property ladder. The target to replace every home sold would not have stemmed the losses either, since there was no obligation for replacement homes to be offered on a 'like-for-like' basis. A home for social rent could be replaced by two starter homes, and the government would have considered this a net increase in the supply of 'affordable' housing.

Other proposals that ended up on the scrap heap include the controversial 'pay to stay' measure, in which social housing tenants could face rent rises if they started earning too much, and the phasing out of lifetime tenancies in council housing, to be replaced with two to five year 'fixed term' tenancies.[4] That these measures were quietly abandoned is cold comfort to many in the social rented sector. The 2016 law successfully managed to rewrite the planning rulebook in a way that made it easier for private developers to further steamroller the democratic process.[5]

Several council estates in London have been bulldozed and replaced with private housing by councils and developers working hand-in-hand to 'improve' inner-city areas. The Architects for

Social Housing (ASH) campaign group detailed this gentrification process in a case study on its blog entitled: *Regenerating Hackney's Estates: Dirty Tricks of a Dirty Council*. It visited three estates in the Labour-run Hackney borough and discovered disturbing signs that the sites were being prepared for demolition, to make way for a 'white, wealthy, middle-class clientele of home buyers.'

The first was the installation of bollards blocking access to the estate via the main road. They were purportedly there to 'reduce traffic,' however, in reality, they served little purpose other than to make it much more onerous for residents with cars to access their homes. Next came restrictions on parking and hikes to permit prices. Then, 'thousands of pounds' were 'spent on gardening carried out by an outside company working to improve the external appearance of the estate for prospective investors' – despite the fact that the homes themselves have long been neglected, and residents' requests for repairs and maintenance work were ignored.

The blog goes on to post a series of images featuring disused garages and padlocked-shut parking spaces, which had been 'allowed to fall into a state of disrepair' by the council. These spaces, the post explains, can now be considered 'brownfield land,' thanks to the 2016 Housing and Planning Act. This means that 'any developer that proposes a housing development on its land will automatically receive planning permission in principle' – a form of planning permission that can be granted before 'technicalities' like tenure type, the number of units and the size of each unit have been agreed upon. 'Once built, even a smallish block of private homes will attract further investors, assured that the Labour council is docile and accommodating,'[6] the blog reads.

While councils are obliged by statute to hold consultations with local residents about planned regeneration works, accusations of 'sham consultations' designed to 'wrong foot' opponents have long been documented by activists. According to author and journalist Anna Minton, holding ballots early or at short notice is 'a favoured tactic' of councils working in partnership with private developers, keen to push through unpopular but highly lucrative new redevelopment projects. Another tactic is to deploy a kind of 'class war' narrative, which Minton illustrates with the example of Lambeth council, who sought to categorise opponents of plans to demolish the Cressingham Gardens estate as middle-class homeowners with a 'Not in My Back Yard' mentality. In fact, they were a predominantly working-class community fighting to hold onto their homes.[7]

A BBC report in 2018 revealed that dozens of social housing estates across London have been listed for demolition, with campaign groups warning that more than 7,000 social rented homes are on course to be lost over the next decade in the capital alone.[8] The Mayor of London, Sadiq Khan, has ruled that developers must secure the approval of the majority of existing tenants in a regeneration area via a ballot before any work can go ahead, but this only applies to large-scale projects that require mayoral funding.[9]

You'd think the law would make it mandatory for developers to replace social housing stock on a like-for-like basis. However, thanks to the 'viability' rules introduced to the National Planning Policy Framework in 2012, developers have a trump card up their sleeves. The rules allow them to promise replacement stock (and secure both planning permission and the consent of existing residents on the back of these promises), then turn around half way through a project and claim that it is no longer 'economically viable' for them to replace the social housing stock in the same quantities as before.[10]

In her book, *Big Capital*, Minton reveals how consultants have sprung up to cater specifically to the needs of developers wishing to skirt affordable housing provision obligations. One advert even boasts that developers can 'go on a nice holiday with the money [they've] saved' after employing the consultancy's loophole-exploiting services.[11] By this point there's very little local authorities can do to challenge such claims.

'A new deal for social housing'

When the government's much-awaited Social Housing Green Paper was published in August 2018, it promised to set out 'a fundamental rethink of social housing in this country.' It was announced in response to the deadly fire at Grenfell Tower the year before, which brought into sharp relief the lack of accountability in the social housing sector, and the dismissive attitudes and stigma many social housing tenants face.

But it also marked a clear departure from the Cameron-Osborne era. Theresa May, the new prime minister, had already made fixing the housing crisis her 'personal mission,' and in her foreword to the green paper she set out her vision for 'a new deal for social housing,' in which she expressed views that would have been anathema for a Conservative politician just a couple of years earlier.[12] For example, she wrote that 'by providing homes based on individuals' needs rather than solely their ability to pay, social housing helped to keep neighbourhoods diverse and integrated' – as if it were a universally accepted fact, and not a hotly contested idea within the ranks of her own government. All the upheaval caused by the Brexit vote, David Cameron's sudden departure, a rapid succession of housing ministers (averaging one per year since 2010) and a drastically weakened government had started to shift the political conversation on social housing.

At the time of writing, with yet another new government at the helm, this time sitting on a comfortable majority, the future of social housing remains more uncertain than ever. When the Secretary of State for Housing, Communities and Local Government Robert Jenrick spoke at the Conservative Party conference in October 2019, all the familiar rhetoric about reinvigorating the homeownership dream had returned. He described homeownership as the 'bulwark of individual freedom, bringing security, dignity and independence.' He then went on to espouse the virtues of shared ownership, and his plans to extend a version of the scheme to social housing tenants.[13]

It all comes down to the relentless drive to turn housing into profit, and to attempt to solve the housing crisis in a way that the Conservative Party deems ideologically acceptable – via private housebuilders and property developers. As research by the academic Alan Murie shows, 'cost renting,' where rents merely meet local authority expenses, is a more economical use of public funds,[14] and gives tenants the chance to take a break from the gridlocked 'free' market altogether. It affords people the opportunity to build some savings, join a community, and escape the trap of low-skilled 'survival jobs.'

But this inclusive vision for low-cost housing is not possible if the government regards social housing as a dumping ground for social problems. Because then the escape becomes the trap, and the 'virtuous circle of dependency' becomes a reality – and social housing itself gets the blame for being the physical place in which violence, drug use, vandalism and gangs fester.

If the spirit of the Housing and Planning Act 2016 is resurrected, it won't be long before the overwhelming majority of renters have to rely exclusively on private landlords. I decided to meet them, face to face.

SECTION VI. WITH THE LANDLORDS

29. 'Is anybody here a socialist?'

Historically, private landlords have been small-scale investors. As far back as 1893, estate agents were advising that 'larger capitalists had better leave [private landlordism] alone.'[1] Letting property was too messy, too granular, and too headache-inducing for hands-off, big investors.

Fast forward to 2018, and all of that was about to change.

'What are you doing this for? There are far easier ways to make money.' – was Tony Gimple's message to all small, barely-profitable 'accidental landlords' in the room who weren't willing to professionalise. The message was clear: either scale up, or ship out.

Mr Gimple is an entertaining character. He's the co-owner of Less Tax for Landlords, an advisory firm that, unsurprisingly, helps landlords pay less tax. He was giving a seminar at the National Landlord Investment Show, so I thought I'd drop in and see what he had to say. He began his talk with a question for the audience: 'Is anybody here a socialist? Put your hands up.' No hands were raised. 'And is anybody here easily offended?' Again, nothing. 'Right, because if you are...' he pointed to the fire escape, 'DOOR.'

His little quips about shopping on Savile Row and buying Rolexes were tempered by his tell-it-like-it-is, London cabbie style delivery. It somehow allowed him to sound like he was railing against the elites, despite ostensibly being one of them. When he'd finished listing the political threats the Labour Party poses to landlordkind, Tony declared that he was unperturbed by the forthcoming purge of amateur landlords. In fact, for the 'savvy landlord,' the new regulations would present a golden opportunity to make 'highly sustainable profits' by turning their property portfolio into a 'professional property business.'

'And the good news is,' he added, 'that's exactly what the government wants you to do.'

The government is snatching away some of the tax perks associated with letting out property, under rules first announced by George Osborne in 2015. A lesser-known raft of changes from the Prudential Regulation Authority, which forms part of the Bank of England, has also placed new obligations on landlords who own four or more mortgaged rental properties, known as 'portfolio landlords.'

While the Bank of England is technically independent from the government, its aims are very much in tune with those of the Treasury – to keep the economy ticking over, and head off risks that might trigger another financial meltdown. In effect, 'scale up or ship out' isn't just a smart business strategy, it's the message coming straight from our most senior governing institutions.

As highlighted by mortgage broker Mortgages for Business, portfolio landlords are now going to be treated like corporations: they will be expected to produce business plans, tax returns, income and expenditure statements; the list goes on.

What's more, while buy-to-let lending remains largely unregulated, portfolio landlords will face tougher scrutiny on the overall profitability of their portfolio, and their creditworthiness as individuals.[2]

What's the upshot of all this for generation rent?

It would be easy to characterize Tony as a direct threat to the interests of generation rent. When he tells a roomful of budding property tycoons: 'You're entitled to be a narcissistic psychopath. If all you want is a nice house on a hill, a Maserati, a Rolex, or you know, a wardrobe full of fancy shoes, so what? Your choice,' it doesn't exactly inspire confidence that the lot of private renters is going to improve any time soon.

But then again, he's also very on board with the idea of booting rogue landlords out of the market. Curiously, for a self-described '19th century free trade liberal,' he's a fan of tightening some regulations in the private rented sector. He even called the idea of a 'tenant right to buy' 'not necessarily a bad thing' (later that year, centre-right think tank Onward suggested it could work by cutting capital gains tax for landlords who sell to a sitting tenant[3]). He also described landlord licensing – a proposal that was so viciously opposed by landlords in Sheffield – as 'marvellous.'

He said: 'Why does the government want to tax you? Because it's a *vibrant business sector*. Licensing is good. You do it properly, you increase capital values: high demand, better rents, better resale.'

He was even in favour of social housing. Not only can it 'save your conscience,' it 'has a really good business model.' As Tony explained: 'Some of my successful clients in Bristol in particular run social housing for addicts and what have you.' It's 'hard bloody work,' but in return you get 'guaranteed rent' and a 'guaranteed tenant.' Then he reiterated: 'Compliance works to your advantage commercially, and you get to sleep at night as well.'

Perhaps this is a sign that the classical liberals were right all along. 'Greed is good' acolytes tend to draw their inspiration from Adam Smith, who wrote in *The Wealth of Nations*: 'It is not from the benevolence of the butcher, the brewer, or the baker that we expect our dinner, but from their regard to their own interest.' Is it possible that the impulses of a narcissistic psychopath portfolio landlord with a penchant for designer shoes and supercars – moderated by regulation – could achieve a comfortable, secure and even pleasant existence for tenants?

Reading between the lines, there's a sense that the weeding out of smaller, weaker landlords will ultimately make the large ones stronger. As small landlords go bust or get fed up of the bureaucracy and sell up, portfolio landlords can pick up the pieces. For the landlords with mid-sized portfolios, negotiating the sales of three, four or five different properties may prove much more of a headache than simply doing a one-shot deal with a bigger portfolio landlord. As Tony told his audience: 'Those of you with access to capital, who can recycle the capital and prepare to operate and run as a business: You will see phenomenal long-term growth, like launching balls up a vacuum.'

Some of this growth will come from capital appreciation, but given that property prices have been flatlining for some time now despite mortgage lenders offering some of the lowest interest rates on record, it's unlikely that the capital gains of the past two decades are going to be replicated. If phenomenal growth is on the horizon, then it's more likely to come from the pockets of the privately renting population.

Landlords are not charities. Tony said this himself: 'You're all businesses, yes? And businesses only exist to make a profit...

There's no such thing as excess profit either, only profit.' In other words, better-quality, and more professionally-run private rentals are going to come at the highest price the market can get away with.

It's not just that charging the maximum amount of rent possible is preferable. It's that there is no 'business case' to provide low-cost housing, unless you're able to secure state subsidy and become a 'social landlord.' For private landlords, there is no material reward for attempting to fill the hole in the social rented sector left by Right to Buy, and plenty of risk.

What's more, many landlords grossly underestimate the responsibilities the government now expects them to shoulder, as I was about to find out.

30. At the Landlord Advice Roadshow

On a balmy evening in April 2018, I reluctantly declined an invitation from friends to enjoy the weather in a beer garden. I'd signed up to attend the Residential Landlords Association's 'Landlord Advice Roadshow' in Sheffield, and I decided to go there wearing my fake property investor hat. If anyone asked, my cover story was that my dad had a buy-to-let property portfolio and was considering passing its management to me. I wasn't trying to catch anyone out or 'expose' anybody (the identities of the people I spoke to are concealed). I simply wanted to understand what landlords were really thinking without putting anyone on the defensive.

The event was held in the nave of an old church, which doubled as a conference venue. A cling-filmed buffet was laid out at the back of the room, and the delegates sat around several large round tables facing a makeshift stage. There, a panel of speakers was seated in front of a large projector screen, bathed in the evening light streaming in through a stained-glass window.

A local councillor was giving a talk to approximately 40 landlords on the latest rules and regulations being adopted by Sheffield city council in the private rented sector. Faced with such a bone dry topic, the councillor had opened with a light-hearted bid to get the audience engaged. 'No rogue landlords here?' No hands went up. 'Good, good. Just checking.'

Of course, no landlord was going to confess to being a rogue in a room full of peers. It's also true that those who attended a Residential Landlords Association seminar probably represented the more conscientious property owners.

During the break, however, an unexpected sentiment started to emerge: resentment. The landlords felt that they were a persecuted group, and that the government had them over a barrel. None of them wanted to breach whatever new regulations were conjured up by Westminster. Yet a landlord's life had become a constant battle to prove you *weren't* a 'rogue landlord' – by dodging the innumerable regulatory traps laid out for you by the authorities.

'You just live in constant fear of being sued' one told me, as we queued for a sandwich at the break.

'Have you ever had an issue with tenants complaining?' I asked. 'Oh no. Never,' he said.

When I sat back down at the table, the lady across from me began to reel off the packed calendar of training events and qualifications she had accumulated in recent years. She had travelled the length and breath of the UK to become an accredited expert in every aspect of landlord law and regulation imaginable. Something about her manner called to mind a documentary I had seen about people in the US who stockpile tinned food, firewood and ammunition to prepare for an apocalypse. 'You've got to cover yourself,' she explained.

She went on to reminisce over the blissful simplicity of her mother's time as a landlady in charge of a batch of student rental properties a few decades back. Before the beginning of term, landlords in the most popular student areas would open up their doors, and bright-eyed students would wander in off the street to request lodgings. If the landlord thought they seemed nice enough, a tenancy agreement would be signed there and then – no fuss. There were rarely any problems, and perfectly amiable landlord-tenant relationships were the norm.

While she acknowledged that it would never be possible to go back to such a carefree era, her nostalgia did raise a valid point: It's always been possible to avoid becoming a rogue landlord. If all you've ever done is treat your tenants with respect, never deducted money from a deposit, and committed no crime more heinous than charging interest on a late rent payment, then the gradual onslaught of rules, obligations and penalties that have crept up over the years must be bewildering and frustrating.

But there are more than a few rogues. Exact figures are hard to come by partly because, by its very nature, the rogue end of the market is unregulated. But London councils investigating the matter have turned up some surprising results.

In his book *Housing Politics in the United Kingdom*, Brian Lund recounts how Newham council introduced landlord licensing in 2013 to tackle its slums. Its mayor, Sir Robin Wales, told the Communities and Local Government Select Committee: '[The sector overall] is much bigger than we thought. We thought we had 5,000 landlords; we now know we have 15,000 and those are just the ones who have registered.'

Since shining a light on the sheer size of the private rented sector, Sir Robin said:

'We are discovering a lot of what we think is fraud,' and 'cash-in-hand criminal landlords.'[1]

The housing journalist Anna Minton recalled how a Southwark councillor informed her that '[the council] thinks that broadly a third of landlords are well-meaning and do a good job, a third are well-meaning and do a bad job and a third are rogue landlords, and at the fringes of that you have slum landlords and criminal human trafficking.'[2] These figures will of course vary throughout the country, and London boroughs are likely to be among the worst affected. But the true answer to the question of what proportion of UK landlords are rogues is that no-one really knows.

What we do know is that in 2017 an investigation by *The Independent* found that more than a quarter of all housing benefit payments, around £2.5 billion of public money, was ending up in the pockets of landlords whose properties were considered to be 'non-decent,' i.e. homes with 'inadequate heating,' 'outdated sanitation,' 'in a state of serious disrepair' or 'unsafe, for example due to a dangerous boiler, vermin infestation or faulty wiring.'[3]

Later in the evening at the Landlord Advice Roadshow, the case for strict legal protections for tenants' rights was made inadvertently. Most questions at the concluding Q&A session with the speakers centred on technical matters, such as about square footage requirements for bedrooms in multiple-occupancy houses. But one caught my attention. A landlord asked:

'We have a problem tenant. She's on housing benefit, got kids, but pays rent on time and everything... that's not the problem. She's given us this long list of ridiculous complaints, and she reckons we need to sort them in the space of 14 days or she's going to report us to the council. It's causing us no end of stress. It's things like, she claims there's a damp problem, but we've told her time and again that she needs to open a window when she puts her clothes out to dry. She's even asked us to remove the chimney breast because 'it's too draughty.' Anyway, what I want to know is, where do we stand with serving Section 21? We've had enough, and we just want her out.'

The panel responded tentatively, stressing that being a landlord comes with responsibilities, and that you would need to tread very carefully so as not to invalidate a Section 21 notice by meeting the criteria for a 'retaliatory eviction.' 'I can't advise you on this without seeing that list,' said one panellist. 'The tenant might not have a leg to stand on with some of those issues, but she might well have a point with some of the others. I would have to go through it point by point before I could say either way whether you'd be able to serve that Section 21.'

Perhaps the tenant really was a troublemaker, and the landlord a beleaguered victim. Asking the landlord to remove a chimney breast does seem quite extreme. But 'you need to open a window' is the textbook argument used by landlords who refuse to resolve systemic issues with mould and damp in their properties.

Browse through any tenant support group on social media, and you'll find post upon post of tenants who've complained about black mould, spongy walls, and even mushrooms sprouting from the plasterwork... only to be told that it's their fault for causing 'condensation.' When #ventyourrent was trending on Twitter, the *Daily Mail* covered the story of a tenant who was told she'd 'caused mould by breathing.'

Responding to a tenant's query over chronic mould posted in the Tenants' Voice Group on Facebook, veteran landlord and property consultant Julian Maurice was sympathetic. 'This is such a big problem and it's mainly down to the fact that a lot of older houses weren't designed to have double glazing and efficient gas heating,' he said.

'Opening windows rarely helps and everyone, from the landlord to the agent to the occupier are clueless as to how to deal with the issue.' The only lasting solution, he said, is for the landlord to call in a mould and condensation specialist, who will recommend the solutions necessary to alleviate the problem. Failing that, the best thing the tenant can do is attack the mould with a bottle of bleach and find somewhere else to live as soon as possible.

There is a wider issue here, in that many landlords seem not to realise the weight of responsibility they have taken on. The BBC's *Panorama* programme, *Evicted for No Reason*, looked at the impact Section 21 was having on the nation's renters. At one point, presenter Richard Bilton interviewed a landlady struggling to evict an intransigent tenant.

The tenant was undeniably in breach of his contract. Not only was he behind on the rent, but he had also made unauthorised alterations to the property, such as installing a satellite dish. The landlady was clearly not an all-powerful millionaire. She was just an ordinary woman who had decided to invest in a buy-to-let property. Being stuck with a loss-making asset while having to go through a protracted legal battle to regain possession of said asset was certainly not what she signed up for.

But she realised what she had let herself in for when she tried to grasp for the words to express her dismay at her tenant's behaviour. 'He's treating the place like it's his...' she said, before trailing off. The presenter picked her up on it: 'But it is his home,' Bilton said.

This lack of awareness of what a rental property really meant to a tenant – and the lengths to which they would go to hold onto it – proved to be her undoing. I am not suggesting that her tenant was right to take liberties with his tenancy agreement or to stop paying the rent. But watching this incident unfold made me wonder: have landlords been sold a lie? Namely, the idea that 'property is just an investment, like any other?'

Having been impressed with his helpful advice to tenants on Facebook, I spoke to Julian Maurice on the phone not long after the Residential Landlords Association event. He said: 'So many landlords don't see themselves as business owners. It drives me mad. I think, don't you realise you're supposed to be providing a service?'

His current venture involves giving interior design advice to landlords, and his aim is to help bring about a shift in mindset in the sector. 'Personally, I think we need to do away with the term 'tenant' altogether,' he said. 'We need to start calling them what they are: 'customers,' who deserve a decent service for the money they pay.' He went on: 'Equally, customers who don't pay shouldn't be entitled to a service. You know, if you're a tenant, and you stop paying the rent, it can take months and months for the landlord to get you out. That's wrong. It's got to be fair on both sides.'

The conversation became slightly uncomfortable at this point, as I pondered where the many people who simply can't afford to pay market rents are supposed to live. He explained: 'Look, if you go into a café, and you order some cake, then you eat the cake and say, oh sorry, I can't afford to pay for that... then that's theft. Landlords aren't charities. There's got to be a profit motive, otherwise it's not a business.'

I was starting to understand what makes being 'a good landlord' so fraught with difficulty. In a country where there is a chronic affordable housing shortage and a fraying social safety net, perhaps the only real way of avoiding awkward ethical dilemmas in the private rented sector is to not become a private landlord in the first place.

If you're already a landlord, there's a very real possibility that your business needs will call on you to carry out some deeply unpleasant tasks, such as evicting people who've lost jobs, fallen into arrears due to Universal Credit delays or gone through relationship breakdowns.

And if the private rented sector were to suddenly collapse, millions of people would be homeless. Private landlords are not equipped to deal with society's ills, but society needs them all the same.

I commend Julian for promoting an attitude shift among landlords, but he faces an uphill struggle. An investigation by Citizens' Advice found that tenants who complain are twice as likely to be served with an eviction notice than those who simply grin and bear their struggles.[4]

What all of this points to is a fundamental mismatch between what tenants need from landlords, and what landlords want from tenants. We already know what tenants need: a secure, affordable and safe home. But what exactly are today's landlords trying to achieve?

31. Nest egg: property as a pension

It would be remiss to talk about 'what landlords want' without touching upon the subject of pensions. The 'get-rich-quick' accusations are only fair for a certain subsection of the landlord population. The fact is, a large proportion of people getting into small-time landlordism do it because they want to top up or create from scratch a healthy retirement income.

This is borne out in the typical age profile of a private UK landlord. Some 59 per cent of private landlords in England are aged 55 or over according to government data, while one in three are retired.[1] It's also part of the national psyche. In 2010, the Office for National Statistics started an annual survey asking non-retired adults: What method of retirement saving makes the most of your money? In 2016-17, more people answered 'property' (49 per cent) than in any other year since the survey began. For comparison, the next biggest segment – employer pensions – was favoured by just under a quarter of respondents. Personal pensions lagged way behind, trailing after stocks & shares and Individual Savings Accounts (ISAs).[2]

Arguably the survey is somewhat nonsensical, given that you can hold collective property funds, stocks, shares and cash *inside* a personal pension and in an ISA. ISAs and pensions are actually just 'wrappers' that determine the tax treatment of whatever's inside them, rather than investments in themselves. But given that many people probably won't know this, we can still glean an important insight: when Brits take the DIY approach to retirement planning, they overwhelmingly pick property.

Where does this fetish for property come from? Every so often, Merryn Somerset-Webb, *Moneyweek* magazine editor-in-chief, calls out yet another celebrity being interviewed in the *Sunday Telegraph* professing their confidence in property as a retirement pot, and their disdain for the 'scary,' 'risky' or 'complicated' stock market.[3]

Many of the financial advisers I've worked alongside have told me that one of the most common responses they hear from new clients when pressed on their retirement plans is 'my property is my pension', as if that's the only sort of investment worth owning. For some, this means one or two (or more) buy-to-let properties. For others, it means downsizing and using the equity released from their home as a retirement fund.

You would be hard-pressed to find a regulated financial adviser happy to recommend pinning all your hopes on residential property as a retirement strategy. For starters, they can take ages to sell. If you need to access the money tied up in your property quickly (without getting into debt), you face having to sell it at drastically below market price. You also can't sell a few bricks; it's the whole lot or none at all. And there's always a chance that your chosen retirement date will coincide with another epic crash in the property market, from which it could take several years to recover.

There's also the risk that, cottoning onto the anger now radiating from tenants stuck in the private rented sector, the government decides to change the rules to make property less attractive as an investment vehicle. For example, legislators could slash mortgage interest tax relief for landlords even further; or tax property in general more harshly – especially empty properties. In spite of this, the general populace is still obsessed with bricks and mortar. Is this obstinate rejection of what the experts think borne out of irrational over-confidence... or something deeper?

The personal pensions bogeyman

Let's look at this from a different perspective: What's causing so many people to reject pensions, and the stock market investments they typically hold?

Pensions are funny creatures, at once tremendously boring and powerfully emotive. They used to be something that workers didn't have to think about. Prior to the 1980s, most employers offered pension benefits on what is known as a 'defined benefit' basis.

This is essentially a credit-based system, where the employee accrues entitlement to a certain level of pension income for every year of service they provide. Usually this is between 1/60th and 1/80th of the employee's final salary before they retire – hence why they're sometimes called 'final salary' pensions.

So, if the employee provides 30 years of service, has an accrual rate of 1/60th and a final salary of £30,000 a year, they will be entitled to an annual pension income of £15,000 a year for the rest of their life. This whole mechanism would have been managed and funded by the employer, on the understanding that pensions were effectively 'deferred salary.'

It is called 'defined benefit' because the benefits you are entitled to are fixed, regardless of the value of what you put in (or what was put in on your behalf). You draw your pension from a huge pool of everybody's contributions, past and present.

Self-employed people could take out Retirement Annuity Contracts and save into their own fund. At the end they could buy a guaranteed income for life from an insurance company, called a lifetime annuity.

Lifetime annuities and defined benefit schemes used to work because they assumed that most annuitants and scheme members would die before they'd depleted their contributions to the fund. This saving would then offset the minority of pensioners who would go on living for much longer.

But advances in medicine coupled with an economic slowdown started wreaking havoc on the sums in the 1970s. People began to live longer, and the entitlements of employees were becoming a growing liability to fund for companies trying to stay profitable in an ailing economy. Margaret Thatcher's solution to this issue was the personal pension. People were strongly encouraged by the government to transfer out of generous defined benefit schemes into personal pension plans. For an estimated two million people who were misled by dodgy financial salespeople, the results were catastrophic.[4]

Through the 1990s and the early 2000s, millions of people were either facing decimated pension savings, knew someone who was, or were reading about all the people who got scammed in the news. These events explain why personal pensions are so badly thought of by many in the general public. Today, personal pensions are tightly regulated, and come with generous tax incentives that make them one of the best options for retirement saving available. But the stigma of scams, mis-selling, and stolen futures still lingers around them like a bad smell.

There were also other high-profile financial advice scams bubbling to the surface around the same time, such as mis-sold endowment mortgages, investment bonds and other, more obscure products such as 'split-cap investment trusts' and 'precipice bonds.'[5] The final nail in the coffin for public trust in the financial world came when the dot.com bubble burst, which for many was a first foray into stock market investing.

The problem wasn't helped, either, by a measure introduced by Gordon Brown in 1997, which abolished the tax credits payable on dividends within pension schemes. When the market was rallying, the effects were barely noticeable. But after the dot.com collapse, many schemes began to run up deficits; others were wound up.[6] Some commentators went so far as to claim that Gordon Brown was responsible for triggering the buy-to-let boom by choking off the growth potential of pension funds, thus driving ordinary investors into the arms of the buy-to-let industry.[7] This is undoubtedly an overstatement, but the measure likely fed into mounting public distrust towards pensions.[8]

In the early 2000s, savers were looking for somewhere 'safe as houses' to put their money. Picture the scene: it's 2004, your hugely promising pets.com shares have long since evaporated into the ether, your pension looks like a student bank account, and your employer doesn't have any reason to pitch in for your future anymore, because the government told you a personal pension would be better.

Then you spot the headline: two former maths teachers turned property tycoons Fergus and Judith Wilson make *Sunday Times* rich list with buy-to-let property portfolio valued at over £75m[9]...

32. Inside the buy-to-let industry

When I arrived, hordes of people were still piling into the Olympia exhibition centre, an hour after the event was supposed to start: the 2018 National Landlord Investment Show. I wanted to see for myself the state of play in the buy-to-let market. Was it a side-business? A passive investment? Was it doomed, and if so, who – or what – would be its replacement?

According to the marketing literature, the event would play host to investment consultants, councillors, lawyers, estate agents and mortgage brokers, all giving their thoughts on the outlook for the private rented sector. Most importantly, there would be hundreds of landlords. I wanted to hear what they had to say.

I surveyed the exhibition hall. The only person under 30 appeared to be a young woman serving overpriced coffee and salads at the pop-up café in the corner. Most people looked to be 45-65. Other than the age demographic, it was reasonably diverse, although there were slightly more men than women. A stand was advertising a women-only networking group, to 'empower' female investors to smash gender stereotypes by building their own property empire.

I guessed that revealing I was writing about the generation screwed by the financialisation of the property market might not elicit the best response from a roomful of property investors. So, I introduced myself as a finance blogger doing some research on the future of buy-to-let. (NB: All names of private individuals have been changed).

Browsing the stalls, I felt like a gatecrasher at a secret underground convention. Every product or service on offer in this room was framed as either a money-spinning or loss-limiting opportunity. There was a 'smart energy' company whose services could produce energy usage stats for landlords of Houses in Multiple Occupation: 'It really strengthens your case during the dispute resolution process if you want to withhold deposits from tenants for excess use of energy.' An insurance broker was pitching insurance products to landlords as tools to 'maximise your profits.'

Everyone wanted to convince you that their offering was the next big thing:

- 'Serviced apartments: they're the future for property investors. You've got your business-trippers, your international tourists... these guys are willing to pay top whack...'

- 'The buy-to-let slowdown means now is the time to diversify, and buy-to-let cars are a great way of doing that...'

- 'To be honest, what we're saying to London landlords now is that they're not going to get better yields in this market – the market's topped out. If you're looking for yield [rent as a percentage of property value], you want to be investing in up-and-coming UK cities, Liverpool, Leeds, Sheffield...'

– 'Have you considered turning your property into an AirBnb? We can take all the hassle away with a completely hands-off management service...'

The only exhibitor not to mention the profit-maximising, yield-generating, growth unleashing possibilities of its offering appeared to be a French polishing company, which was displaying a beautifully buffed selection of hardwood flooring. It was selling 37 years of experience and expertise. It didn't seem to be very busy. The interior design company in the next room which made explicit the link between providing a nice place and generating better returns – 'increase rents by up to 20 per cent with differentiated design' – was having more success.

The 'back-to-front' vibe I was getting emanated in large part from the overt pursuit of the greatest amount of profit, coupled with a strong distaste for and reluctance to provide customer service.

I couldn't help but compare the experience to an entrepreneurship festival I went to in Sheffield in 2017, where I watched a talk by Jim Cregan, the larger-than-life founder of Jimmy's Iced Coffee. Cregan was a ball of energy on the stage, and he had a slightly mad backstory of how he went from being 'a casual labourer by day, and a mermaid MC by night' to creating a multimillion-pound company in just a few years with his sister. He was genuinely obsessed with iced coffee.[1] Only after this performance did he begin to talk profits, growth, targets and balance sheets. The order of events was clear: focus first on the quality of the product and the needs of the customer; then focus on maximising profits.

The 'business model' of the landlord on the other hand seemed to run in reverse: focus on maximising profits and meeting your own personal investment goals, *then* think about the needs of the customer and delivering quality products and services (if you must). Based on some of the horror stories I heard from private tenants, some landlords never make it past the stage of meeting their own personal investment goals. The very fact that interior designers have to coax landlords into refurbishing their rental properties by dangling the carrot of 20 per cent rent hikes is a strong indication that trying to please your tenants – the supposed 'customer' in this market – is optional.

What's more, the marketing messages seemed to be designed to amplify the alienation between landlords and tenants. When I decided to sit down and peruse the small rainforest's worth of leaflets in my goody bag, what took me by surprise was how unabashed the advertisers were about glossing over the fact that tenants are human beings, let alone customers. The gravity of taking on the responsibility for providing someone's home was buried under anonymous facts and figures about yields and capital gains.

For example, one company boasted that its clients were 'achieving' an 'average net return of 16.2 per cent per annum,' as if the money fell out of the sky. Another claimed to provide 'the easiest way to let your property,' promising 'no calls, no visits, 100 per cent online bookings for mid to long-term rentals.' Both adverts neglected to mention the word 'tenants' at any point, nor gave any hint that the property would be inhabited by real-life people.

Others still were downright comical. For example, Landlord Action was advertising its eviction services with a large cartoon boot set against a red background, as if a Loony Tunes character was being kicked offstage. In a seeming bid to out-rank its competitors, the Sherriff's Office ad featured a great big lion, captioned with the words: 'fast and effective eviction of tenants.'

Of course, not all tenants facing eviction are helpless victims and many landlords are nothing like Peter Rachman, the notorious slum landlord of the 1950s. But you would expect that removing a human being from their home would be advertised with more sensitivity than an image of a boot. Especially given that Assured Shorthold Tenancy eviction is the second most common cause of homelessness, after 'family or friends can no longer accommodate.'[2]

Fundamentally: if the adverts and exhibitors are anything to go by, what landlords really want is the most hands-off, hassle-free way of generating a consistent level income. In other words, they want an annuity, the guaranteed income for life that was a common feature of pensions, but which now have very low payouts.

Nowadays, a £300,000 pot will buy a healthy 65-year-old an annuity of less than £10,000 a year according to research from pension provider Aegon,[3] less than the gross income of a full-time worker earning the minimum wage. Said 65-year-old would have to live past the age of 95 to make buying an annuity worth her while.

So, while the healthy levels of guaranteed income once provided by annuities are now off the table, demand for reliable, automated cashflow is fiercer than ever.

From the looks of it, tenants in the private rented sector have unwittingly become the next-best source of passive income in the investment market.

The existential landlord

By lunchtime I'd struck up a conversation with a landlady called Rose. Rose was 54 and had been a landlady for 15 years. The only trouble she'd ever had with her rented properties was when a friend she was letting to fell into rent arrears. She explained: 'Because I am too nice, I ended up letting her stay for three months without paying rent. If she was someone I didn't know, I would have done something about it sooner.'

Other than that, it'd been plain sailing: 'The only time my tenants call me is when they ring to say they are leaving! They are never any trouble. That's why I dread phone calls from them. Not because they have problems, but because they only call when they want to move out.'

Rose's properties were mostly homes for young families and professional couples in the London commuter belt. I asked how she got started.

'I had a job in senior management in the City. The money was good, but oh my God, the stress was crazy. I didn't have a life. And business was not going well – they had to make a lot of cutbacks. Eventually I found out I was going to be made redundant. That was the turning point for me. If I hadn't already paid my mortgage off by then, I would have been in trouble. But it was a time to stop and look at my life and think: do I want all this stress? So that's when I got started in buy-to-let.'

Since then she'd escaped the rat race, got married, and begun living exclusively off the rental income from her property portfolio. She had the freedom and the money to jet off to Italy for four days on a whim; she could afford to buy luxury brands, dine at expensive restaurants, and generally live life on her own terms. She was also child-free, which certainly assists wealth accumulation.

But all was not well. She told me: 'I want to get out.' She explained: 'I prefer experiences to things. What do I need another pair of shoes for? It's just stuff. I want to travel, see the world… but this isn't enough. I want to do something else.'

You'd think being able to live off the rental income from a property portfolio would suit a burnt-out high-earner. But Rose's existential ennui seems to have been brought on by the relatively undemanding nature of letting out residential property.

'It's not a full-time job,' she admitted, before wondering aloud, '…maybe I'll try property developing – that seems like it would be interesting. But then again, I don't want to be in property when I'm older. I want to invest in a pension, but I don't trust the stock market to not go down in value.'

Rose wanted to do something more fulfilling with her life, but she was also accustomed to a lifestyle and an income that seemingly couldn't be attained anywhere other than through renting out property. What does it mean for the economy if it makes more financial sense to remain idle and live off the yield from a portfolio of investment properties than it does to work in a high-powered corporate job? Rose isn't doing anything wrong; she is merely behaving rationally in a profoundly dysfunctional system.

And this is the crux of the matter. For all the glossy adverts touting the 16 per cent-plus yields you can 'achieve' in buy-to-let, what no-one talks about is where the property's 'yield' really comes from. With shares you buy on the stock market, the yield (or the 'dividend') comes from the profits of the company that sold the share. With bonds – a fancy term for the debts held by large companies and governments – the yield is derived from the rate of interest paid by the organization that issued the bond. In both cases, the capital and the income both come from the same source.

But, unlike a business or a government, property is inert. Being an inanimate object, it produces nothing, changes nothing and goes nowhere of its own accord. Property 'yields' don't leak out of the taps, rain down from the light fittings or come up through the floorboards. They come from the pay packets of tenants, who have no choice but to spend a third or more of their gross income on rent if they want to avoid sleeping on the streets.

In their book *The Rent Trap,* Rosie Walker and Samir Jeraj dub this phenomenon 'trap and tap,' illustrating how today's rental market will naturally take the maximum it can get away with from private renters.[4] Also, given that roughly 22 per cent of private tenants are in receipt of housing benefit, a good chunk of the aggregate rental yields generated in the private rented sector come out of the public purse.[5]

Out of the entire exhibition hall, I found one stall for a company whose selling point was that they sought to provide good quality customer service to tenants. It was called the Happy Tenant Company, and described itself as a 'residential asset management' company for landlords.[6]

Something about the company name struck me as odd, until I realised it reminded me of the Happy Egg Company – which pitches itself as an ethical alternative to farmers who use battery hens. The Happy Tenant Company's stated reason for improving tenants' private renting experience was that 'a happy tenant will better look after your investment and so improve long-term returns.'[7] Compare this to the Happy Egg Company's pitch: 'We believe happy hens lay tasty eggs!' In both scenarios, the tenants and the hens' wellbeing is not a moral imperative, but a variable to be optimised for financial gain.

The financialisation of property is, at root, the financialisation of people. Tenants are not just unfortunate bystanders caught in a speculative housing bubble that got out of control. They are not the customers. They are the livestock.

33. Now for the 'crackdown'

George Osborne was explicit about his intentions when he launched his tax crackdown on buy-to-let in 2015: 'Frankly, people buying a home to let should not be squeezing out families who can't afford a home to buy.'[1] But exactly how much ordinary families will benefit from the squeeze on private landlords remains to be seen. For a prime example, in 2018, an entire portfolio of 46 'traditional residential units' located 'in towns and villages on the whole throughout the North East' popped up for sale on Rightmove.co.uk for an all-in price of £1,850,000. The 'units' comprised a range of 'semi-detached and terraced housing' and contained a 'mixed tenure of families and DSS tenants.' The portfolio reportedly generated a 'rental income £235,584 per annum,'[2] or a gross yield of nearly 13 per cent.

Perhaps the existing landlord was prompted to sell his or her properties by the shifting of the winds in buy-to-let. But the idea that any of these homes will end up in the possession of first-time buyers is laughable, which is good news for the 46 households who would otherwise be displaced by the removal of these properties from the private rented sector.

This exposes an uncomfortable truth: before the advent of buy-to-let, we weren't dependent on private landlords as a last line of defence against mass homelessness. Now that social housing has been decimated (with around 40 per cent of ex-council houses now in the possession of private landlords[3]), we are.

Finding people from within the property world to speak to about the inner-workings of the buy-to-let industry proved surprisingly tricky. Time and again, I came up against the firewall of PR departments. Eventually, I managed to get in contact with a marketing executive at a property investment company that builds urban apartment blocks. He asked not to be named and to chat via email so as not to put his job in jeopardy. We'll call him Chris and the company Gray Quay.

To paint a picture of just how lucrative the buy-to-let industry remains, Chris gave me some figures: at Gray Quay, £40k a month goes on 'third party emails and banners' and £30k a month goes on pay-per-click advertising, on top of which the cost of 'running a marketing agency, printing brochures and all the rest' ends up costing many hundreds of thousands of pounds a year.

Gray Quay also holds events across the globe: whether by attending 'property expos' (for £15,000 a pop), or by holding their own seminars (for £70,000 a pop), in places ranging from Western Europe to South Africa and across East Asia. 'It works,' he said, 'especially in China.'

Chris assured me that these figures are a drop in the bucket compared with the profits there are to be made. 'Bear in mind we are only a single company,' he added. 'The scale of this industry is off the charts.'

Even if the old model of buy-to-let is dying, a new-and-improved version – one that taps into a pool of global wealth – is already poised to step in and take its place.

Gray Quay isn't (yet) in on the sexy build-to-rent scene in the strictest sense, in that its 'units' do get sold off, and the buildings it creates don't have rooftop terraces and in-house activity organisers to help residents feel as if they're at summer camp.

That said, it does sell its developments primarily to buy-to-let landlords. Chris told me: 'We sell unbuilt off-plan flats in city centre markets, mainly in northern cities. Our clients are probably what you would expect – investors aged 50 plus from around the world. We're not really fussy and have sold to people from more than 100 countries.'

I browsed its website, and the flats themselves were modestly priced considering their central locations and luxurious interiors. You could snag a swanky one-bed flat in an up-and-coming northern city centre for around the £100,000 mark, or a two-bed apartment of similar quality for just under £145,000. A twenty-something earning £25,000 a year who'd managed to scrape together £10,000 in savings (or even £5,000, now that the banks have started to loosen their lending criteria), could potentially afford a one-bed flat without bankrupting themselves. For a couple eyeing up the two-bed on two salaries with two pots of savings to draw upon, it would have been even easier. So why were all of these new-builds going to investors?

Chris explained: 'People can buy our flats to live in if they want, but realistically not many people know where they want to move two years in advance, are willing to wait that long and can pay in cash up front. Off-plan properties are generally not mortgageable as no-one will lend on something that isn't built. Once the development is complete you will normally see *some* owner-occupiers (as opposed to absentee buy-to-let landlords) buying flats and moving in, but the vast majority of the units we take to market are bought by investors.'

Again, we come up against the access versus affordability conundrum. Buying off-plan developments is inherently risky, since the builder could go bankrupt before the property materialises. Thus, properties that seem affordable on paper are actually only available to those who can afford to take a £100,000 risk.

Risk is often overlooked in public debates about the property development and housebuilding sector. For starters, it's a loss-leader: the point at which a housebuilder makes a profit is at the point of sale. Before that can happen, sites must be sourced, planning permission secured, plans drawn up, materials bought, construction completed, snagging issues resolved and finally marketing and sales operations launched. All the while a small village of staff and contractors must be paid. To ensure they don't go bust, housebuilders need to maintain a steady production line of sales and land acquisitions. This is no small feat when every stage of the pipeline is wracked with uncertainty.

Against this backdrop, it's easy to see why the Gray Quay model – selling unbuilt homes for upfront cash – is so appealing. The risk is shared by a solvent third-party, and with cash in the bank from the start there's less reliance on a never-ending production line. However, despite the strong business case for this approach, Chris has huge reservations about its ethical implications. He explains:

'The bosses sometimes like to put up the illusion that we are providing homes and thereby helping to solve the housing crisis, but quite frankly that is a fantasy. In truth, the company doesn't really see itself as either a contributor to or an alleviator of the housing crisis. It does not see itself as a housing company at all, much like every other buy-to-let sales company.'

This naturally gives rise to the question: what *do* buy-to-let companies see themselves as, if not as housing companies?

This is where Chris becomes especially scathing: 'Buy-to-let is so safe and stable that people around the world put their money into it to keep it safe from wars, political scandals and all the rest... Buy-to-let is nothing, nothing, nothing to do with housing.'

This function of buy-to-let as a safety deposit box for global wealth hasn't escaped the attention of the media in recent years, especially in the capital. In 2018, the UK Foreign Affairs Committee released a damning report on the London property market, calling it a 'laundromat' for dirty Russian money.[4]

What's more, it's not just Russian money – ill-gotten or otherwise – that finds its way into UK property development. In September 2015, *Private Eye* magazine created an interactive map which revealed the startling extent of just how much UK property is owned by offshore-registered companies.[5]

The Money Observer puts this down to three factors. The first is that 'investors, often from politically or economically less-stable countries, are attracted to the relative stability of the UK property market.' Secondly, the UK's comparatively strong commitment to property rights makes its property attractive. And finally, there's the Brexit-induced weak sterling, making UK property look like a tidy bargain for investors with pockets full of strengthening foreign currencies.[6]

Chris is confident that, because of its usefulness as a safe haven for international wealth, the UK buy-to-let industry will emerge from Brexit and the Treasury's tax changes unscathed. He points out: 'Buy-to-let survived the banking crisis, it has survived years of negative research, it has survived impassioned pleas from people who just want to be able to have a house of their own... Property investors are chameleons who shift with the winds.'

'People like me aren't going to go away'

His observations certainly ring true with my experience at the National Landlord Investment Show. One particular attendee caught my attention, because among the bustling crowds, he was reclining on a bench in the lobby looking vacant and haughty. Everyone around him was either hunched over a brochure, squinting at the signs on seminar room doors, or otherwise chatting animatedly about what they thought of the talk on speeding up eviction. I went over and asked how his day was going.

'Ah, I'm just exhausted by the enthusiasm of people thinking they've got something new. If you've just got some guy going: 'Oh, I offer advice on the whole of the market, I'm doing this, I'm doing that... I offer a bespoke service.' I don't want a bespoke service, you know? You need creative people in this industry to move the business on.'

His name was Gordon, and he looked to be in his mid-50s. Early on in our conversation, he alluded to having amassed immense wealth over the years as a veteran of the property investment scene. I was curious to learn what, in his opinion, constituted a creative idea in the property industry.

He explained: 'Newbies to the business might be happy buying property at 20 per cent below market rate, and that's fine. But if you've been in the business for as long as I have, the last thing you want to do is spend money.'

I learned that when my new acquaintance spoke of creativity, he meant creative ways to make money while spending as little as of it as possible. He shared a few of the strategies he'd adopted over the years: getting in with housebuilders who 'if they knew you,' would give you a 25 per cent discount on a property, dabbling – naturally – in buy-to-let, then moving onto lease purchase options, which landlord software provider PropertyHawk warns are often 'used to exploit vulnerable homeowners' by people who 'don't have a great moral compass.'[7]

Were 'lease purchase options' the latest thing? No, they were all the rage a few years back. The hot new thing at the moment, he said, was property education. In other words, the serious money these days is not in doing what the likes of Tony Gimple or even Robbie Fowler tell you to do. The serious money is in being the person selling the knowledge. Somehow this idea tickled me: that the biggest winner of all was the National Landlord Investment Show itself.

Now that all the low-hanging fruit is gone, the buy-to-let industry has started to cannibalise itself. And yet, in spite of this, to use Gordon's own words, 'people [i.e. property speculators] like me aren't going to go away.' The climate is ripe for existing winners to scale up and consolidate their gains, while generation rent must increasingly rely on anomalies, handouts and loopholes to get a foot on the ladder, or otherwise face a lifetime of paying an increasing proportion of their earnings in rent to a landlord.

SECTION VII. WHAT SHOULD WE DO?

34. Some ways to make the system work

When I started writing this book, I thought it would be about the private rented sector. What I've learned is that the private rented sector is a bit player in this whole sorry saga.

In its 2019 election manifesto, Boris Johnson's triumphant Conservative Party committed itself to abolishing Section 21 no-fault evictions and introducing a Lifetime Deposit for renters, so that a deposit from a previous tenancy could be 'passported' to the next one.[1] These are important steps in the right direction, but I can't help but remain sceptical over the fate of the proposal to end Section 21. Loopholes lie ahead. Despite the abolition of no-fault evictions in Scotland, Scottish landlords can still evict contract-abiding rent-paying tenants from their homes with less than three months' notice, so long as one of seven grounds for eviction is met.

These are:

- Ground 1: Landlord intends to sell
- Ground 2: Property to be sold by lender
- Ground 3: Landlord intends to refurbish
- Ground 4: Landlord intends to live in the property
- Ground 5: Family member intends to live in the property
- Ground 6: Landlord intends to use for non-residential purposes

- Ground 7: Property required for religious purposes

There are 11 other grounds for eviction on the basis of the tenant's conduct and eligibility, and on the legal status of the landlord and his or her property.[2] It's much better than it was, but it's hardly a giant leap forward for tenantkind.

This is why, when it comes to reforming the private rented sector, I'm reluctant to reduce my conclusion to a list of policy demands. As a result of both my research findings and my direct experience of talking to tenants, landlords, politicians and activists, I have lost faith in the viability of the private rented sector as a mainstream, long-term provider of housing.

As we saw with Jess and her experiences renting in Exeter, the private rented sector can provide a good service at a reasonable price. But not, as in Leamington Spa, when it's the only option in a fiercely competitive market. Such markets reward rogues, and leave ethical landlords feeling cheated out of the additional profits they have forgone because they have a conscience. The rental market functions best when it's at the fringes: it's ideally suited to students, job hoppers, foreign workers only temporarily in the country, and mobile young professionals who don't want (rather than can't afford) to settle down and buy a house yet.

As a place in which to build a life and raise a family, the private rented sector is inexorably inadequate. The reforms tenants need aren't compatible with the profits buy-to-let landlords expect in exchange for the risk they assume. For the most part, the private rented sector should be replaced. It cannot do the job that council housing once did (which, as we have seen, was the entire reason for its rescue from the brink of oblivion in the first place). Institutional private landlords moving into the up-and-coming 'build to rent' sphere cater mostly to the wealthiest tenants.

And even though there's enough money in the housing benefit and universal credit coffers to deliver secure, so-called 'ethical' returns in the region of five per cent for private investors and fund managers in the social rented sector, there's not enough money left over to house the one million plus people stuck on social housing waiting lists.[3] In short, private investors and affordable housing don't mix.

Small private landlords and large institutional investors alike have no economic reason to provide low-cost housing. They don't want to be 'ethical' if it means reducing profits. They aren't charities. They don't want to be lenient on tenants who get into rent arrears because the government has messed up the roll-out of a new benefit, or because local housing allowances don't begin to cover market rents.

Even Ali, the disabled private renter who has been exiled from her hometown of Bristol by the private rented sector, doesn't blame landlords for her predicament: 'Why should they care? They aren't social housing providers.'

The only system that has ever successfully done the job of housing the nation's non-homeowners over the long term is social housing, before Right to Buy. The reasons for not bringing it back are ideological. Social housing purportedly creates 'dependency' and discourages 'self-reliance.'

These arguments are supposedly good enough reason to write a blank cheque for housing benefit and for support for 'mixed tenure' private developments,[4] no matter how much more expensive they are than councils providing rented homes.

The reasons for bringing back social housing on the other hand are empirical. Social housing is more cost-effective for government (and the taxpayer). It's cheaper, more secure, higher quality[5] and therefore more conducive to fostering strong communities for tenants than the private rented sector ever will be.

Germany is often held up as a shining example of how a well-regulated private rental market can function. But in April 2019, protesters took to the streets of Berlin to call for the nationalisation of the city's corporate landlords. They were fed up of rising rents triggered by monopolistic landlords who could skirt rules on rent controls.[6] According to *The Guardian*, if the campaign is a success, it will establish housing as a human right and could 'affect real estate companies as far away as London.'[7] Regardless of the outcome, the implications are clear: if tenants in the so-called 'renter's paradise' are being driven to protest, maybe the problem lies with privately rented housing itself. Isn't it time we stop sacrificing the health, happiness and economic prospects of swathes of society on the altar of a failed ideology?

Local authorities and housing associations

The bodies that currently provide social housing leave much to be desired. Housing associations are riddled with perverse incentives and enjoy an unacceptable level of immunity from their abuses. Granted, not all housing associations are the same. But much as the private rented sector rewards rogue landlords and squeezes ethical ones, housing associations are struggling to survive in a cut-throat economic environment. The easiest course of action is to dump the social conscience and invest in a good PR department.

Local authority housing departments can also be toxic. They

have given rise to nasty ideas like buying one-way train tickets out of town for homeless people,[8] and denying access to homelessness support services for people who flee bullying landlords on the grounds that they made themselves 'intentionally homeless.'

But much of the poison infecting local authorities arises from the fact that they have been systematically stripped of funds, resources and skilled personnel. Further, Right to Buy has acted as a huge deterrent for councils to build more of their own social housing, as new homes run the risk of being sold off at a discount before the council has recouped its costs.

The saving grace of the local authority is that councillors are elected, and the activities of local government come under the jurisdiction of the Freedom of Information Act. Housing associations on the other hand are able to act under a veil of secrecy, picking the pockets of their shared ownership tenants and other 'customers' to paper over the fact that they can't afford to provide social housing without government cash.

As we have seen, government cash without equity, democratic accountability and transparency all too often leads to leeching. This is borne out in the case studies of Help to Buy, shared ownership horror stories and successive rounds of government funding for 'affordable' housing that most cannot afford.

An entity should be run as a public good or service, paid for by taxes, or run privately and paid for by customers. The mixed model, where a public service is paid for by a small number of customers who've been snared in a contractual spider's web, and where taxes fatten the pay packets of unaccountable individuals, is surely the worst of both worlds.

Can housing associations be reformed?

In 1966, Ken Loach's drama *Cathy Come Home* was aired on BBC One. While fictional, it delivered a stark insight into the realities faced by homeless families in Britain, and its gritty documentary style deeply affected viewers. By pure fluke, the film coincided with the launch of housing charity Shelter, and the latter began to receive generous donations from audiences who were moved by Cathy's story. The housing associations that were inspired (and often financed) by this outpouring of support were dubbed 'the new philanthropists,' and they explicitly set out on a social mission to end the scourge of homelessness.[9]

At this point, housing associations' motives were pure and un-encumbered. If we can find a way to return them to this state, then perhaps they could play a powerful role in the battle to end the housing crisis.

But following a series of legislative changes that began in the 1980s, housing associations have been co-opted by governments in their aim to privatise social housing. Housing associations' social mission has been muddied by brutal government cutbacks designed to morph them into something more commerical, more profitable, more investor-friendly.[10] Many are now Frankenstein versions of their former selves.

To improve matters, we could make housing associations subject to the Freedom of Information Act,[11] and properly investigate the allegations of misbehaviour made by leaseholders like Ryan. In fact, this should be done as a matter of urgency. What's more, executive pay at housing associations could be brought back into line with the pay grades imposed on the rest of the public sector.

If we were to ban housing associations from using their customers to cross-subsidise a social housing sector starved of funds, then the true extent of government underfunding and mismanagement of the social housing sector would be laid bare. Housing associations would have to do what they should have done in the first place, and fight tooth and nail for adequate government funding on the grounds that they refuse to rinse their customers in the name of 'creating social value.'

But if we did all of this, what would we be left with? Something taxpayer funded which operates according to a 'cost renting' model (i.e. without the need for profits or surpluses)? That sounds very much like the housing department of a local authority. Either way, what matters is the way it works, not the name.

Reform of the sector will also require a shift in politics. New Labour, the Lib-Con coalition and the 2015 Conservative government all, to varying degrees, felt that direct state provision of public goods and services was a thing of the past. Instead they believed the state should provide funding to allow the market to deliver solutions. In housing, this meant taking steps to subsidise the demand for homes (giving people rent money and help with mortgage deposits) in the hope that the market would spontaneously decide to supply them.

By feeding and celebrating the property boom, then propping up the market with state subsidy once the bubble burst, governments of the past 20 years have demonstrated that demand-led solutions to the housing crisis do not work. Social landlords and aspiring homeowners cannot thrive alongside speculators and property tycoons. Government has to pick a side. Currently, social housing providers must compete for land in a system that rewards speculation and punishes attempts to deliver long-term social benefits. Until that changes, perverse incentives for housing associations and private property developers alike will remain.

Reinstating the rights of the commons

Challenging the status quo begins with a rethink of how we perceive commonly-owned assets. The prevailing ideology is that state ownership is wholly bad, while private ownership is wholly good. This has given way to what can only be described as a fire sale of public land over the past 40 years. In 1979, 20 per cent of Britain's landmass belonged to the commons. Now, that figure stands at just 10.5 per cent.[12]

In his review of *The New Enclosure* by Brett Christophers, Ian Jack notes how we used to own school playing fields, railway arches, forests, parks, farms and moors – the list goes on. Since 1979, £400 billion worth of publicly-owned land (with just one tenth of this comprising Right to Buy housing stock) has been sold without our consent.[13]

This may have helped raise funds for governments past, and brought some idle pastures into productive use. But these quick wins came at a steep cost: there is now a severe shortage of land for affordable housebuilding. The demand for developable land is now so acute that land accounts for 70 per cent of the value of a typical UK home.[14]

If the public owns something, we all have the opportunity to benefit from it, both now and for generations to come. If a private individual owns something, it is only accessible if we pay rent to a private gatekeeper. The planning system was supposed to solve this problem by democratising land use, but it is powerless to stop developers from drip-feeding new properties onto the market to keep prices artificially high. Since 2012-13, local authorities have approved nine out of ten planning applications, and since 2009-10 permission has been granted for over 2.6 million units. Of these, over 40 per cent – 1.1 million units – are yet to be completed.[15] Still more developable land has been tied into option and promotion agreements by strategic land investors, who are poised to pocket vast planning gains as soon as the local authority approval comes through. As a result, affordable housing and local amenities are squeezed out in favour of 'luxury' developments that deliver maximum resale value.

Despite all this, as Brett Christophers' book highlights, accusations of 'land hoarding' are still largely directed at local governments[16], who remain under constant pressure to dispose of their landholdings thanks to ongoing funding cuts.

Private property development undoubtedly has its place when it comes to solving the housing crisis. Especially if the planning and land acquisition process can be reformed so that it's easier and cheaper for smaller developers to enter the market. But Britain's most, and arguably only, successful affordable housebuilding programme to date was spearheaded by massive public sector investment in social housing.

As Josh Ryan-Collins and his colleagues show, social and other non-market housebuilding can counteract the volatility of private sector development by sustaining a steady level of demand for skills and building materials during market slumps.[17] When the property development industry imploded post-2008, the pain was compounded by the loss of many small- to medium-sized housebuilders and a shortage of bricks.[18] A strong public sector housebuilding programme might have helped keep greater numbers of construction workers and suppliers in business in those post-crash years, which could have greatly sped up the recovery.

It's worth mentioning as well that private housebuilding reached its peak alongside the peak in council housebuilding.[19] So the idea that the private sector only thrives when the state retreats is not borne out in the housing sector. If anything, the opposite is true.

To recreate the housebuilding successes of the post-war period, some reform of the compulsory purchase process will be necessary. Government must no longer be compelled to pay landowners the speculative 'hope value' of an empty field, and should instead be able to acquire land at closer to its current 'use value,' as recommended by Shelter's former head of policy (and, for a brief period, No 10 housing adviser) Toby Lloyd. This measure is likely to be politically controversial,[20] but it must be re-emphasised here that land speculation is not about entrepreneurship, creativity or innovation, since landowners do not create land values. Remuneration at or near existing 'use value' would also be a fair trade, as it would be in line with the sum the landowner originally paid to acquire the land.

Currently, the bulk of the value created by a new housing development can be siphoned off by an idle landowner before a single brick is laid. This is madness. A government-sanctioned right to collect windfall gains through ownership of land titles is not capitalism; it is feudalism. It has no place in a 21st century society.

Beyond the broken market

In a landmark move in 2018 Theresa May, removed the borrowing cap that prevented local authorities from accessing finance to build homes.[21] It was a tacit acknowledgement that the market had failed to solve the housing crisis, and that social housing might be a part of the solution.

But for this move to have the desired impact, all forms of Right to Buy must be scrapped. All variations on Help to Buy must be wound up as soon as possible, and the byzantine system of determining what constitutes 'affordable' housing needs to be binned and rethought, with affordability linked instead to actual local earnings. The planning system should be overhauled in favour of local communities and their needs, and away from central planners and corporate housebuilders. The feudalistic leasehold tenure must either be radically reformed or abolished. Ditto for housing sold as 'freehold' which is actually bound by restrictive covenants that leave homeowners on the hook for endless fees and management charges.[22] Funding for social housing, community-led housing and Community Land Trusts, which keep homes permanently out of the hands of speculators, should take priority over funding for trendy build to rent and urban regeneration projects, which often end up catering to wealthier tenants and buyers while forcing out those on lower incomes.

More broadly, it's not enough to say 'we need more social and community-led housing.' We've also got to define who it's for and what role it should play in society. History shows that social housing in particular works best when it is for ordinary working people as well as for the underprivileged.

As we have seen, in just a few decades the council house has gone from being a desirable place to live to a cultural emblem for crime, fecklessness and social degeneracy. This transformation occurred, not because state-provided housing itself engenders the so-called 'virtuous circle of dependency,' but because of policy changes designed to kill off social housing. Right to Buy started the rot. Then the compounding effects of the priority need system and a spate of other social asset-stripping policies contrived to make sure that:

a) There wasn't enough social housing to go around; and

b) The social housing that was available was the least desirable, situated in the worst areas, and selectively allocated to those with the most 'complex needs.'

Rekindling the post-war 'golden age' in social housing would require an attitude change as much as it would require policy changes. We need to stop seeing homes as trophies for personal success. Society loses when high rent costs make it impossible for millions of people to afford to challenge low pay and precarious work conditions; let alone do something better.

We need policymakers to acknowledge that successful towns and cities rely on more than a handful of wealthy elites to prosper. We also need nurses, street cleaners, schoolteachers, waiting staff, street food chefs, market stallholders, office administrators, artists, plumbers, musicians, receptionists, police officers, window cleaners and the rest.

With some landlords now turning to the more lucrative opportunities of short-term letting made possible by Airbnb, homes for local people are being lost to the tourism industry. But the irony is that the rich cultural mix of a given location is what tends to pull in tourists in the first place.

Culture is a living, breathing thing that is made by the community. Property developers, who are wont to pounce on locations that can be marketed as trendy, creative hotspots for young professionals, risk killing off the social capital that makes a location valuable in the first place. A development in Hackney Wick called the Bagel Factory that keeps cropping up on my Twitter feed is a prime example. In an ad for one of their luxury apartments, the developers write: 'Stray away from mainstream living with Bagel Factory apartments – inspired by the artists of Hackney Wick.'

The accompanying picture is of an open-plan living area with floor to ceiling windows, exposed brickwork, Scandi-inspired furnishings and an abundance of large potted plants – what you might call a 'sterilised bohemian' aesthetic. In smaller text below the image are the words 'Help To Buy from £580,000.'

Beneath this tweet, someone called Lewis Heriz writes: 'As an artist of Hackney Wick whose studio is now rubble thanks to redevelopment, I have to ask that you don't use us to sell your eye-wateringly overpriced apartments. How many studios are you providing for the displaced artists that have 'inspired' you?'

'Who's being helped to buy, millionaires?' says another critic. 'DO NOT USE PEOPLE YOU HELP DISENFRANCHISE AS CLICKBAIT!!' reads another. Someone also points out that, despite the heart-stopping price tag, the apartment is 'next to the A12 and a great stinking recycling yard.'[23]

Many of the sites acquired for these sparkling new developments are former council estates. According to the BBC, as of September 2018, 'more than 31,000 residents will be affected in 118 sites undergoing or facing regeneration' across London, with activists fearing that the majority of the homes on these estates will not be replaced.

These fears are justified by precedent. When the Heygate Estate in Southwark was demolished between 2011 and 2014 and replaced by a luxury development called Elephant Park, just 82 homes out of 3,000 on the new development were for social rent. Before the site was torn down, the number of socially rented homes stood at 1,200.[24] None of this would have been possible without a rich stock of commonly-owned wealth for private developers to ransack.

If we're going to have a social and community-led housing renaissance, it's got to be ambitious enough to make access to cities, jobs, culture and thriving social and professional networks possible for all the people who give an area not just its wealth, but its soul too. It's got to push the private rented sector to the fringes, where the latter will be able to do what it does best: cater to the needs of students, tourists and affluent individuals who prefer not to buy. Above all, it's got to drive out the greed that not only killed the housing dream, but gave birth to it in the first place.

There is also one other big idea – much bigger than the rest – which could transform the property market for the good.

35. Time for a land value tax

Henry George is the most influential American economist you've probably never heard of. His ideas won the support of everyone from Albert Einstein, Leo Tolstoy and Bertrand Russell to swathes of the working class. Published in 1879, his book, *Progress and Poverty*,[1] begins with a groundbreaking observation: the richer a geographical area becomes, the poorer its have-nots become.

Undeveloped regions, George observed, tend to start out with most inhabitants living in humble yet adequate conditions. Economic advancements then shunt people in both directions, with fewer and fewer remaining in the middle as time goes on. In other words: it isn't just that economic progress leaves some people behind – it actively plunges the poor deeper into poverty.

George agonised over this paradox after he visited New York for the first time in 1860s. Despite the city's grandeur and op-ulence, he couldn't fathom why it had more deprivation and squalor than the less-wealthy West coast of the United States. After years of research, he finally identified an underlying cause.

His conclusions owed much to the work of a political econ-omist called David Ricardo. Ricardo formulated his well-known Law of Rent around the time of the Napoleonic Wars, when corn and land prices rose steeply. Many blamed high corn prices on rising agricultural rents. However, Ricardo argued that the reverse was true: that demand for corn was swelling the rental value of land. Moreover, the amount of rent a landlord could charge was roughly equal to the surplus profits his land could generate, relative to the profitability of the best available rent-free or 'marginal' land. This concept was known as 'economic rent.' Ricardo showed how, in agriculture, economic rent is not something landlords or farmers can control. It is a surplus made possible by the land's natural attributes and the market demand for its produce (i.e. corn). Invariably, this naturally occurring wealth would flow, not to the farmers who worked the land, but to the landlords who sat back and did nothing.

George's breakthrough was to apply this theory to the wider economy. In doing so, he exposed how an outsized proportion of all the new wealth being created was flowing to idle landowners, while industrious tenants and workers were getting ripped off. He saw that technological advancements, free enterprise and investments in infrastructure did little to boost the prosperity of the working classes, as the economic benefits of progress were often sucked up by soaring rents.

Progress and Poverty purportedly sold more copies in 1890s America than any other book except the Bible,[2] and George quickly amassed a tremendous following around the globe. As the 20th century progressed however, his ideas fell out of favour. The role of land was sidelined by the academic establishment and 'capital' was given pride of place as the most important factor of production.

But Ricardo's Law of Rent, with a few tweaks, does a decent job of describing the mechanisms that drive today's housing crisis. In truth, the landlord's yield is made up of two elements – 1) a charge for the tenant's use of the building, and 2) the 'economic rent'; the surplus income a tenant can earn by living in an area of high economic activity (relative to an area where there's hardly any work). It's the latter component that has ballooned in the last 20 years, driving up the profitability of private landlordism.[3]

What is a land value tax?
Henry George's proposed solution to this problem was a land value tax (LVT).

LVT would be levied on the 'unimproved' value of land, i.e. the bit that wasn't created by the landowner. This distinguishes it from a property tax. A property tax disincentivises productive activities like building and renovation, because improving a dwelling increases its tax burden.

LVT, on the other hand, makes sitting on land not only futile, but expensive. If implemented in London, the wealth-incubating powers of prime London real estate would dissolve. Thousands of silent luxury ghost towers would have to be released onto the real 'open market': the one that responds to the purchasing power of the majority of Londoners, and not just the uncountable fortunes of a handful of elites.

LVT would stop the retirement savings of the entire nation from pouring into land and property. Instead, millions of UK citizens would avoid property as a retirement nest-egg – and instead invest in productive enterprises that stimulate the economy, create jobs, and spur technological innovation.

While this might lead to a virtuous circle of jobs raising spending and spending increasing jobs, it is also unlikely to produce the levels of unbridled land speculation that drive the destabilising 'boom and bust' cycle, because the more valuable the land becomes, the more it will be weighed down by tax levies.

Because UK land can't be hidden in a complex warren of shell companies in Panama, LVT would be practically impossible to evade. If you don't pay your taxes, you forfeit your land. Therefore, the bulk of economic rents would be captured by the government, to be spent or redistributed for the benefit of citizens.

For purists like George himself, LVT would be the tax to replace all other taxes – hence why it's sometimes known as 'the single tax.' Income tax, national insurance, VAT, council tax, corporation tax, and a long list of stealth taxes… all could be consolidated into one periodic payment, levied on the freeholders of land. The large bill that LVT would produce for millions of ordinary homeowners would be offset by the lifting of all other forms of taxation.

Even if an idea this radical would be unthinkable at the moment, many economists from all points on the political spectrum agree that taxes on land values are the fairest form of tax.[4] They cause the fewest market distortions and neutralise many of capitalism's self-destructive tendencies. The same cannot be said for taxes on earnings and consumption. As ever, the barriers to change lie, not in the technicalities, but in politics.

The Stern cover-up

From 2003 to 2007, the economist Nicholas Stern headed the Government Economic Service. During this time, he wrote three reports. The first was on climate change and the second was for the Commission for Africa: both influenced government policy. The third report never saw the light of day. Instead, it was, in Lord Stern's words, 'promptly buried in the Chancellor's drawer' as soon as it was submitted. According to a *Financial Times* article written by Stern in 2014, the report recommended overhauling the UK taxation regime with the introduction of a land value tax.[5]

Fred Harrison, an economist and journalist, wrote about the cover-up in his 2015 book, *As Evil Does*. A long-time proponent of LVT, he made a Freedom of Information request for the government to publish Lord Stern's report. The response he got was surprising. The government reported that it could 'neither confirm nor deny' the report's existence.[6] After reading this, I emailed Lord Stern to ask for a copy of the report. Within days, I received a gracious response from his assistant: unfortunately, he was not at liberty to share it with me because it was an 'internal document.' Existence: confirmed. Contents: still a state secret.

Ever since Henry George first advanced the idea, land value tax has been repeatedly suppressed, mocked and disparaged. After the inclusion of a mild form of it in the Labour Party manifesto in 2017, Theresa May warned that it amounted to a 'devastating tax on homes and gardens.'[7] Without a shred of evidence, sections of the press issued dire predictions that people might be forced to sell their gardens if the law came to pass.[8]

A 'Georgist' economist Mason Gaffney argues that the entire neoclassical school of economic thought came into being to oppose the threat posed by Henry George and his 'single tax propaganda.'[9] It's fair to say that throughout its existence LVT has been a highly charged and controversial topic.

But how come? To find out, I spoke to Laurie Macfarlane, an economist who co-wrote *Rethinking the Economics of Land and Housing* with Josh Ryan-Collins and Toby Lloyd. The book successfully managed to talk about landownership, economic rent, and bank lending without raising the hackles of academics or the eyebrows of the media. On the contrary, *The Financial Times'* Martin Wolf named it one of the 'best books of 2017.'

I wanted to know how Laurie and his colleagues had pulled off this feat without being marginalised as raving loonies who dream of taxing everyone's flowerbeds. We met on a bright and blustery afternoon outside the British Library. I began with a vital question: Could LVT deliver the factory reset our housing market needs?

His blunt answer was: probably not. 'It's no magic bullet,' he said. Firstly, it would be difficult to bring in a land value tax without creating 'gigantic winners and losers overnight.' As we've seen, land prices under the rules of the current market account for the future potential of a piece of land as well as its current use value. Current homeowners therefore have already paid for an LVT-free future. LVT would depress house prices, because all those future LVT payments would need to be factored into today's prices. 'It would literally wipe out the wealth of large parts of the population,' Laurie explains, 'it's not just the rich, it's the middle class.'

Of course, the flipside of the above argument is that homeowners across the class spectrum have 'benefited a huge amount through house price inflation,' as Laurie put it. As a consequence, millions of young and disenfranchised people have been robbed of their hope of ever attaining the same level of financial security as their parents' generation, condemning them to a lifetime of instability as private renters. If we are to balance the conflicting interests of homeowners and renters, how can we find a way forward?

Repeating past mistakes

Land value tax doesn't have to be the sledgehammer proposed by

Henry George. The classical LVT would be a 100 per cent tax on the rental value of all land, effectively reducing its capital value to zero. But reforming the incentives surrounding landownership wouldn't require such extreme action.

For the last half century, successive governments have ploughed billions into subsidising homeownership and propping up the land and housing markets. The market is already distorted by government intervention, and merely rolling back or rethinking these interventions would go a long way towards fixing the problem.

Sadly, it looks like the lessons of the past have not been learnt. The housing policy with the most damage potential in the 2019 Conservative Party manifesto was not the commitment to extend Right to Buy to 'spread the dream of homeownership to even more people.' Nor was it the promise to 'review new ways to support home ownership' following the scheduled wind-up of Help to Buy in 2023. It was the pledge to 'encourage a new market in long-term fixed rate mortgages' for first-time buyers, which, the manifesto claimed, would 'slash the cost of deposits.'[10]

This proposal was based on a report released by the Centre for Policy Studies entitled *Resentful Renters*. This identified the Financial Policy Committee's strenuous 'stress test' as a key barrier to getting on the property ladder. As I discussed earlier, the fact that aspiring homeowners are assessed on their ability to afford mortgage repayments following a three-point hike to interest rates makes many ineligible for a mortgage.

The solution proposed by the Centre for Policy Studies is for the government to 'play a powerful role' in supporting mortgage providers to offer fixed low-rate mortgages over a period of 25-40 years. According to its analysis, this would enable an extra '1.83 million' people to afford a mortgage.[11] A flurry of mortgage credit creation has helped drive house prices to current unaffordable levels. And yet here we are, with house prices on the life support of ultra-low interest rates, and the government is backing more mortgage credit creation.

When the report was announced, I tweeted about the likelihood that further house price inflation would price out even more renters in the long run. Robert Colevile, director of the Centre for Policy Studies, shot back that my argument was 'a point we address thoroughly.'[12] Indeed, the report accepts that the policy will help bid up prices, and runs the risk of 'potentially stoking another bubble.' It suggests that this inflationary potential could be mitigated in two ways. Somewhat vaguely, the first is to 'continue housebuilding efforts.' The second is to 'gently persuade' private landlords 'to park their money elsewhere' with further tax changes.[13] While I endorse both of these to a degree, the Centre for Policy Studies overlooks the reality that, because of the scarcity of social housing, hundreds of thousands of low-income households rely on the private rented sector as a last line of defence against homelessness. Chasing private landlords out of the market before reinvigorating the social rented sector risks exacerbating an already severe problem.

We need to wake up to the fact that our economy is far too dependent on an ever-expanding supply of mortgage credit. The current banking system pumps up house prices. Banks channel roughly five times more money into secured lending to individuals (mostly mortgages) than they do into businesses that grow the economy.[14] Most new money that is created is therefore being soaked up by the land and property markets, when it ought to be fuelling the nation's start-ups and small businesses.

The former Shadow Housing Secretary, John Healey, has suggested that the Bank of England should take a more proactive role in monitoring house price inflation with an annual house price inflation target,[15] in much the same way as it aims to maintain general inflation at two per cent. Regulatory bodies could then prick growing property bubbles before they blow up.

However, even if we were to ban banks from lending against property altogether and revert to the pre-1980s system of mortgages funded by savers' deposits, this wouldn't change the attractiveness of property to speculators. People with capital will still use residential property to generate a low risk return, especially while interest rates on cash deposits are so dismal. Thus, banking system reform without land-use reform would probably hoist the property ladder up even further.

The first port of call in breaking the land-finance cycle therefore is to focus on land. Is it possible to capture unearned wealth locked within the land without crashing the property market and triggering a recession?

This was the aim of *Land for the Many*, a report on land reform commissioned by the Labour Party and written by Laurie Macfarlane, Robin Grey, Tom Kenny, Anna Powell-Smith, Guy Shrubsole and Beth Stratford. In the introduction, its editor, the journalist George Monbiot, makes clear that political sensitivities are no excuse for letting the land problem go unaddressed, arguing that the issue needs to be 'at the heart of the political agenda.'

The report's headline-grabbing idea is to set up what the authors call a Common Ground Trust, which would be a non-profit, commonly-owned institution dedicated to helping people buy homes. Aspiring homebuyers would apply to the trust for assistance, and once a price had been agreed for a particular home, the trust would be able to buy the land beneath the property. The buyers would therefore only have to secure finance for the building itself, significantly lowering the bar of entry into the housing market. The new homeowner would then pay a mortgage on the building and rent to the trust. In this way, 'land rents can be socialised,' while existing homeowners would still be able to sell their homes at current market values. The property market would stay afloat for those who have their net worth locked in bricks and mortar, while the rent paid to the trust would effectively function as a form of LVT.

The report also recommends reforming council tax. The current system relies on property valuations dating back to 1991, just after the 1990 crash. As a result, rates are now well below the true value of dwellings. Council tax reform has been previously proposed by the left-wing think tank, the Institute of Public Policy Research, which highlighted that in London, the poorest residents pay 8.1 per cent of their household earnings in council tax, while the top 10 per cent pay just 1.3 per cent.[16]

By scrapping the banding system, levying taxes on owners rather than residents, and basing the taxes on current property values, the system could be made fairer for everyone, while raising revenues for local government. *Land for the Many* also suggested ramping up surcharges for empty dwellings and residences owned by people domiciled outside the UK for tax purposes.[17]

These proposals are highly unlikely to be implemented any time soon, thanks to Labour's crushing defeat in the 2019 general election. Even so, if there is one thing the *Land for the Many* report makes absolutely clear, it's that 'the land problem' is not going to go away on its own. Socially created land values enrich some and impoverish others, and we need more informed, nuanced public debate on the topic.

For Laurie Macfarlane, understanding the political forces at play should be central to any resolution to the housing crisis: 'Previously, we had a situation where homeownership became the dominant tenure by far, and homeowners tended to be the people who would turn out to vote,' he said. 'Therefore it [the situation] was always going to be self-reinforcing, in that politicians wrote more policies to protect and enhance the wealth of homeowners, at the expense of non-homeowners – who are in the minority, and less likely to vote.' As such, so long as homeownership remains the dominant tenure, a progressive idea like LVT is likely to stay, as Lord Stern puts it, safely 'buried in the chancellor's drawer.'

But how long is this state of affairs going to last? Homeownership nationwide stands at 65 per cent of total households, and has been forecast to dwindle over the next 20 years.[18] NatWest bank predicts that, by 2025, more people will be renters than mortgagees.[19] It's true that first-time buyer activity has increased slightly since 2018, but a substantial portion of this is underwritten by the Bank of Mum and Dad, loosening mortgage credit, and various government schemes. Increasing numbers of first-time buyers are also finding themselves trapped in exploitative leasehold contracts which amount to little more than a tenancy agreement strapped to a mortgage.

In London, the balance has already tipped, with more than 50 per cent of the population renting as of 2016.[20] 'This is why I think the Tories are worried about housing now,' said Laurie, 'It was explicitly recognised in the 80s by the Thatcher government that promoting a 'property owning democracy' was about eroding social sentiment. Giving people a stake in private property made them more likely to vote Tory, that was always the plan.'

It's impossible to say at which point the nation's priorities will change. But if the struggles faced by generation rent go unaddressed, eventually there will be a critical mass of voters who suffer substantially from the special status in society afforded to homeowners. At this point, the idea of a full-blown land value tax could win mass approval.

As discussed in Chapter 4, fending off popular support for ideas that run counter to landed interests was the whole point of Noel Skelton's original vision for a 'property owning democracy' in 1923. Politicians can wring their hands and talk nonsense about the threat posed by 'garden taxes,' and how homes that don't hoover up all your disposable income 'create social dependency.' But in resisting change, they ignore the cost of failing to act, and refusing to compromise. As a result, the eventual resolution to the housing crisis could end up being far more radical and profound than current politicians expect. There is too much pent up frustration and anger to ignore.

'We are not your assets'

The real dream is to live a life where you can forget about housing. Where a secure, genuinely affordable home is no longer a privilege, nor is it nirvana. It is simply somewhere safe and warm to eat, sleep, wash, relax and store your belongings, ideally close to friends, family and work.

This humble ambition won't be realised without a fight. The financialisation of land and housing has turned a generation of renters into an asset class. Tenants now save more into their landlords' retirement funds than they do into their own pensions.[21] It's time for generation rent to get angry, and not be fobbed off with 'affordable' housing that promises to take away 'only' one third of their pre-tax salary – closer to 40 per cent after tax. Mortgaged homeowners typically pay just 18 per cent of their earnings for a home they will eventually own outright.[22]

The value of private rented sector housing stock exceeded £1.5 trillion in 2019, having grown by £61 billion in 2018 alone.[23] That's about £22,500 worth of buy-to-let property wealth per person in the UK.[24] Those riches grew at the expense of generation rent, who now face an uncertain and precarious future.

Stephen Hill was right: It's a war out there. Human beings are exploited when they become someone else's assets. Groups become powerful when they feel that so much is taken from them that they have nothing left to lose.

Acknowledgements

The genesis of this book was a bit unusual: it began life as a competition entry. In December 2017, I had just started a blog on the politics of land and property ownership (as you do), when I saw a call out on Facebook for a young writer to tell the story of 'generation rent'. I refashioned my ideas for the blog into a book proposal, thinking nothing would come of it. The blog is now defunct, and the book you are currently holding is far better than anything I could have produced by myself, thanks to the support and expertise of the people around me.

First and foremost, I owe a huge debt to Martin Hickman, my publisher and editor. Martin thankfully looked past my stylistic quirks and lack of formal training in journalism and saw enough potential to offer me a book deal. His patience and wisdom have been invaluable. He helped me see the bigger picture and separate the wheat from the chaff.

My partner Rowan kept me sane with a steady supply of pep talks and caffeine. He also did the bulk of the housework while I wrote, for which I will be forever grateful. My mum, dad and sister Rose gave indispensable moral and practical support. My friends managed not to glaze over during umpteen conversations about housing. Rowan, Rose and Emma also helped me to transcribe interview recordings, saving me hours of tedious, painstaking work. My cousin Alex proofread the manuscript and gave valuable feedback in record time, and Allie and Steve also helped check for factual and other errors. You are all appreciated more than you know.

I owe a heartfelt thank you to the people who agreed to share their stories with me. This includes everyone who took part in the online surveys I put out, those who spoke to me via social media, and those who were willing to be interviewed. Whether or not your story made the final cut, your contributions gave life to this book; the story falls flat without you.

I am especially grateful to those who spoke to me despite possible legal or professional ramifications. Thank you for reviewing the sections in which you appear and giving me your blessing to publish. Your willingness to speak out makes it possible to hold the powerful to account.

I owe a massive thank you to ACORN's Sheffield branch, who welcomed me into their ranks and helped me see first hand the struggles faced by private renters today. Jonny Butcher and Jo Hiley deserve a special mention – thank you both for the time and attention you gave.

Thank you to Dan Wilson Craw, the Director of the Generation Rent campaign organisation, for taking the time to speak to me and share your insights. In the time it's taken me to write this book, you and your colleagues have been instrumental in securing a government promise to end Section 21 evictions and introduce tenancy 'deposit passporting', as well as raising awareness of the plight of UK private renters. I hope you feel this book has done its title justice.

The Leasehold Knowledge Partnership was a vital resource,

and I am particularly grateful to journalist and campaigner Harry Scoffin for helping me find answers and deepen my understanding of the leasehold scandal.

I'm thankful to the politicians who offered their time and assistance, notably Labour MP and Sheffield City Region Mayor Dan Jarvis, who tabled a question on my behalf in parliament, and Conservative MP Bob Blackman, who not only shared his expertise but offered to help when a single parent I was interviewing was about to become homeless. I'd also like to thank an aide (who did not wish to be named) to the former Shadow Housing Secretary and Labour MP John Healey, who provided valuable insights and information.

Intellectually, this book rests on the work and assistance of too many people to name, but a handful stand out. Graham Hodges, a volunteer researcher for think tank Positive Money, helped me to understand the mechanics of money creation and how the mortgage market changed dramatically in the 1980s. Economist Laurie Macfarlane gave a stellar account of the political backdrop to the homeownership dream, and historian Christopher England sharpened my understanding of the historical milieu of Henry George, and provided vital feedback.

I am also indebted to the members of the LVT Facebook group, who proved that respectful and well-reasoned debate on social media is still possible. Thank you to everyone who challenged and enlightened me there (especially fellow author and LVT enthusiast Phil Anderson*).

*Not to be confused with Philip J Anderson, who is noted for his work on the land and credit cycle. He also inspired me, though I have never met him.

The economist Akhil Patel introduced me to Henry George and the concept of economic rent in his monthly newsletter *Cycles, Trends and Forecasts*. Various books and articles by Josh Ryan-Collins, Laurie Macfarlane and Toby Lloyd (especially *Rethinking the Economics of Land and Housing*) have formed the bedrock of my understanding of the UK housing crisis and the banking system that feeds it.

Books by journalist Anna Minton (chiefly *Big Capital*) also had a major influence on my work, particularly on the subjects of estate regeneration and the 'domino effect' of the spread of housing inequality. The leading housing solicitor Giles Peaker's blog *Nearly Legal* was my go-to resource on all things housing law. Lastly, books by academics Brian Lund (*Housing Politics in the United Kingdom*), Alan Murie (*The Right to Buy?*) and Duncan Bowie (*Radical Solutions to the Housing Supply Crisis*) were essential resources on the history of housing and housing policy in the UK.

Thank you all for being giants on whose shoulders I stand.

I must also thank my first writing coaches Steve Dearden and Danny Broderick. Steve and Danny accepted me into their young writers' development scheme, The Writing Squad, back in 2011, and Steve supported me in the early stages of drafting this book. He was also the one who shared the original call out for a writer to work on a book about generation rent, so without him (and The Writing Squad, and in turn the support of Arts Council England) I would not be a published author today.

Finally, I can't write the acknowledgements of my first book without a nod to my Year 7 English teacher Jim McKeown, who was kind enough to take me seriously when I told him my goal was to publish a book by the age of 13. Thank you for believing in me, even if it took me 16 years longer than planned.

UK housing is a vast and complex subject, spanning the fields of finance, economics, law, politics, business, history, sociology and public policy. I've tried my best to defer to the experts on technical and scholarly matters, and represent people, groups and ideas fairly and accurately. In spite of this, it's entirely possible that errors and omissions remain. If you spot a mistake, or feel I have misrepresented something, please feel free to let me know, and I will do my best to make amends. You can email me at generationrentbook@gmail.com, or send me a direct message on Twitter; my handle is @GenRentBook.

On a final note, this book was written and edited before the 2020 outbreak of the novel coronavirus, which sent much of the globe into state-enforced lockdown. The resulting economic jolt is bound to shake house prices, making ownership more affordable to those lucky enough to keep their jobs. Just as in previous downturns, however, the deep structural problems in the UK's housing market – the fiscal bias towards ownership and paucity of rights for renters – will persist without determined reform. My hope is that support for that will grow, helped by this book.

NOTES

SECTION I. TRYING TO BUY A HOME

1. Can't buy, won't buy

1. The average tenancy... lasts about four years: *English Housing Survey 2018 to 2019: headline report*, MHCLG, accessible at: https://assets.publishing. service.gov.uk/government/uploads/system/uploads/attachment_data/ file/860076/2018-19_EHS_Headline_Report.pdf

2. on average... 60 per cent faster than wages between 2011 and 2017: *Rentquake: Change in private rents from 2011 to 2017*, Shelter, accessible at: https://england.shelter.org.uk/support_us/campaigns/rising_rents

3. homes in England and Wales now cost... before tax: *House price to residence-based earnings ratio* [March 2019], ONS, accessible at: https:// www.ons.gov.uk/peoplepopulationandcommunity/housing/datasets/ ratioofhousepricetoresidencebasedearningslowerquartileandmedian

4. In Scotland... 7 times average incomes: *The state of Scotland's housing market in four charts*, BBC News, accessible at: https://www.bbc.co.uk/ news/uk-scotland-46945882

5. The ratio in Northern Ireland... at 4.8: *Northern Ireland should see house prices rise again in 2019*, Danske Bank, accessible at: https://danskebank. co.uk/business/economic-analysis/opinion/northern-ireland-should-see-house-prices-rise-again-in-2019

6. in Northern Ireland house prices... as of October 2019: *Northern Ireland house prices soar as rest of UK remains stagnant, Belfast Telegraph*, accessible at: https://www.belfasttelegraph.co.uk/news/northern-ireland/northern-ireland-house-prices-soar-as-rest-of-uk-remains-stagnant-38550834.html

7. in 2007, 73 per cent... born in the late 1980s onwards: *Home ownership falls more in UK than any other EU country, The Independent*, accessible at: https://www.independent.co.uk/news/business/analysis-and-features/ uk-home-ownership-falls-more-than-eu-country-france-poland-property-market-a8501836.html

2. 'Refusing to leave home'

1. *The Daily Mail... before they turned 26: How to become a property developer in your twenties, Daily Mail*, accessible at: https://www.dailymail. co.uk/news/article-6683857/Three-millennials-debunk-myth-home-ownership-building-property-portfolio-worth-750k.html

2. Metro... first home aged 19: Property: *Meet the 29-year-old who built a*

property empire before she hit 30, Metro, accessible at: https://www.metro. news/property-meet-the-29-year-old-who-built-a-property-empire-before-she-hit-30/1240168/

3. In 2005... 'hand-outs and a spare bed': The article concedes 'soaring house prices' are partly to blame, but is nonetheless unsympathetic. *The Boomerang Generation, The Independent*, accessible at: https://www. independent.co.uk/news/uk/this-britain/the-boomerang-generation-kidults-move-back-home-489964.html

4. After the 2008 crash... 'keeping themselves entertained': *Generation who refuse to grow up, Daily Mail*, accessible at: https://www.dailymail. co.uk/news/article-2176281/Generation-refuse-grow-No-mortgage-No-marriage-No-children-No-career-plan-Like-30-somethings-Marianne-Power-admits-shes-.html

5. overall... 8 per cent of the economically active population: *UK unemployment rate drops to 7.7%, BBC News*, accessible at: https://www.bbc. co.uk/news/business-24045546

6. while youth unemployment stood at 21.9 per cent: *Youth unemployment across the OECD, The Guardian*, accessible at: https://www.theguardian. com/news/datablog/2012/may/16/youth-unemployment-europe-oecd

7. 'My parents... sacrifices need to be made': MoneySavingExpert. com Forums, accessible at: https://forums.moneysavingexpert.com/ showthread.php?t=5832478&page=3

8. This idea was summed up in 2017 by Tim Gurner... owning a home: *Millionaire to millennials: Lay off the avocado toast if you want a house, CNN Money*, accessible at: https://money.cnn.com/2017/05/15/news/ millennials-home-buying-avocado-toast/index.html

9. Elle Hunt, a journalist... 'lose a bit of the moral argument': *Can you really save for a deposit by ditching coffee and avocado toast? I tried to find out, The Guardian*, accessible at: https://www.theguardian.com/money/2018/ jan/29/can-you-really-save-for-a-deposit-by-ditching-coffee-and-avocado-toast-i-tried-to-find-out

10. Several months... owning a home wasn't a priority: *'A reader told me I was wasting my life': what I learned after my money diary went viral, The Guardian*, accessible at: https://www.theguardian.com/lifeandstyle/2018/ dec/18/what-i-learned-after-my-money-diary-went-viral

11. everyday 'luxuries' are much cheaper... in the past: All prices in today's money (except 'Flights') were calculated using the Bank of England inflation calculator as of 2nd February 2020, accessible at: https://www. bankofengland.co.uk/monetary-policy/inflation/inflation-calculator

12. Flights... costs just £686: *How far have fares really fallen since the golden age of flying? The Telegraph*, accessible at: https://www.telegraph.co.uk/travel/ comment/how-airfares-have-fallen-since-golden-age-of-flying/

13. Cinema... in 1989 cost £2.20: Bower, Anne L. ed. *Reel Food: Essays on Food and Film* (Oxfordshire: Routledge, 2012), p. 319

14. Mobile phone... cost £1,765: *How much did mobile phones cost in the 80s and 90s?* accessible at: https://www.mobilephonehistory.co.uk/lists/phones_by_price.php

15. Samsung smartphone... costs £250: *Samsung Galaxy S7 review,* accessible at: https://www.techradar.com/uk/reviews/phones/mobile-phones/samsung-galaxy-s7-1315188/review

16. Average home... £216,805: Figures taken from Q3 each year for consistency. *UK House Prices since 1952,* Nationwide, accessible at: https://www.nationwide.co.uk/about/house-price-index/download-data#xtab:uk-series

17. According to the Resolution Foundation... over-65s: *Home ownership in the UK*, Resolution Foundation, accessible at: https://www.resolutionfoundation.org/data/housing/

18. Sebastian Burnside... mortgage by 2025: *More People will Rent than Own their Homes in 8 Years, Economist Believes, Landlordnews.co.uk*, accessible at: https://www.landlordnews.co.uk/people-will-rent-homes-8-years/

19. English Housing Survey found that 27 per cent... (HHSRS): *English Housing Survey 2017 to 2018: private rented sector,* MHCLG, accessible at: https://assets.publishing.service.gov.uk/government/uploads/system/uploads/attachment_data/file/817630/EHS_2017-18_PRS_Report.pdf

20. Shelter found that renters... a master bedroom and a kitchen: *Renting in England: Paying more for less, Shelter Blog,* accessible at: https://blog.shelter.org.uk/2018/10/renting-in-england-paying-more-for-less/

21. Shelter warns... 'nearly nomadic.': *Renting families move so often they are nearly nomadic - new research,* Shelter, accessible at: https://blog.shelter.org.uk/2016/02/renting-families-move-so-often-they-are-nearly-nomadic-new-research/

22. 'a private tenant in the UK typically spends...' or 14 per cent in London: *Where does rent hit young people the hardest in Britain? BBC News,* accessible at: https://www.bbc.co.uk/news/business-45559456

23. Furthermore, for the very poorest... cost of privately renting: *Families on housing benefit unable to afford 94% of rental homes, research finds, The Independent,* accessible at: https://www.independent.co.uk/news/uk/home-news/housing-crisis-benefit-freeze-renting-families-affordable-homes-lha-shelter-a9143531.html

24. In 2015-16, local authorities... address the underlying problems: *Homelessness*, NAO, accessible at: https://www.nao.org.uk/press-release/homelessness/

25. In 2018-19, councils... accommodation alone: *Homelessness crisis costs councils over £1bn in just one year,* Shelter, accessible at: https://england.

shelter.org.uk/media/press_releases/articles/homelessness_crisis_costs_councils_over_1bn_in_just_one_year

26. Lifetime renters... on a Mortgage: *Renters spend £1.1m more than buyers in their lifetime, research finds, The Independent,* accessible at: https://www.independent.co.uk/money/spend-save/uk-renting-cost-spending-lifetime-buyers-homeowner-savings-a8409671.html

3. A short history of British homes

1. Fundamentally... belongs to the Crown: HC Daily Hansard – Written Answers, 11 Feb 2009: Col 2093W, accessible at: https://publications.parliament.uk/pa/cm200809/cmhansrd/cm090211/text/90211w0027.htm#09021110000019

2. Following these conquests... 'William the Conqueror': *Duke of Westminster dies, The Financial Times,* accessible at: https://www.ft.com/content/57f2dec2-5e7d-11e6-bb77-a121aa8abd95

3. 90 per cent of the population rented privately: All stats on population and housing tenure in Great Britain: Murie, Alan. *The Right to Buy?* (Bristol: Policy Press, 2016), p. 18

4. In Glasgow... protections were enhanced: *Lund, Brian. Housing Politics in the United Kingdom,* (Bristol: Policy Press, 2016), pp. 95-96

5. Many landlords were actually in favour... 'bloodsuckers, profiteers and despots': Wilson, Wendy. *A Short History of Rent Control,* Commons Library Briefing, 30 March 2017, accessible at: https://researchbriefings.parliament.uk/ResearchBriefing/Summary/SN06747

6. In the years between 1919... to 33 per cent: Murie (2016), p.18

7. spurred on... a housebuilding boom in the 1930s: *How housebuilding helped the economy recover, The Guardian,* accessible at: https://www.theguardian.com/housing-network/2013/apr/19/1930s-house-building-economic-recovery

8. Between 1939 and 1953... social housing: 'Chapter 1: Trends in Tenure,' *English Housing Survey-Households 2013-14,* DCLG, p.23, accessible at: https://assets.publishing.service.gov.uk/government/uploads/system/uploads/attachment_data/file/461440/Chapter_1_Trends_in_tenure.pdf

9. Most public sector housing... poorest households: Murie (2016), p. 27

10. council house building... new homes per year: *Table 244, Live Tables on house building,* MHCLG, accessible at: https://www.gov.uk/government/statistical-data-sets/live-tables-on-house-building

4. Selling off council homes

1. Noel Skelton... 'property-owning democracy': O'Neill, Martin and Williamson, Thad. eds. 'Property-Owning Democracy: A Short History,' in *Property-Owning Democracy: Rawls and Beyond*, (Chichester: Wiley, 2012), pp. 33-52
2. 'huge municipal domains'... broken up: Murie (2016), p. 20
3. Council tenants...maximum of 50 per cent: Murie (2016), p. 34
4. Rather than fund like-for-like replacement stock... Treasury: Murie (2016), pp. 36-37
5. in 1982... higher private rents: *Bricks or benefits?* Shelter, accessible at: https://england.shelter.org.uk/__data/assets/pdf_file/0009/436275/Bricksorbenefitsfullreport.pdf
6. Labour MP Clive Soley... 'take the strain': HC Deb, 30 January 1991, Vol 184 Col 940, accessible at: https://publications.parliament.uk/pa/cm199091/cmhansrd/1991-01-30/Orals-2.html
7. As Right to Buy expert... even produces surpluses: Murie (2016), p. 108
8. Housing benefit... many whole departments: *Doubling of the housing benefit bill is sign of something deeply wrong*, IFS, accessible at: https://www.ifs.org.uk/publications/13940
9. The Centre for Social Justice... treble to £70bn: *A SOCIAL JUSTICE HOUSING STRATEGY*, CSJ, accessible at: https://www.centreforsocialjustice.org.uk/core/wp-content/uploads/2018/10/CSJJ6574-Housing-Commission-2-Housing-Supply-181025-WEB.pdf
10. Government raised £6.25 billion... in England alone: *Table 692, Live tables on social housing sales*, MHCLG, accessible at: https://www.gov.uk/government/statistical-data-sets/live-tables-on-social-housing-sales#right-to-buy-sales
11. The homes... average discount of 45 per cent: Table 682, *Live tables on social housing sales*, MHCLG, accessible at: [see above]
12. Between 1980 and 2019... sold under Right to Buy: *Right to Buy homes made £2.8m in profit 'in weeks,'* BBC News, accessible at: https://www.bbc.co.uk/news/uk-47443183
13. 40 per cent... private landlords: *Exclusive: 7% rise in former Right to Buy homes now rented privately, Inside Housing*, accessible at: https://www.insidehousing.co.uk/news/news/exclusive-7-rise-in-former-right-to-buy-homes-now-rented-privately-53507

5. Boom! The impact of credit

1. Between 1997 and 2007... homes were built: Frisby, Dominic. *Life After the State*, (London: Unbound, 2013), p. 85

2. UK house prices more than tripled: *WHY ARE HOUSE PRICES SO HIGH?* Positive Money, accessible at: https://positivemoney.org/issues/house-prices/

3. money creation... by a commercial bank: *Money creation in the modern economy*, BoE, accessible at: https://www.bankofengland.co.uk/-/media/boe/files/quarterly-bulletin/2014/money-creation-in-the-modern-economy

4. 'two phenomena quite unlike other commodities'... more difficult to access: Ryan-Collins, Josh. *Why can't you afford a home?* (Cambridge: Polity Press, 2019), pp. 31-33

5. Big banks were unshackled... On demand: Ryan-Collins, Josh, Lloyd, Toby, Macfarlane, Laurie. *Rethinking the Economics of Land and Housing*, (London: Zed Books Ltd, 2017), pp. 132-133

6. Say hello to the landlord

1. During the 1980s and 1990s... private landlord: *English Housing Survey 2018 to 2019: headline report*, MHCLG, accessible at: https://assets.publishing.service.gov.uk/government/uploads/system/uploads/attachment_data/file/860076/2018-19_EHS_Headline_Report.pdf

2. Figures from... households across the UK: *UK private rented sector: 2018*, ONS, accessible at: https://www.ons.gov.uk/economy/inflationandpriceindices/articles/ukprivaterentedsector/2018

3. Judith and Fergus...over 900 properties: *The king and queen of buy-to-let*, *The Guardian*, accessible at: https://www.theguardian.com/money/2008/oct/04/buyingtolet.property

4. In 2014... his properties at the time: *Fergus Wilson: The landlord who wants to put 200 families out on the street, The Independent*, accessible at: https://www.independent.co.uk/news/uk/home-news/fergus-wilson-the-landlord-who-wants-to-put-200-families-out-on-the-street-9052651.html

5. guilty of... estate agent: *Property tycoon found guilty of assaulting estate agent, The Telegraph*, accessible at: https://www.telegraph.co.uk/news/uknews/crime/10760917/Property-tycoon-found-guilty-of-assaulting-estate-agent.html

6. a court found... discriminatory: *Landlord's ban on 'coloured' tenants is unlawful, court rules, The Guardian*, accessible at: https://www.theguardian.com/money/2017/nov/08/landlord-ban-coloured-tenants-unlawful-court-rules-equality-watchdog

7. In 2006, the government set up... 'social benefits being delivered by the [BTL] sector': Buy-to-let mortgage lending and the impact on UK house prices: a technical report, NHPAU, accessible at: https://webarchive.

nationalarchives.gov.uk/20120920065246/http://www.communities.gov.uk/documents/507390/pdf/684943.pdf

8. In 2014... 'respond to this demand': *Reshaping housing tenure in the UK: the role of buy-to-let*, IMLA, accessible at: http://www.imla.org.uk/perch/resources/imla-reshaping-housing-tenure-in-the-uk-the-role-of-buy-to-let-may-2014.pdf

9. to quote Susan Dyson... 'housing stock in the UK': *Landlords Quit the Buy to Let Sector*, Landlord Vision, accessible at: https://www.landlordvision.co.uk/blog/landlords-quit-the-buy-to-let-sector/

10. property developer Knight Frank... for generation rent: *Tenant Survey 2017: Meet the Tenants*, Knight Frank, accessible at: https://www.knightfrank.co.uk/research/article/2017-06-29-tenant-survey-2017-meet-the-tenants-research

11. A 2016 whitepaper by... built before 1945: *Whitepaper: UK Private Rented Residential Sector*, Invesco, accessible at: https://www.invesco.co.uk/dam/jcr:c92499af-9b88-416c-afad-fe716bb5db37/inv-uk-private-rented-residential-whitepaper.pdf

12. Tom Entwistle... 'into [the] sector': *'Yet another blow for landlords,'* Landlord Investor Magazine, p. 6, accessible at: https://issuu.com/landlordinvestor/docs/li_magazine_38th_edition

7. Caught in the mortgage trap

1. In 2018... renting: *Owning a home is cheaper than renting in all areas of the UK*, Santander, accessible at: https://www.santander.co.uk/about-santander/media-centre/press-releases/owning-a-home-is-cheaper-than-renting-in-all-areas-of-the-uk

2. First came the Mortgage Market Review... in 2014: *The Mortgage Market Review (MMR)?* Uswitch, accessible at: https://www.uswitch.com/mortgages/guides/mortgage-market-review/

3. Then, in 2015... first five years of the mortgage: *The Financial Policy Committee's powers over housing policy instruments*, BoE, accessible at: https://www.bankofengland.co.uk/-/media/boe/files/statement/2016/the-financial-policy-committee-powers-over-housing-policy-instruments.pdf?la=en&hash=9449FF251302F5529C4EFAF0E821828FC43A1488

4. The average 'starter home'... £207,500: *How much?! First-time buyers will need this staggering sum to buy a home in years to come...* Ideal Home, accessible at: https://www.idealhome.co.uk/news/average-first-time-buyer-house-price-2052-221396

5. 2.46 per cent: This was the average 2-year fixed initial rate for UK first-time buyers in September 2019. *Fixed Rate Mortgages*, Moneyfacts, accessible at: https://moneyfacts.co.uk/mortgages/fixed-rate-mortgages/

6. 4.90 per cent: This was the average Standard Variable Rate as of January 2019. *Standard variable rate mortgages*, Which? accessible at: https://www.which.co.uk/money/mortgages-and-property/mortgages/types-of-mortgage/standard-variable-rate-mortgages-a6rfd6j1j0bg

7. the monthly repayments…: All monthly repayments in this chapter have been calculated using the Moneyfacts Mortgage Repayment Calculator, and have been rounded to the nearest pound, accessible at: https://moneyfacts.co.uk/mortgages/mortgagerepayment-calculator/

8. £800 a month in rent… in England: 2018/2019 (Biannual 1), *Average monthly private sector rent for a 2 bedroom property (gross) in England*, LG Inform, accessible at: https://lginform.local.gov.uk/reports/lgastandard?mod-metric=3477&modarea=E92000001&mod-group=AllRegions_England&mod-type=namedComparisonGroup

9. Bank of England… in March 2009: *Official Bank Rate history*, BoE, accessible at: https://www.bankofengland.co.uk/boeapps/database/Bank-Rate.asp

10. According to Bank of England data… 6 per cent: Average bank rate Oct 1694 to Aug 2018, *Official Bank Rate history Data from 1694*, BoE, accessible at: https://www.bankofengland.co.uk/-/media/boe/files/monetary-policy/baserate.xls?la=en&hash=EEB8729ABFFF4B947B85C328340AE5155A99ADoF

11. At its peak in 1979… 17 per cent: Official Bank Rate history Data from 1694, BoE, accessible at: [see above]

12. As a report in 2010… 'upward interest rate movement': *Mortgage Market Review: Responsible Lending*, FSA, accessible at: https://www.fca.org.uk/publication/consultation/fsa-cp10-16.pdf

13. which argues that… on the property ladder: *Stress tests for mortgages too stringent, FTAdviser*, accessible at: https://www.ftadviser.com/mortgages/2019/06/07/stress-tests-for-mortgages-too-stringent/

14. in 2008… on record: *House prices 'fell 15.9% in 2008,' BBC News*, accessible at: http://news.bbc.co.uk/1/hi/business/7812108.stm

15. £375 billion of quantitative easing: *EVERY UK CITIZEN COULD HAVE RECEIVED £6,834*, Positive Money, accessible at: https://positivemoney.org/2017/02/qe-for-people/

16. House prices… 7.83: England and Wales ratios are used here because no UK-wide data using median income (not average income, which is skewed by extreme high earners) in the date range could be located. *House price to residence-based earnings ratio* [28 March 2019], ONS, accessible at: https://www.ons.gov.uk/peoplepopulationandcommunity/housing/datasets/ratioofhousepricetoresidencebasedearningslowerquartileandmedian

17. trade bodies... unleashed once more: *Building on the Bank of Mum and Dad*, BSA, accessible at: https://www.bsa.org.uk/BSA/files/da/da1a7288-7755-43db-9a5d-69687ef84416.pdf

SECTION II. HELP FOR BUYERS

8. The Bank of Mum and Dad

1. research from Legal & General... in 2017: *THE BANK OF MUM AND DAD* [2017], L&G, accessible at: https://www.legalandgeneral.com/landg-assets/personal/retirement/_resources/documents/more-money-in-retirement/reports/bank-of-mum-and-dad-report-2017.pdf

2. Legal & General has estimated... buy a home: *THE BANK OF MUM AND DAD* [2019], L&G, accessible at: https://www.legalandgeneral.com/bank-of-mum-and-dad/bomad-report-2019.pdf

3. Millennials... property ladder: Nearly two thirds (62%) of homeowners under 35 had relied on family help for their last home purchase. More than a third of 35 to 44 year olds and one fifth of 45 to 55 year olds had also done the same. *THE BANK OF MUM AND DAD* [2019], L&G, accessible at: [see above]

4. Laurie MacFarlane... 'trolling millennials': Tweet by @L__Macfarlane, July 17, 2018, accessible at: https://twitter.com/L__Macfarlane/status/1019163007363026944

5. A journalist... 1,000 likes: Tweet by @LouiseRidley, Nov 4, 2018, accessible at: https://twitter.com/LouiseRidley/status/1059007992509673472

6. In January 2019... '£30,000': *My 2-bed terrace has earned more than me, Daily Mail*, accessible at: https://www.dailymail.co.uk/femail/article-6637837/My-2-bed-terrace-earned-me.html

7. As an article in *The Economist* points out: *There is more to high house prices than constrained supply, The Economist*, accessible at: https://www.economist.com/finance-and-economics/2018/11/24/thereis-more-to-high-house-prices-than-constrained-supply

8. In his book... for this reason: Bowie, Duncan. *Radical Solutions to the Housing Supply Crisis*, (Bristol: Policy Press, 2017), p.165

9. Rudge's circumstances... hard work: *Top 10 areas where homes 'earn' more than their owners*, Zoopla, accessible at: https://www.zoopla.co.uk/discover/property-news/house-prices-vs-earnings/

10. financial columnist John Stepek... catch up: *More good news from the UK property market – house prices aren't going anywhere, MoneyWeek*, accessible at: https://moneyweek.com/514078/uk-house-prices-not-going-anywhere

9. Official Help to Buy

1. International Monetary Fund... inflationary potential: *IMF adds to growing criticism of 'Help to Buy' mortgage scheme, The Financial Times*, accessible at: https://www.ft.com/content/64bdfe24-c309-11e2-9bcb-00144feab7de

2. The Council for Mortgage Lenders... 95 per cent mortgages: *Help to Buy loan guarantee scheme comes to an end, BBC News*, accessible at: https://www.bbc.co.uk/news/business-38418289

3. *Analysis... surge in house prices: Help to Buy scheme is inflating house prices, The Independent*, accessible at: https://www.independent.co.uk/news/uk/home-news/help-to-buy-scheme-is-inflating-house-prices-10124042.html

4. The personal finance blog... thousands of pounds: *The Lifetime ISA*, Monevator, accessible at: https://monevator.com/lifetime-isa/

5. However, the National Audit Office... afforded a home anyway: *Help to Buy: Equity Loan scheme – progress review*, NAO, accessible at: https://www.nao.org.uk/press-release/help-to-buy-equity-loan-scheme-progress-review/

6. the trend that saw... in 2016: *The decline of homeownership among young adults*, IFS, accessible at: https://www.ifs.org.uk/uploads/publications/bns/BN224.pdf

7. North East... £131,000: *UK House Price Index*, [November 2019] Land Registry, accessible at: https://landregistry.data.gov.uk/app/ukhpi/browse?from=2018-12-01&location=http%3A%2F%2Flandregistry.data.gov.uk%2Fid%2Fregion%2Fnorth-east&to=2019-12-01

8. the government leg-up... anywhere in the country: the 2021-2023 scheme however will be subject to 'regional property price caps': https://www.helptobuy.gov.uk/equity-loan/further-guidance/

9. as journalist Claer Barrett...'why shouldn't I?': *Don't be a loser with your Lifetime Isa, The Financial Times*, accessible at: https://www.ft.com/content/7731aa08-1876-11e7-9c35-0dd2cb31823a

10. In the five years since... by around half: *£230m windfall for top builders since start of Help to Buy, This is Money*, accessible at: https://www.thisismoney.co.uk/money/markets/article-6364383/230m-windfall-builders-start-Help-Buy.html

11. the Facebook group... 'problems with their homes': *Persimmon defends shutting Facebook group to 'gag critics,' The Times*, accessible at: https://www.thetimes.co.uk/article/persimmon-defends-shutting-facebook-group-to-gag-critics-ohzcjn38l

12. Help to Buy recipients... introduction of Help to Buy: *Persimmon scrambles*

to stop the brickbats, The Times, accessible at: https://www.thetimes.co.uk/article/persimmon-scrambles-to-stop-the-brickbats-bkb9moqno

13. assembled a £500 million bonus package... 'a distraction': *Persimmon boss asked to leave amid outrage over bonus, The Guardian*, accessible at: https://www.theguardian.com/business/2018/nov/07/persimmon-boss-asked-to-leave-amid-ongoing-outrage-over-bonus

14. In 2019, analysis... price hike of 22 per cent: *BRICKS AND MORTAR: First time buyers using Help to Buy 'pay up to 22% more for new homes', The Sun*, accessible at: https://www.thesun.co.uk/money/10089081/first-time-buyers-help-to-buy-pay-more-new- homes/

15. Another red flag... rising local house prices: *Exclusive: one in seven Help to Buy homes lose value despite local house prices soaring, Which?* accessible at: https://www.which.co.uk/news/2020/06/exclusive-one-in-seven-help-to-buy-homes-lose-value-despite-local-house-prices-soaring/

16. This is especially worrying... in February 2020: *Help to Buy dream could become a nightmare for thousands of homeowners, The Telegraph*, accessible at: https://www.telegraph.co.uk/business/2020/02/22/help-buy-dream-could-become-nightmare- thousands-homeowners/

17. Recent figures... underpinned by Help to Buy: *Help to Buy demand surges to 40% of new-build homes sales, The Financial Times*: accessible at https://www.ft.com/content/52edc21c-f4bb-11e8-ae55-df4bf40f9d0d

10. Sharing a home

1. Shared ownership arrangements... since the 1970s: *Shared Ownership 2.0: Towards a Fourth Mainstream Tenure*, CIH, accessible at: http://www.cih.org/resources/PDF/Policy%20free%20download%20pdfs/Shared%20Ownership%202.0%20towards%20a%20fourth%20mainstream%20tenure.pdf

2. The aim... 'housing market': *HomeBuy Direct Buyers' Guide*, Homes and Communities Agency, accessible at: https://www.myfirsthome.org.uk/wp-content/uploads/2018/05/5.-HomeBuy-Direct_Buyers-Guide.pdf

3. Ryan lives... each month: *Where does rent hit young people the hardest in Britain? BBC News*, accessible at: https://www.bbc.co.uk/news/business-45559456

4. shared ownership schemes... known as 'leasehold': Except in Scotland.

5. Even when... uncapped fees and service charges: Leasehold is the default arrangement for shared ownership flats after full staircasing. For shared ownership houses it can differ, for example, many will automatically be converted to freehold after staircasing to 100%. However, this doesn't mean the problems end – ex-shared ownership freeholders can remain on the hook in perpetuity for fees for the maintainance of the housing

estate and its communal areas.

6. *In Inside Housing...* no choice but to pay: *Social landlords must be stopped from abusing their power over leaseholders, Inside Housing*, accessible at: https://www.insidehousing.co.uk/comment/comment/social-landlords-must-be-stopped-from-abusing-their-power-over-leaseholders-60865

11. Mortgaged tenants

1. General note on this chapter: The leasehold scandal is largely limited to England and Wales. In Northern Ireland the rules are much more favourable to leaseholders, and a succession of laws passed by the Scottish Parliament since 2000 have all but abolished leasehold in Scotland.

2. Once... reverts to the freeholder: *Freeholder,* The Leasehold Advisory Service, accessible at: https://www.lease-advice.org/lease-glossary/freeholder/

3. In the last 25 years... one in three for new builds: *Leasehold and commonhold reform,* HC Library, accessible at: https://researchbriefings.parliament.uk/ResearchBriefing/Summary/CBP-8047

4. all shared ownership... on the housing ladder: See: '1. General note on this chapter.'

5. The national conversation... in 2016: *The ground rent scandal that is engulfing new home buyers, The Guardian,* accessible at: https://www.theguardian.com/money/2016/nov/05/ground-rent-scandal-engulfing-new-home-buyers-leasehold

6. Government figures... was leasehold: Perplexingly, the commonhold tenure, in which flat owners collectively manage shared buildings and spaces, was not allowed under *Help to Buy. Help to Buy (Equity Loan scheme) Data to 31 March 2019, England,* MHCLG, accessible at: https://assets.publishing.service.gov.uk/government/uploads/system/uploads/attachment_data/file/820479/Help_To_Buy_Equity_Loan_statistical_release_Q1_2019.pdf

7. As pointed out... were houses: *To have or to leasehold? Inside the scandal rocking the new homes industry,* Which? accessible at: https://www.which.co.uk/news/2018/06/to-have-or-to-leasehold-inside-the-scandal-rocking-the-new-homes-industry/

8. Labour MP Clive Betts...'could not justify them': *SELECT COMMITTEE INQUIRY EVIDENCE,* NLC, accessible at: https://nationalleaseholdcampaign.org/select-committee-inquiry/

9. In April 2017... 'are causing': *Taylor Wimpey sets aside £130m to cover ground rent disputes, The Financial Times,* accessible at: https://www.ft.com/content/2dcc761a-2b20-11e7-9ec8-168383da43b7

10. Later that year... homes with escalating ground rents: *Implementing reforms to the leasehold system in England*, MHCLG, accessible at: https://assets.publishing.service.gov.uk/government/uploads/system/uploads/attachment_data/file/812827/190626_Consultation_Government_Response.pdf

11. The Law Commission's forays... not violated: *Leasehold reform plans branded 'nothing more than tinkering,'* The Guardian, accessible at: https://www.theguardian.com/money/2020/jan/09/leasehold-reform-plans-branded-nothing-more-than-tinkering-law-commission

12. The bind for leaseholders is further complicated... vastly higher prices: *Leasehold Voices – NLC*, National Leasehold Campaign, accessible at: https://www.youtube.com/watch?v=o7EgBbB5_iA

13. Thousands of freeholds... pension funds: *Pensions at risk from Law Commission's leasehold reforms*, The Telegraph, accessible at: https://www.telegraph.co.uk/pensions-retirement/news/pensions-risk-law-commissions-leasehold-reforms/

14. squirrelled away... British Virgin Islands: *John Lewis Partnership Pensions Trust tells leaseholder it will 'disinvest' in doubling ground rents*, LKP, accessible at: https://www.leaseholdknowledge.com/john-lewis-partnership-pensions-trust-tells-leaseholder-will-disinvest-doubling-ground-rents/

15. They have become an 'asset class' in their own right: *Ground rent scam 'creates new asset class,' says Ruth Cadbury*, LKP, accessible at: https://www.leaseholdknowledge.com/ground-rent-scam-creates-new-asset-class-says-ruth-cadbury/

12. The homeownership dream sours

1. In a last-ditch bid... control of your own destiny: *David Cameron manifesto speech in full, Politics.co.uk*, accessible at: https://www.politics.co.uk/comment-analysis/2015/04/14/david-cameron-manifesto-speech-in-full

2. In 2017, The Guardian... 'don't know how hard it is,' she said: *The bank of Mum and Dad: 'It's such a huge amount of money. And guilt,'* The Guardian, accessible at: https://www.theguardian.com/money/2017/nov/11/generation-rent-property-borrowing-from-mum-and-dad-guilt

3. In June 2019... 40,000 per year: *Internal migration: by local authority and region, five-year age group and sex*, ONS, accessible at: https://www.ons.gov.uk/peoplepopulationandcommunity/populationandmigration/migrationwithintheuk/datasets/internalmigrationmovesbylocalauthoritiesandregionsinenglandandwalesby5yearagegroupandsex

4. Academics Nick Gallent and Mark Scott... struggle to find staff: Scott, Mark, Gallent, Nick and Gkartzios, Menelaos. eds. 'Housing and

299

Sustainable Rural Communities,' in *The Routledge Companion to Rural Planning*, (Oxfordshire: Routledge, 2019), pp. 261-272

5. David Cameron thought that... priced out of the property market: David Cameron's speech, *Conservative Party Conference 2013: Full text, New Statesman*, accessible at: https://www.newstatesman. com/staggers/2013/10/david-camerons-speech-conservative-party-conference-2013-full-text

6. renters are more likely... than for a house: *Tenants Prioritise Saving for a Holiday over a Home Deposit*, Landlordnews.co.uk, accessible at: https:// www.landlordnews.co.uk/tenants-prioritise-saving-holiday/

7. One of Barker's main recommendations... affordable to first-time buyers: Barker also recommended spending £1.2 - £1.6 billion annually on social housing and a levy on the 'planning gain' unlocked by an award of planning permission, but these ideas were ignored by the Labour government. Minton, Anna. *Big Capital: Who is London for?* (Penguin Random House UK, 2017), pp. 39-40

8. In an article for the *Mail on Sunday*... wanted to upsize: *'Second steppers' caught in new home loans - the families who would need to double their mortgage to move home, This is Money*, accessible at: https://www.thisismoney. co.uk/money/mortgageshome/article-3190406/Second-steppers-caught-new-home-loans-trap-moving-double-mortgage-Ten-steps-make-hap pen.html

9. Research from Lloyds Bank... their first home: *Almost one in three Second Steppers need financial support from family and friends to move up the property ladder*, Lloyds Bank, accessible at: https://www.lloydsbankinggroup. com/Media/Press-Releases/press-releases-2017/lloyds-bank/240617_Sec ond_Steppers_2/

10. roughly two thirds... helping hand from family: *Bank of Mum and Dad* [2019], L&G, accessible at: https://www.legalandgeneral.com/bank-of-mum-and-dad/bomad-report-2019.pdf

11. around a third... Help to Buy ISA: Calculated using estimates from the Yorkshire Building Society on the number of First Time Buyers in 2018 (353,130), and government data on the number of Help to Buy ISA bonuses paid out in the same year (114,725). *Number of first-time property buyers 'at highest level since 2007'*, The Independent, accessible at: https://www.in-dependent.co.uk/news/business/news/housing-market-first-time-buy ers-record-property-ladder-a9266476.html and *Help to Buy: ISA Scheme Quarterly Statistics*, HM Treasury, accessible at: https://assets.publishing. service.gov.uk/government/uploads/system/uploads/attachment_data/ file/848918/Official_Statistics_Publication_-_June_2019.pdf

SECTION III. HOW HOMES ARE BUILT

13. Why can't we just build more new homes?

1. Big developers take...keys to buyers: Letwin, Rt Hon Sir Oliver, *Independent Review of Build Out: Final Report*, accessible at: https://assets.publishing.service.gov.uk/government/uploads/system/uploads/attachment_data/file/752124/Letwin_review_web_version.pdf

2. As the Home Builders' Federation... 'zero ecology issues': *Pre-Commencement Conditions*, HBF, accessible at: https://www.hbf.co.uk/documents/6854/Pre-Commencement_Conditions.pdf

3. Paul Smith... 'somewhere between three to four years': *Landbanking - an inconvenient truth*, Building.co.uk, accessible at: https://www.building.co.uk/communities/landbanking-an-inconvenient-truth/5092801.article

4. In 2018, the Conservative MP Sir Oliver Letwin... 'the economy as a whole': Letwin, Rt Hon Sir Oliver, *Independent Review of Build Out: Final Report*, accessible at: [see above]

5. In 2017, Shelter reported... 'faults with utilities': *'Rigged' housebuilding system means eight in ten families cannot afford new home, says Shelter*, Shelter, accessible at: https://england.shelter.org.uk/media/press_releases/articles/rigged_housebuilding_system_means_eight_in_ten_families_cannot_afford_new_home,_says_shelter

6. That same year... poor workmanship: *Bovis to pay £7m to compensate customers for poorly built*, The Guardian, accessible at: homeshttps://www.theguardian.com/business/2017/feb/20/bovis-to-pay-7m-to-compensate-customers-angry-at-poorly-built-homes

14. Shipping containers: cheaper homes

1. I first came across him... housing crisis: *Meet the Sheffield social enterprise using shipping containers to tackle the housing crisis, CityMetric*, accessible at: https://www.citymetric.com/fabric/meet-sheffield-social-enterprise-using-shipping-containers-tackle-housing-crisis-4144

2. shipping containers are... 8ft wide: Shipping Containers for Storage, Mr Box, accessible at: https://www.mrbox.co.uk/shipping-containers/

3. In 2019, a trade magazine... 'next ten years': *Planning system sparks modular construction housing revolution, PBC Today*, accessible at: https://www.pbctoday.co.uk/news/modular-construction-news/planning-system-modular-construction/58247/#

4. 'about 100 million tonnes'... 'at the moment': *"Uber moment for construction": Deal signed for 750 modular homes in UK, GCR*, accessible

at: http://www.globalconstructionreview.com/news/uber-moment-cons truction-deal-signed-750-modular-h/

5. Code for Sustainable Homes scrapped: *Goodbye to the Code for Sustainable Homes,* Homebuilding.co.uk, accessible at: https://www.homebuilding. co.uk/fairwell-code-we-hardly-knew-ye/

6. It was on this matter... the housing crisis: *I was 'temporarily' housed in a shipping container when I was pregnant and homeless. 18 months later, I'm still here,* i news, accessible at: https://inews.co.uk/opinion/comment/i-was-temporarily-housed-in-a-shipping-container-when-i-was-pregnant-and-homeless-18-months-later-im-still-here-256219

7. Community Interest Company... benefit of the community: 'Chapter 6: The Asset Lock,' in *Office of the Regulator of Community Interest Companies: Information and guidance notes,* Dept for BEIS, accessible at: https:// assets.publishing.service.gov.uk/government/uploads/system/uploads/ attachment_data/file/605418/14-1089-community-interest-companies-chapter-6-the-asset-lock.pdf

8. In a housing co-op... in the current market: *Types of housing co-operative,* Shelter, accessible at: https://england.shelter.org.uk/legal/security_of_ tenure/housing_co-operatives/types_of_housing_co-operative

9. Community Land Trust... private rented sector: Wilson, Wendy. *Briefing Paper: Community Land Trusts,* HC Library, accessible at: http:// researchbriefings.files.parliament.uk/documents/SN04903/SN04903. pdf

10. While the government... access plots for building affordable housing: '8 Access to land,' in *Modern methods of construction,* Housing, Communities and Local Government Select Committee, accessible at: https://publications.parliament.uk/pa/cm201719/cmselect/cmcomloc/ 1831/183111.htm

11. the process continues to favour... national affordable housing shortage: *Public land sell-off branded a 'massive missed opportunity' to fix the housing crisis,* Inside Housing, accessible at: https://www.insidehousing. co.uk/news/news/public-land-sell-off-branded-a-massive-missed-opportunity-to-fix-the-housing-crisis-63375

15. Selling planning permission

1. Option agreements sound complex... can be offset: *In plain English: Option Agreement price negotiations,* Savills, accessible at: https://www. savills.co.uk/blog/article/242968/residential-property/in-plain-english-option-agreement-price-negotiations.aspx/

2. The land is currently worth... an agricultural field: *Farmland hits £1m/ acre for housing, Farmer's Weekly,* accessible at: https://www.fwi.co.uk/

business/housing-need-pushes-farmland-1macre

3. An option contract: A sample option agreement can be found here: https://onlinelibrary.wiley.com/doi/pdf/10.1002/9780470690710.app1

4. Land promoters... developers and landowners: *Strategic land promotion – key points for land owners*, Stephens Scown Solicitors LLP, accessible at: https://www.stephens-scown.co.uk/property/strategic-land-promotion-key-points-land-owners/

5. free webinar... no experience needed: The form of words for the advertising copy has been changed to conceal its origin. The underlying meaning has been preserved as far as possible.

6. small-to-medium developers... pre-2008: *Reversing the decline of small housebuilders: Reinvigorating entrepreneurialism and building more homes*, HBF, accessible at: https://www.hbf.co.uk/documents/6879/HBF_SME_Report_2017_Web.pdf

7. 'strategic' land... or promotion agreement: *The missing numbers behind land options - the little-known contracts used to control land*, Missing Numbers, accessible at: https://missingnumbers.org/land-options-the-little-known-contracts-used-to-control-land/

8. Legal & General... 'Luton to Cardiff': *Who owns the country? The secretive companies hoarding England's land, The Guardian*, accessible at: https://www.theguardian.com/environment/2019/apr/19/who-owns-england-secretive-companies-hoarding-land

9. Others generating generous... its portfolio in May 2017: *Real assets strategies boosts Church Commissioners' returns, IPE Real Assets*, accessible at: https://realassets.ipe.com/real-assets-strategies-boosts-church-com missioners-returns/10019027.article

10. Grosvenor estate: *Grosvenor to triple size of its Strategic Land business* Grosvenor, accessible at: https://www.grosvenor.com/news-and-insight/all-articles/grosvenor-to-triple-size-of-its-strategic-land-bus

11. the bulk of which... passed away: *One of Britain's richest men inherits billions and avoids paying inheritance taxes, The Independent*, accessible at: https://www.independent.co.uk/news/uk/home-news/duke-of-westminster-son-avoids-inheritance-tax-billions-britains-richest-men-family-trusts-rules-a7998246.html

12. 6 per cent of UK land mass is built on: It's true the remaining 94% isn't all land with development potential. Even so, developed land (chiefly comprising 'discontinuous urban fabric') is dwarfed by pastures and arable land, more of which could be converted to residential use. See: Cole, B. King, S. Ogutu, B. Palmer, D. Smith, G. Balzter, H. *Corine Land Cover 2012 for the UK, Jersey and Guernsey*. NERC Environmental Information Data Centre, (2015) accessible at: https://doi.org/10.5285/32533dd6-7c1b-43e1-b892-e80d61a5ea1d

13. What about compulsory purchase orders?: Much of this section is indebted to Bentley, Daniel. *The Land Question*, (London: Civitas, 2017), accessible at: https://www.civitas.org.uk/content/files/thelandquestion. pdf

14. Its aim… reconstruction effort: HC Deb 29 January 1947 vol 432 col 947-1075, accessible at: https://api.parliament.uk/historic-hansard/commons/1947/jan/29/town-and-country-planning-bill

15. The idea was to allow builders to… not from land speculation: Bentley (2017), p. 42

16. the 'raw deal' they were getting in *The Times*: Bentley (2017), p. 44

17. Unsurprisingly, land prices surged… (in 2016 money): Bentley (2017), p. 48

18. by the 1970s… continue to the present day: *The housebuilding records of the major parties, graphed*, Full Fact, accessible at: https://fullfact.org/economy/housebuilding-records-major-parties-graphed/

16. Letting the local economy

1. In 2018, Direct Line…25 per cent higher than rebuild costs: *Bricks and mortar account for only 59 percent of a property's market value*, Direct Line, accessible at: https://www.directlinegroup.co.uk/en/news/brand-news/2018/bricks-and-mortar-account-for-only-59-percent-of-a-property-s-ma.html

2. in her book… 'Yours truly, Fay Lewis': Raworth, Kate. *Doughnut Economics: Seven Ways to Think Like a 21st-Century Economist*, (United States: Chelsea Green Publishing, 2017), p.152

3. In a report in 2016… higher disposable income: *Scottish workers have more disposable income than London earners, The Guardian*, accessible at: https://www.theguardian.com/uk-news/2016/jan/17/scottish-workers-more-disposable-income-london-earners

4. Toby Lloyd, co-author… six and a half times: *Where's all the money gone?* Shelter, accessible at: https://blog.shelter.org.uk/2017/12/wheres-all-the-money-gone/

5. Even in Silicon Valley… productive endeavours of landlords: *Peter Thiel: Majority of capital poured into SV startups goes to 'urban slumlords,' SFGATE*, accessible at: https://www.sfgate.com/expensive-san-francisco/article/peter-thiel-silicon-valley-capital-landlords-12759450.php

6. 'Roads are made'… 'enrichment is derived': *Winston Churchill said it all better then* [sic] *we can*, Land Value Taxation Campaign, accessible at: http://www.landvaluetax.org/current-affairs-comment/winston-church ill-said-it-all-better-then-we-can.html

SECTION IV. A NATION OF RENTERS

17. Helping out the landlords

1. 'the private landlord'... 'done about it': Lund, Brian. *Housing Politics in the United Kingdom*, (Bristol: Policy Press, 2016), p.102

2. Often in times of crisis... even dangerous: Jones, Owen. *The Establishment*, (Penguin Random House UK, 2015), pp. 294-295

3. The intellectual groundwork... free-market enterprise: Jones (2015), pp. 20-21.

4. 70 per cent... 15 years or more: Murie, Alan. *The Right to Buy*, (Bristol: Policy Press, 2016), p.38

5. Private landlordism has a long tradition... [private renting] at all: Lund (2016), p. 115

6. The Act lavished... considerably lower than 'market rents': *Regulated Tenancies*, DCLG, accessible at: https://assets.publishing.service.gov.uk/government/uploads/system/uploads/attachment_data/file/11445/138295.pdf

7. thanks to the 1977 Rent Act... the next generation: *Succession: Regulated tenancies*, Shelter, accessible at: https://england.shelter.org.uk/legal/security_of_tenure/succession/succession_regulated_tenancies

8. 'We have done much'... 'the deserving landlord': HC Deb, 08 July 1974, Vol 876 Col 1038, accessible at: https://hansard.parliament.uk/Commons/1974-07-08/debates/ec210655-4f7a-447e-b5a3-2ab642b089cf/CommonsChamber

9. Assured Tenancies were made the default tenure: *What's The Housing Act 1988 and what rights does it give Landlords?* HomeLet, accessible at: https://homelet.co.uk/landlord-insurance/tips/whats-the-housing-act-1988-and-what-rights-does-it-give-me

10. However, that's not the whole picture... rather than opt into: *Assured Shorthold Tenancies 25 years on – time for a change?* Landlord Law Blog, accessible at: https://www.landlordlawblog.co.uk/2013/10/28/assured-shorthold-tenancies-years-on-time-for-a-change/

11. A 2018 blog post... 'vintage year' for landlords: *Game changer – what the '88 Housing Act did for us*, RLA, accessible at: https://news.rla.org.uk/game-changer-what-the-88-housing-act-did-for-us

18. The house of landlords

1. It meant that... than their dog: The Animal Welfare Act 2006 explicitly states that pets are entitled to 'a suitable environment.' The Housing Act 2004 gave local authorities powers to crack down on landlords letting

out hazardous homes, but tenants could not use this legislation to take their landlord to court. For further info, see: Wilson, Wendy. *Homes (Fitness for Human Habitation) Bill 2017-19*, HC Library, accessible at: http://researchbriefings.files.parliament.uk/documents/CBP-8185/CBP-8185.pdf

2. commentator highlighted... 'Western Europe': *Tories vote down law requiring landlords make their homes fit for human habitation, The Independent*, accessible at: https://www.independent.co.uk/news/uk/politics/tories-vote-down-law-requiring-landlords-make-their-homes-fit-for-human-habitation-a6809691.html

3. Overall, privately rented homes... housing stock on average: *English Housing Survey, Stock profile and condition*, 2017, MHCLG, accessible at: https://assets.publishing.service.gov.uk/government/uploads/system/uploads/attachment_data/file/817408/EHS_2017_Stock_Condition_Report.pdf

4. The legislation... effectively defunct: Wilson, Wendy. *Homes (Fitness for Human Habitation) Bill 2017-19*, HC Library, accessible at: [see above]

5. 'Look – it's OK for my generation'... 'reach your dreams': *David Cameron's Conservative Party Conference speech: in full, The Telegraph*, accessible at: https://www.telegraph.co.uk/news/politics/conservative/9598534/David-Camerons-Conservative-Party-Conference-speech-in-full.html

6. At the 2015 Conservative Party Conference... 'actually own': *Tory Party Conference 2015: David Cameron's speech in full, The Independent*, accessible at: https://www.independent.co.uk/news/uk/politics/tory-party-conference-2015-david-camerons-speech-in-full-a6684656.html

7. 200,000 'starter homes'... was zero: *Election 2019: Liz Truss told 'zero' starter homes built by Tories, BBC News*, accessible at: https://www.bbc.co.uk/news/av/election-2019-50507342/election-2019-liz-truss-told-zero-starter-homes-built-by-tories

8. a drive the *Architect's Journal* called 'a bonfire of regulations': *Cameron claims victory in bonfire of the Building Regulations, Architect's Journal*, accessible at: https://www.architectsjournal.co.uk/cameron-claims-victory-in-bonfire-of-the-building-regulations/8658068.article

9. Nick Clegg... 'Labour voters': *Tories refused to build social housing because it would 'create Labour voters,' Nick Clegg says, The Independent*, accessible at: https://www.independent.co.uk/news/uk/politics/tories-refused-to-build-social-housing-because-it-would-create-labour-voters-nick-clegg-says-a7223796.html

10. In 2018, the Homes (Fitness for Human Habitation) Bill... had garnered: HC Deb 19 January 2018, Vol 634 Col 1203-28, accessible at: https://hansard.parliament.uk/Commons/2018-01-19/debates/0DA962E4-7E56-4588-91DE-48C68715C5F8/Homes(FitnessForHumanHabitation.

AndLiabilityForHousingStandards)Bill

11. It later emerged... giant tinderbox: *Grenfell Tower fire: Firms 'knew cladding would fail in fire' BBC News*, accessible at: https://www.bbc.co.uk/news/uk-51279906

12. In November 2016... 'ineptitude and incompetence': *KCTMO – Playing with fire!* Grenfell Action Group, accessible at: https://grenfellactiongroup.wordpress.com/2016/11/20/kctmo-playing-with-fire/

13. the issue of poor housing standards... in January 2018: HC Deb 19 January 2018, Vol 634 Col 1215, accessible at: [see above]

14. Sajid Javid... 'a change in attitude': *Number of tower blocks with combustible cladding rises to 11, government says – as it happened, The Guardian,* accessible at: https://www.theguardian.com/politics/blog/live/2017/jun/22/hammond-suggests-brexit-transitional-period-could-last-up-to-four-years-politics-live

15. Since the incident... 'yet to be remediated': *Building Safety Programme: Monthly Data Release, Data as at 30 September 2019*, Coverage: England, MHCLG, accessible at: https://assets.publishing.service.gov.uk/government/uploads/system/uploads/attachment_data/file/838050/Building_Safety_Data_Release_September_2019.pdf

19. Get out of my house

1. if you rent a residential property... whatever the reason: *Section 21 eviction*, Shelter, accessible at: https://england.shelter.org.uk/housing_advice/eviction/section_21_eviction

2. In Northern Ireland... length of the tenancy: *Right to evict*, Housing Rights, accessible at: https://www.housingadviceni.org/advice-land lords/right-evict

3. Scotland outlawed... renovate the property: *If you're being evicted – private tenant,* mygov.scot, accessible at: https://www.mygov.scot/private-tenant-eviction/grounds-for-eviction-assured-and-short-assured-tenancies/

4. ASTs... right to a secure home: *Time for reform: How our neighbours with mature private renting markets guarantee stability for renters*, Shelter, accessible at: https://england.shelter.org.uk/__data/assets/pdf_file/0005/1289615/Time_for_reform_FINAL.pdf

20. Revenge evictions

1. the Deregulation Act... well-behaved, rent-paying, contractually-compliant tenants: *What you need to know to avoid an invalid section 21*, NLA, accessible at: https://landlords.org.uk/news-campaigns/blogs/what-you-need-know-avoid-invalid-section-21

2. Under the 2015 Consumer Rights Act... potential to cause damage: *Could tenants win the right to keep pets in their rental property?* mydeposits, accessible at: https://www.mydeposits.co.uk/blogcat/could-tenants-win-the-right-to-keep-pets-in-their-rental-property/

3. research from rental listings website SpareRoom.co.uk... refused to let to pet-owners: *Pet Think Tank Report 2018*, SpareRoom, accessible at: https://static.spareroom.co.uk/downloads/reports/SpareRoom_Pet_Think_Tank_Report.pdf

4. In Germany... pets are 'generally allowed': *Reality Check: How does renting a home in the UK compare? BBC News*, accessible at: https://www.bbc.co.uk/news/uk-43075176

21. The reality of renting

1. One tenant called Amy Wilson... who 'did absolutely nothing': Tweet by @ms_wilson, Aug 20, 2018, accessible at: https://twitter.com/ms_wilson/status/1031517128170643456

2. Daniel Sparrow... 'if you're not careful': Tweet by @DanielDeathtrap, Aug 23, 2018, accessible at: https://twitter.com/DanielDeathtrap/status/1032682252088627201

3. Rachel Collinson... '40 and still renting': Tweet by @rachel_shares, Aug 20, 2018, accessible at: https://twitter.com/rachel_shares/status/1031550758146244608

4. Ciara McKibbin... 'evidence/tenancy law': Tweet by @ciaramckibbin, Aug 29, 2018, accessible at: https://twitter.com/ciaramckibbin/status/1034766649616998401

5. As a Twitter user... you're 'a serf': Tweet by @consol8ion, Jul 3, 2018, accessible at: https://twitter.com/consol8ion/status/1014016106514788359

6. A Uswitch report from 2015... to change provider: Even if such terms are technically unenforceable, the landlord's Section 21 trump card makes violating unfair terms in a tenancy agreement a risky move. *One in Ten Landlords Stop Tenants Changing Energy Supplier, Landlordnews.co.uk*, accessible at: https://www.landlordnews.co.uk/one-in-ten-landlords-stop-tenants-changing-energy-supplier/

7. In a Facebook support group for private tenants... during the winter: A similar story emerged in November 2019 and made headlines, so the practice is clearly not a one-off. See: *Can my landlord lock my thermostat in a box? BBC News*, accessible at: https://www.bbc.co.uk/news/uk-50294404

8. An anonymous user on the London Assembly discussion forum... even the police can't': Post by Amgrealis in thread 'Problems with private rental properties,' Talk London, accessible at: https://www.london.gov.uk/talk-

london/housing/problems-private-rental-properties?page=1&action=

9. Another tenant... 'photos taken were unnecessary': *Can the landlord's agents take all these photos?* The Landlord Law Blog, accessible at: https://www.landlordlawblog.co.uk/2015/04/15/can-the-landlords-agents-take-all-these-photos/

10. By law, tenants do have the right... in need of urgent attention: Landlord and Letting Agent Access to Your Property, The Tenants' Voice, accessible at: https://www.thetenantsvoice.co.uk/advice_from_us/landlord-access/

11. As Tessa Shepperson... 'quiet enjoyment': *Can the landlord's agents take all these photos?* The Landlord Law Blog, accessible at: [see above]

12. Writing in *The Guardian*... 'No blacks, no Irish, no dogs': *Housing benefit claimants increasingly shut out of private rental market, The Guardian*, accessible at: https://www.theguardian.com/money/2017/jan/21/housing-benefit-claimants-shut-out-private-rental-no-dss

13. Since 2012, socially rented homes... lost by 2020: *More than 165k social homes lost in six years, says CIH, PublicFinance*, accessible at: https://www.publicfinance.co.uk/news/2019/02/more-165k-social-homes-lost-six-years-says-cih

14. In the UK, average rents... rising by just 10 per cent: *Private rents have risen faster than pay since 2011, says Shelter, The Guardian*, accessible at: https://www.theguardian.com/society/2018/aug/03/soaring-rents-rose-60-faster-than-pay-since-2011-shelter

15. Savills... unlikely to be resolved any time soon: *Savills forecasts UK residential market in the next 5 years*, Savills, accessible at: https://www.savills.co.uk/insight-and-opinion/savills-news/170245-1/savills-forecasts-uk-residential-market-in-the-next-5-years

16. *The Huffington Post*... still affordable on local wages: *This Is The Most Affordable Place To Rent In England (And The Least), Huffpost*, accessible at: https://www.huffingtonpost.co.uk/entry/this-is-the-most-affordable-place-to-rent-in-england-and-the-least_uk_5d9af9b8e4b0fc935edcf98c

17. Adzuna's widely cited list of Worst Cities to Find a Job: *The Best And Worst Places In The UK To Get A Job, Grazia*, accessible at: https://graziadaily.co.uk/life/real-life/best-worst-places-uk-get-job/

18. In her 2017 book *Big Capital*... and so on: Minton, Anna. *Big Capital: Who is London for?* (Penguin Random House UK, 2017), pp. 7-9

19. Bristol is among the least affordable areas... in the country: *Private renting unaffordable for working families on low wages in 67% of the country*, Shelter, accessible at: https://england.shelter.org.uk/media/press_releases/articles/private_renting_unaffordable_for_working_families_on_low_wages_in_67_of_the_country

20. It is also among... for homelessness: *320,000 people in Britain are now homeless, as numbers keep rising*, Shelter, accessible at: http://england.

shelter.org.uk/media/press_releases/articles/320,000_people_in_
britain_are_now_homeless,_as_numbers_keep_rising

21. Following a Freedom of Information request... 'waiting list is very long': The true extent of Bristol's housing crisis: *Council home wait list numbers and times revealed, Bristol Post*, accessible at: https://www.bristolpost. co.uk/news/bristol-news/true-extent-bristols-housing-crisis-1573863

22. Zoopla revealed that... any other city in the country: *House Prices Are Soaring In This UK City & It's Not London*, Refinery29, accessible at: https://www.refinery29.com/en-gb/2018/02/191498/house-prices-uk-london-sheffield

23. totallymoney.com's 'Buy-to-Let Yield Map'... London-based landlords are currently getting: *UK Buy-to-Let Yield Map 2019/2020*, accessible at: https://www.totallymoney.com/buy-to-let-yield-map/

22. Regulating the rental market

1. the rogue landlords' register... a single name: *Government's rogue landlord list empty after six months, The Guardian*, accessible at: https://www.theguardian.com/business/2018/oct/23/governments-rogue-landlord-list-empty-after-six-months

2. The Mayor of London, Sadiq Khan... local average income: *Khan finds support for rent controls in London, The Financial Times*, accessible at: https://www.ft.com/content/f432c7aa-16bd-11e6-b197-a4af20d5575e

3. The Labour party... curbs to rent rises: *The Labour Party Manifesto 2019*, p. 79, accessible at: https://labour.org.uk/wp-content/uploads/2019/11/Real-Change-Labour-Manifesto-2019.pdf

4. in April 2019... 'no-fault' eviction: *Short-notice evictions face axe in tenant rights victory, The Guardian*, accessible at: https://www.theguardian.com/society/2019/apr/15/short-notice-evictions-face-axe-in-tenant-rights-victory

5. Housing lawyer Giles Peaker... 'still taking a moment': *The End of Section 21*, Nearly Legal Blog, accessible at: https://nearlylegal.co.uk/2019/04/the-end-of-section-21/

6. Exeter... with its population of 57,812: 2018 estimates. See: *UNITED KINGDOM: Countries and Major Cities*, City Population, accessible at: https://www.citypopulation.de/en/uk/cities/

7. According to Indeed.co.uk... job opportunities as Exeter: It is difficult to document the number of job openings at a given time and location, but I re-ran this exercise on the 22nd February 2020, and the numbers continue to hold true: 4,927 job listings in Exeter versus 18,512 job listings in Leamington Spa.

8. countries where... heavily regulated markets in the world: *Time for*

reform: How our neighbours with mature private renting markets guarantee stability for renters, Shelter, accessible at: https://england.shelter.org. uk/__data/assets/pdf_file/0005/1289615/Time_for_reform_FINAL.pdf

9. the Netherlands... social housing associations: *Basics on Dutch housing, Government of the Netherlands*, accessible at: https://www.government.nl/ topics/investing-in-dutch-housing/basics-dutch-housing

10. In the social sector... rent reduction: [accessed via Google Translate] *Rental price and point counting*, Government of the Netherlands, accessible at: https://www.rijksoverheid.nl/onderwerpen/huurprijs-en-puntentelling

11. getting thrown out... following such an eviction: *In Amsterdam, most rents are capped, revenge evictions illegal and affordable housing quotas are enforced*, CityMetric, accessible at: https://www.citymetric.com/politics/ amsterdam-most-rents-are-capped-revenge-evictions-illegal-and-affordable-housing-quotas-are

12. a report by Dutch real estate investment company Bouwinvest... qualify for social housing: *Dutch Real Estate Market Outlook 2020-2022*, Bouwinvest, accessible at: https://www.bouwinvest.nl/media/4305/ bouwinvest-dutch-real-estate-market-outlook-2020-2022.pdf

13. A report in 2015 by Civitas... long-term commitment to a property': Bentley, Daniel. *The Future of Private Renting Shaping a fairer market for tenants and taxpayers*, Civitas, accessible at: http://www.civitas.org.uk/ pdf/thefutureofprivaterenting.pdf

14. problems in German cities... corporate landlord monopolies: *Berlin's grassroots plan to renationalise up to 200,000 ex-council homes from corporate landlords, The Conversation*, accessible at: https://theconversation.com/ berlins-grassroots-plan-to-renationalise-up-to-200-000-ex-council-homes-from-corporate-landlords-112884

23. With the community activists

1. 'Recovering in the pub'... 'experiences of renting': Public Facebook post by Jonny Butcher, 21 February 2018, accessible at: https://www.facebook.com/photo.php?fbid=532327687151208&set=a.2601132377059 89&type=3&theater

2. The license costs £750 over five years... selective licensing area: *Selective Licensing of privately rented properties and Apply for a Selective Licence in London/ Abbeydale/ Chesterfield Road*, Sheffield City Council, accessible at: https://www.sheffield.gov.uk/selectivelicensing/ and https://www. sheffield.gov.uk/home/housing/selective-licence-london-abbeydale-chesterfield-road/

3. Selective licensing... directly above takeaways and restaurants: *Selective*

Licensing Proposal – London Road, Abbeydale Road and Chesterfield Road Consultation Report – June 2018, Private Housing Standards, Sheffield City Council, accessible at: https://www.sheffield.gov.uk/content/dam/sheffield/docs/housing/selective-licensing-of-privately-rented-properties/Selective%20Licensing%20Consultation%20Report%20June%202018%20London%20Abbeydale%20Chest....pdf

4. The area is populated... ethnically diverse in Sheffield: based on local knowledge and data from https://www.streetcheck.co.uk/

5. Some 70 per cent of the properties... excessive cold: *Selective Licensing Proposal – London Road, Abbeydale Road and Chesterfield Road Consultation Report – June 2018*, Private Housing Standards, Sheffield City Council, accessible at: [see above]

6. Michelle Houston... 'bucket on a corridor': *Council plan clampdown on 'high-risk' rented flats in area of Sheffield where inspectors found buckets being used in place of toilets, The Star*, accessible at: https://www.thestar.co.uk/news/council-plan-clampdown-high-risk-rented-flats-area-sheffield-where-inspectors-found-buckets-being-used-place-toilets-441312

7. One landlord warned... £50 a month: *Meeting over controversial landlord proposals in Sheffield 'nearly ends in blows,' The Star*, accessible at: https://www.thestar.co.uk/news/meeting-over-controversial-landlord-proposals-sheffield-nearly-ends-blows-344370

8. Despite the fact... hazards were found by council officers: *Designating an area of London Road, Abbeydale Road and Chesterfield Road for Selective Licensing of Private rented properties*, Private Housing Standards, Sheffield City Council, accessible at: http://democracy.sheffield.gov.uk/documents/s31150/Selective%20Licensing%20Report.pdf

9. 'Hey everyone'... 'or just turn up': Posted in a private Facebook group.

10. Saul Alinksy... 'for the Have-Nots': *Know Thine Enemy, The New York Times*, accessible at: https://www.nytimes.com/2009/08/23/weekinreview/23alinsky.html

11. Barack Obama's younger years... defining phase of his political career: *Obama's Community Roots, The Nation*, accessible at: https://www.thenation.com/article/archive/obamas-community-roots/

12. the Alinskyan idea... 'start a union in the community': *Do you live in shoddy housing that costs a fortune? Time to join the renters' union, The Guardian*, accessible at: https://www.theguardian.com/society/2018/jun/03/renters-union-shoddy-housing-cost-fortune-acorn-bristol

13. contacts in Westminster... against its interests: *Campaigns and NLA meeting with Housing Minister: Tell us what you want us to raise with him*, NLA, accessible at: https://landlords.org.uk/news-campaigns/campaigns/ and https://landlords.org.uk/news-campaigns/news/nla-meeting-housing-minister-tell-us-what-you-want-us-raise-him/

14. ACORN researchers found a clause... 'for some time': *Do you live in shoddy housing that costs a fortune? Time to join the renters' union, The Guardian*, accessible at: [see above]

15. chanting 'NatWest, say yes to DSS!'... Village People: Facebook video by Momentum Sheffield, 24 November 2018, accessible at: https://www.facebook.com/momentumsheffield/videos/2164673313781282/

16. NatWest was next... its lending policies: *NatWest close branches after housing-benefit protests, The Guardian*, accessible at: https://www.theguardian.com/uk-news/2018/nov/24/natwest-close-branches-after-housing-benefit-protests

17. in March 2019, the bank agreed to meet ACORN's demands: *VICTORY: NatWest says Yes to DSS*, GMHA, accessible at: http://www.gmhousingaction.com/victory-natwest-says-yes-to-dss/

18 When Stephen Hill was invited... the Housing Futures collective: I attended the talk in person, but a recording is available on YouTube. See: *02 Housing Futures. Alternative Models of Ownership*, South Manchester News and Events Clubs, 25 Oct 2018, accessible at: https://youtu.be/4uaEYwgll8g?t=2883.

19. According to his bio on The Housing Forum... *'neighbourhood regeneration'*: Stephen Hill, The Housing Forum, accessible at: http://www.housingforum.org.uk/resources/about-us/board_profiles/stephen-hill

20. the work of Elinor Ostrom... its collective wealth: *Elinor Ostrom And The Digital Commons, Forbes*, accessible at: https://www.forbes.com/2009/10/13/open-source-net-neutrality-elinor-ostrom-nobel-opinions-contributors-david-bollier.html#2465d233406a

24. Could build-to-rent help?

1. The British Property Federation... Leeds and Birmingham: BPF BUILD TO RENT MAP OF THE UK, BPF, https://www.bpf.org.uk/what-we-do/bpf-build-rent-map-uk

2. The market has been forecast... 2017 and 2023: *Investors racing to invest in homes for Generation Rent, The Telegraph*, accessible at: https://www.telegraph.co.uk/business/2017/06/11/investors-racing-invest-homes-generation-rent/

3. a British Property Foundation... multilateral endorsement from MPs: *Majority of MPs back growing 'build-to-rent' housing sector*, BPF, accessible at: https://www.bpf.org.uk/media-listing/press-releases/british-property-federation-majority-mps-back-growing-%E2%80%98build-rent%E2%80%99

4 In 2014, it launched the £3.5 billion... purpose-built rental units: *£3.5*

billion funding boost for new rented homes, MHCLG, accessible at: https://www.gov.uk/government/news/35-billion-funding-boost-for-new-rented-homes.

5. Some £65 million funding... homes will be for rent: *£65 million government support for UK's largest Build to Rent site*, MHCLG, accessible at: https://www.gov.uk/government/news/65-million-government-support-for-uks-largest-build-to-rent-site

6. Homes and Communities Agency... heavily oversubscribed: *HAVE WE FOUND THE LISTED PRS VEHICLE WE WERE LOOKING FOR?* The Property Chronicle, accessible at: https://www.propertychronicle.com/found-listed-prs-vehicle-looking/

7. the former Olympic Village flats... Macquarie Capital: *Rent – the next big asset class? The Financial Times*, accessible at: https://www.ft.com/content/812a13bc-d5d8-11e3-83b2-00144feabdc0

8. the increasing numbers of young professionals... a whole lot sleepier: *The UK's rapid return to city centre living, BBC News*, accessible at: https://www.bbc.co.uk/news/uk-44482291

9. the promotional literature of... 'any issue, whether big or small': Essential Living website, accessible at: https://www.essentialliving.co.uk/

10. the FT interviewed... 'knit and natter groups': *Generation Rent finds a new landlord, The Financial Times*, accessible at: https://www.ft.com/content/784a697c-4386-11e6-9b66-0712b3873ae1

11. 'Generation rent and the end'... often have to contend with: *Generation Rent and the end of 'forever furniture,' The Financial Times*, accessible at: https://www.ft.com/content/faacdc0a-3601-11e8-8eee-e06bde01c544

12. *The Times* reported that... pay-as-you-wear' clothing services: *Generation Rent is targeted by pay-as-you-wear fashion firms, The Times*, accessible at: https://www.thetimes.co.uk/article/generation-rent-is-targeted-by-pay-as-you-wear-fashion-firms-7dngkbwx2

13. American investment management company JLL... 'super unaffordable': *Will tenants pay more rent for amenities?* JLL, accessible at: https://residential.jll.co.uk/insights/opinions/will-tenants-pay-more-rent-for-amenities

14. A *Guardian* article in 2018... about half their take-home pay: *Build-to-rent: how developers are profiting from Generation Rent, The Guardian*, accessible at: https://www.theguardian.com/housing-network/2018/apr/11/build-to-rent-developers-profiting-generation-rent

SECTION V. SOCIAL HOUSING NOW

25. Living on a council estate

1. In June 2018, 1.15 million... five years or more: *One year on from Grenfell, millions still stuck on housing waiting lists*, Shelter, accessible at: https://england.shelter.org.uk/media/press_releases/articles/one_year_on_from_grenfell,_millions_still_stuck_on_housing_waiting_lists

2. Right to Buy didn't just affect... high-rise tower blocks: Murie, Alan. *The Right to Buy?* (Bristol: Policy Press, 2016), pp. 70-76

3. To this day... a staggering 50 per cent: *Right to Buy: buying your council home*, Gov.uk, accessible at: https://www.gov.uk/right-to-buy-buying-your-council-home/discounts

4. 'priority need'... armed forces or prison: accessible at: *Rights and wrongs: The homelessness safety net 30 years on*, Shelter, https://england.shelter.org.uk/__data/assets/pdf_file/0015/48012/Briefing_Rights_and_Wrongs_Nov_2007.pdf

5. according to research by Criminology Professor... disproportionately on council estates: *How did the council house sell-off change crime risks?* Centre for Crime and Justice Studies, accessible at: https://www.crimeandjustice.org.uk/resources/how-did-council-house-sell-change-crime-risks

6. American social policy researcher... government handouts: Murray, Charles. et. al. *Charles Murray and the Underclass: The Developing Debate*, (London: The IEA Health and Welfare Unit, 1999), accessible at: https://www.civitas.org.uk/pdf/cw33.pdf

7. rumours began to swirl... turned out to be bogus: *Calling people chavs is criminal*, The Telegraph, accessible at: https://www.telegraph.co.uk/comment/columnists/christopherhowse/3560662/Calling-people-chavs-is-criminal.html

8. John Boughton... 'ever-increasing costs to government': *The White City Estate, Shepherd's Bush: 'I like it but maybe it's not for everyone,'* Municipal Dreams, accessible at: https://municipaldreams.wordpress.com/2017/01/24/the_white_city_estate_part_two/

26. Housing associations under pressure

1. Much to the exasperation... House of Lords: Lund, Brian. *Housing Politics in the United Kingdom*, (Bristol: Policy Press, 2016), p. 190

2. Firstly, the Housing Acts of 1985 and 1988... commercially-oriented social rented sector: Pawson, Hal. and Fancy, Cathie. Maturing assets: *The evolution of stock transfer housing associations*, (Bristol: Policy Press, 2003), pp. 5-6, accessible at: https://www.jrf.org.uk/file/36920/download?token=ioj9TkXE&filetype=full-report

3. In 1988, the Treasury... schemes alike: Lund (2016), pp. 190-191

4. Brumble's customer-facing annual report... in other areas: Source cannot be disclosed for legal reasons.

5. housing associations had their grants... really quite hard: In fact, the cuts were even deeper than this – closer to two thirds. See: *Housing associations' ability to build maybe 'seriously undermined' by cuts, PublicFinance*, accessible at: https://www.publicfinance.co.uk/news/2018/05/housing-associations-ability-build-maybe-seriously-undermined-cuts

6. David Cowans... in 2017/18: *Housing association chief executive salary survey 2018, Inside Housing*, accessible at: https://www.insidehousing.co.uk/insight/insight/housing-association-chief-executive-salary-survey-2018-57896

7. more than double that of the highest earning civil servant: Simon Bollom was the highest-paid individual in the civil service as of September 2018, with a 'Total Pay Ceiling' of £284,999. See: 'Senior officials 'high earners' salaries as at 30 September 2018,' *Cabinet Office senior officials 'high earners' salaries*, Cabinet Office, accessible at: https://assets.publishing.service.gov.uk/government/uploads/system/uploads/attachment_data/file/858878/Senior_officials__high_earners__salaries_as_at_30_September_2018.xlsx

8. the average earnings... £173,274: *Housing association chief executive salary survey 2018, Inside Housing*, accessible at: [see above]

9. the average salary of an NHS surgeon: This was reported as £59,101 on the 6th January 2020, see: *NHS – Physicians & Surgeons Salaries in the United Kingdom*, Indeed.co.uk, accessible at: https://www.indeed.co.uk/cmp/Nhs/salaries?job_category=meddr&start=30

10. September 2018... twice the rate of inflation: *Housing association chief executive salary survey 2018, Inside Housing*, accessible at: [see above]

11. vast operating surpluses: *Housing associations' record profits are no reason to rejoice, The Guardian*, accessible at: https://www.theguardian.com/housing-network/2018/feb/28/housing-associations-record-profits-affordable-homes

12. the total number... is in freefall: *Morning Briefing: government under pressure over falling social rent, Inside Housing*, accessible at: https://www.insidehousing.co.uk/news/news/morning-briefing-government-under-pressure-over-falling-social-rent-59232

13. a *New Statesman* report... 'longevity of income': *Investment funds have found a new cash cow: social housing, New Statesman*, accessible at: https://www.newstatesman.com/spotlight/housing/2018/03/investment-funds-have-found-new-cash-cow-social-housing

14. Social housing professionals... build affordable housing: *Seven problems with last night's Dispatches programme, Inside Housing*, accessible at:

https://www.insidehousing.co.uk/insight/seven-problems-with-last-nights-dispatches-programme-57239

15. 'Subsidised housing needs subsidy'... 'housing association surpluses': *Dispatches episode was not a balanced documentary, Inside Housing*, accessible at: https://www.insidehousing.co.uk/comment/dispatches-episode-was-not-a-balanced-documentary-57241

27. 'Intentionally homeless'

1. an anonymous council officer... 'as a matter of course': *Breaking the silence: a council insider shines a light on the homelessness crisis, Inside Housing*, accessible at: https://www.insidehousing.co.uk/insight/insight/breaking-the-silence-a-council-insider-shines-a-light-on-the-homelessness-crisis-57405

2. wait until 'the bailiffs arrive': HC Deb, 27 January 2017, Vol 620 Col 582, accessible at: https://hansard.parliament.uk/Commons/2017-01-27/debates/9B0EADC0-6050-477B-A649-19AEC91BAE33/Homelessness ReductionBill

3. housing solicitor Giles Peaker... 'during the passage of the Bill': *A bluffers guide to the Homeless Reduction Act 2017*, Nearly Legal: Housing Law News and Comment, accessible at: https://nearlylegal.co.uk/2017/05/bluffers-guide-homeless-reduction-act-2017/

4. Homelessness charity Crisis... 'ambition of the legislation': *Crisis response to DCLG's consultation paper on the Homelessness Code of Guidance for Local Authorities*, Crisis, accessible at: https://www.yhne.org.uk/wp-content/uploads/1711-Homelessness-code-of-guidance-response-FINAL.pdf

5. a 2019 survey revealed... under the new law: *UNCOMFORTABLE HOME TRUTHS REVEALED BY NLGN'S LATEST LEADERSHIP INDEX*, NLGN, accessible at: http://www.nlgn.org.uk/public/2019/uncomfortable-home-truths-revealed-by-nlgns-latest-leadership-index/

6. The successful pilot scheme... 'on the severed artery': *New homelessness act fails to address root causes, charities say, The Guardian*, accessible at: https://www.theguardian.com/society/2018/apr/03/homelessness-act-england-councils-legal-duty-fails-address-root-causes-charities-say

28. Social housing: the end game

1. Several of the Act's measures were never actually implemented: *Implementation of the Housing and Planning Act 2016*, HC Library, accessible at: https://researchbriefings.parliament.uk/ResearchBriefing/Summary/CBP-8229

2. Chief among these was the doomed 'starter homes' initiative...

regardless of local housing need: Bowie, Duncan. *Radical Solutions to the Housing Supply Crisis*, (Bristol: Policy Press, 2017), pp. 15-17

3. the extension of Right to Buy... 'high value' council homes had actually been sold: Wilson, Wendy, Bellis, Alexander, Cromarty, Hannah, Garton Grimwood, Gabrielle. *Briefing Paper: Implementation of the Housing and Planning Act 2016*, HC Library, p.11-12, accessible at: https://researchbriefings.parliament.uk/ResearchBriefing/Summary/CBP-8229#fullreport

4. Other proposals that ended up... 'fixed term' tenancies: Wilson, Wendy, et. al. *Briefing Paper: Implementation of the Housing and Planning Act 2016*, HC Library, p. 12 ('pay to stay') & p. 14 (end of secure tenancies for life), accessible at: [see above]

5. The 2016 law successfully managed to... steamroller the democratic process: *A wholesale power grab: how the UK government is handing housing over to private developers, The Guardian*, accessible at: https://www.theguardian.com/artanddesign/architecture-design-blog/2016/jan/05/housing-and-planning-bill-power-grab-developers

6. Architects for Social Housing... 'docile and accommodating': Regenerating *Hackney's Estates: The Dirty Tricks of a Dirty Council*, ASH, accessible at: https://architectsforsocialhousing.co.uk/2016/09/08/regenerating-hackneys-estates-the-dirty-tricks-of-a-dirty-council/

7. While councils are obliged by statute... hold onto their homes: Minton, Anna. *Big Capital: Who is London for?* (Penguin Random House UK, 2017), pp. 72-74

8. A BBC report... capital alone: *Dozens of London council estates earmarked for demolition, BBC News*, accessible at: https://www.bbc.co.uk/news/uk-england-london-45196994

9. The Mayor of London... mayoral funding: *Mayor's ballots requirement for estate regeneration comes into force*, London Assembly, accessible at: https://www.london.gov.uk/press-releases/mayoral/requirement-for-estate-regeneration-ballots

10. You'd think the law would make it mandatory... same quantities as before: *The truth about property developers: how they are exploiting planning authorities and ruining our cities, The Guardian*, accessible at: https://www.theguardian.com/cities/2014/sep/17/truth-property-developers-builders-exploit-planning-cities

11. Anna Minton, in her book... loophole-exploiting services: Minton, Anna. *Big Capital: Who is London for?* (Penguin Random House UK, 2017) pp. 34-35

12. much-awaited 'Social Housing Green Paper'... conversation on social housing: *A new deal for social housing*, MHLG, accessible at: https://assets.publishing.service.gov.uk/government/uploads/system/uploads/

attachment_data/file/733605/A_new_deal_for_social_housing_web_accessible.pdf

13. When the Secretary of State for Housing... social housing tenants: *Secretary of State announces new policies at Conservative Party Conference*, SP Broadway, accessible at: http://www.spbroadway.com/politics-of-planning/secretary-of-state-announces-new-policies-at-conservative-party-conference/

14. As research by the academic Alan Murie... public funds: Murie, Alan. *The Right to Buy?* (Bristol: Policy Press, 2016), p. 164

SECTION VI. WITH THE LANDLORDS

29. 'Is anybody here a socialist?'

1. As far back as 1893... leave [private landlordism] alone': Lund, Brian. *Housing Politics in the United Kingdom*, (Bristol: Policy Press, 2016), p. 92

2. A lesser-known raft of changes... their creditworthiness as individuals: *How the new PRA guidelines for portfolio landlords will affect you, Mortgages for Business*, accessible at: https://www.mortgagesforbusiness.co.uk/news-insight/2017/june/how-the-new-pra-guidelines-for-portfolio-landlords-will-affect-you/

3. centre-right think tank Onward... sell to a sitting tenant: *Make a house a home*, Onward, accessible at: https://www.ukonward.com/wp-content/uploads/2018/10/061018-Make-a-House-a-Home-Final-1-1.pdf

30. At the Landlord Advice Roadshow

1. In his book... 'criminal landlords': Lund, Brian. *Housing Politics in the United Kingdom*, (Bristol: Policy Press, 2016), pp. 108-109

2. Anna Minton... 'criminal human trafficking': Minton, Anna. *Big Capital: Who is London for?* (Penguin Random House UK, 2017), pp. 99-100

3. an investigation by *The Independent*... 'vermin infestation or faulty wiring': *Rogue private landlords given £2.5bn a year of public money, new analysis reveals, The Independent*, accessible at: https://www.independent.co.uk/news/uk/home-news/rogue-landlords-12-billion-25-rentals-property-public-money-housing-benefit-lease-flats-houses-a7926421.html

4. an investigation by Citizens' Advice... grin and bear their struggles: *Nearly half of tenants who make complaint face 'revenge eviction,' The Guardian*, accessible at: https://www.theguardian.com/money/2018/aug/23/uk-rent-groups-deliver-petition-calling-for-ban-on-unfair-evictions

31. Nest egg: property as a pension

1. Some 59 per cent... one in three are retired: *English Private Landlord Survey 2018*, MHCLG, accessible at: https://assets.publishing.service.gov. uk/government/uploads/system/uploads/attachment_data/file/775002/ EPLS_main_report.pdf
2. In 2010, the Office for National Statistics... Individual Savings Accounts (ISAs): *Early indicator estimates from the Wealth and Assets Survey: attitudes towards saving for retirement, automatic enrolment into workplace pensions, credit commitments and debt burden, July 2016 to June 2017*, ONS, accessible at: https://www.ons.gov.uk/peoplepopulationandcommunity/person alandhouseholdfinances/incomeandwealth/articles/earlyindicatoresti matesfromthewealthandassetssurvey/attitudestowardssavingforretire mentcreditcommitmentsanddebtburdenjuly2016tojune2017
3. very so often... 'complicated' stock market: For example, see Tweets by @MerrynSW, Aug 19, 2018 – 8:35 PM, Aug 27, 2018 – 11:24 AM and Aug 27, 2018 – 11:45 AM, accessible at: https://twitter.com/MerrynSW/ status/1031263366801752064, https://twitter.com/MerrynSW/status/1034 023824369573888 and https://twitter.com/MerrynSW/status/1034029 246803529728
4. But advances in medicine... the results were catastrophic: *Fears of 1980s-style pension mis-selling scandal grow*, FT Adviser, accessible at: https://www.ftadviser.com/pensions/2017/10/13/fears-grow-for-repeat-of-1980s-pension-mis-selling-scandal/
5. high-profile financial advice scams... 'precipice bonds': *Scandals eroded trust in financial advisers*, The Financial Times, accessible at: https://www. ft.com/content/5acf5082-6d0e-11e0-83fe-00144feab49a
6. a measure introduced by Gordon Brown... others were wound up: *Savers could have lost £230bn in Brown's pensions raid*, FT Adviser, accessible at: https://www.ftadviser.com/2014/05/07/opinion/tony-hazell/savers-could-have-lost-bn-in-brown-s-pensions-raid-WTQAjLW5DSRp 9HUxwNZN7K/article.html
7. Some commentators... arms of the buy-to-let industry: *Who can blame the buy-to-let landlords? The Guardian*, accessible at: https://www. theguardian.com/money/2007/jun/17/buyingtolet.business
8. This is undoubtedly a gross exaggeration... both employer and private: *FactCheck: Did Gordon destroy our pensions?* Channel 4 Fact Check, accessible at: https://www.channel4.com/news/articles/business_ money/factcheck+did+gordon+destroy+our+pensions/171020.html
9. Fergus and Judith Wilson... valued at over £75m: This wasn't a real headline, but a similar one appeared in 2004, see: *Tales of a Landlady:*

A route to royal riches, The Sunday Times, accessible at: https://www.thetimes.co.uk/article/tales-of-a-landlady-a-route-to-royal-riches-mbnr7octvtj

32. Inside the buy-to-let industry

1. Jim Cregan... genuinely obsessed with iced coffee: *Jimmy's Iced Coffee - Animation Video, Jimmy's Iced Coffee*, 16 Mar 2017, accessible at: https://www.youtube.com/watch?v=cJ8lHfR8dRI

2. Assured Shorthold Tenancy eviction... 'no longer accommodate': *Statutory Homelessness, April to June (Q2) 2019: England*, MHCLG, accessible at: https://assets.publishing.service.gov.uk/government/uploads/system/uploads/attachment_data/file/852953/Statutory_Homelessness_Statistical_Release_Apr-Jun_2019.pdf

3. Nowadays, a £300,000 pot... pension provider Aegon: *Average earners need £300k pension pot for comfortable retirement, YourMoney.com*, accessible at: https://www.yourmoney.com/retirement/average-earners-need-300k-pension-pot-comfortable-retirement/

4. In their book *The Rent Trap*... from private renters: Walker, Rosie, Jeraj, Samir. *The Rent Trap: How We Fell Into it and how We Get Out of it*, (London: Pluto Press, 2016), p. 136

5. roughly 22 per cent of private tenants... out of the public purse: *UK private rented sector: 2018*, ONS, accessible at: https://www.ons.gov.uk/economy/inflationandpriceindices/articles/ukprivaterentedsector/2018

6. a 'residential asset management' company for landlords: Adam Joseph, *The Happy Tenant Company, PropertyInvestorTODAY*, accessible at: https://www.propertyinvestortoday.co.uk/60-second-interview/2017/7/adam-joseph-the-happy-tenant-company

7. a happy tenant will... improve long-term returns: *About Us, The Happy Tenant Company*, accessible at: https://www.happytenant.co.uk/about

33. Now for the 'crackdown'

1. The then Chancellor... 'can't afford a home to buy': Lund, Brian. *Housing Politics in the United Kingdom*, (Bristol: Policy Press, 2016), p. 114

2. an entire portfolio of 46 'traditional residential units'... '£235,584 per annum': The original page is no longer available. It used to be accessible at: https://www.rightmove.co.uk/property-for-sale/property-76819814.html

3. 40 per cent of ex council houses... possession of private landlords: *Forty percent of homes sold under Right to Buy now in the hands of private landlords, new analysis reveals, The Independent*, accessible at: https://www.

independent.co.uk/news/uk/politics/right-to-buy-homes-sold-private-landlords-latest-figures-rent-a8098126.html

4. UK Foreign Affairs Committee... dirty Russian money: *Moscow's Gold: Russian Corruption in the UK*, HC Foreign Affairs Committee, accessible at: https://publications.parliament.uk/pa/cm201719/cmselect/cmfaff/932/932.pdf

5. *Private Eye* magazine... offshore-registered companies: *Selling England (and Wales) by the pound, Private Eye*, accessible at: https://www.private-eye.co.uk/registry

6. *The Money Observer* puts this down to... foreign currencies: British investors cool on UK residential property, but foreign buyers are still bullish, *Money Observer*, accessible at: https://www.moneyobserver.com/news/british-investors-cool-uk-residential-property-foreign-buyers-are-still-bullish

7. landlord software provider PropertyHawk... 'moral compass': *Lease options explained*, PropertyHawk, https://www.propertyhawk.co.uk/magazines/lease-options-explained/

SECTION VII. WHAT SHOULD WE DO?

34. Some ways to make the system work

1. In its 2019 election manifesto... 'passported' to the next one: *The Conservative and Unionist Party Manifesto 2019*, p. 29, accessible at: https://assets-global.website-files.com/5da42e2cae7ebd3f8bde353c/5dda924905da587992a064ba_Conservative%202019%20Manifesto.pdf

2. Scottish landlords can still evict... his or her property: *Grounds for eviction for private residential tenancy tenants*, Shelter Scotland, accessible at: https://scotland.shelter.org.uk/get_advice/advice_topics/eviction/eviction_of_private_tenants/grounds_for_eviction_for_private_residential_tenancy_tenants

3. the one million... social housing waiting lists: *Some 1.15 million households 'stuck' on social housing waiting lists*, 24 housing, accessible at: https://www.24housing.co.uk/news/some-1-15-million-households-stuck-on-social-housing-waiting-lists/

4. support for 'mixed tenure' private developments: It was highlighted as far back as 2003 that 'mixed tenure' development is often used as a 'euphemism' for privatisation. See: Tunstall, Dr Rebecca. *'Mixed tenure' policy in the UK: privatisation, pluralism or euphemism?* in Housing, Theory and Society (2003), Vol 20 Issue 3, pp. 153-159

5. higher quality: according to the English Housing Survey, socially rented homes are on average in better condition than both owner-occupied

and privately rented homes. See: *English Housing Survey 2018 to 2019*: headline report, MHCLG, accessible at: https://assets.publishing. service.gov.uk/government/uploads/system/uploads/attachment_data/ file/860076/2018-19_EHS_Headline_Report.pdf

6. They were fed up... skirt rules on rent controls: *Berlin's grassroots plan to re-nationalise up to 200,000 ex-council homes from corporate landlords*, The Conversation, accessible at: https://theconversation.com/berlins-grassroots-plan-to-renationalise-up-to-200-000-ex-council-homes-from-corporate-landlords-112884

7. in April 2019, protesters took to the streets... as far away as London': *Berlin's rental revolution: activists push for properties to be nationalised*, The Guardian, accessible at: https://www.theguardian.com/cities/2019/apr/04/berlins-rental-revolution-activists-push-for-properties-to-be-nationalised

8. nasty ideas like... for homeless people: *Hundreds of homeless people given one-way tickets to other areas by their local councils*, The Independent, accessible at: https://www.independent.co.uk/news/uk/home-news/homeless-people-reconnection-policies-one-way-tickets-train-bus-councils-local-authorities-cuts-a8005606.html

9. The housing associations that were inspired... the scourge of homelessness: Lund, Brian. *Housing Politics in the United Kingdom*, (Bristol: Policy Press, 2016), pp. 188-189

10. more investor-friendly: For example, see: *Investing in housing associations*, Kames Capital, accessible at: https://kamescapital.com/investing_in_housing_associations.aspx

11. we could make Housing Associations... Freedom of Information Act: a campaign for this is already underway. See: *Bring housing associations and public service contractors under FOI*, Campaign for Freedom of Information, accessible at: https://www.cfoi.org.uk/2017/07/bring-housing-associations-and-public-service-contractors-under-foi/

12 In 1979, 20 per cent... 10.5 per cent: *Why did we not know? LRB*, accessible at: https://www.lrb.co.uk/the-paper/v41/n10/ian-jack/why-did-we-not-know.

13. In his review... without our consent: *Why did we not know? LRB*, accessible at: [see above]

14. The demand for developable land... a typical UK home: *The UK's market for land is broken but it can be fixed*, The Telegraph, accessible at: https://www.telegraph.co.uk/business/2019/11/17/uks-market-land-broken-can-fixed/

15. Since 2012-13... yet to be completed: *Beautiful homes on sunlit uplands? Not once the developers are in charge*, The Guardian, accessible at: https://www.theguardian.com/society/2020/feb/21/beautiful-homes-on-sunlit-

uplands-not-once-the-developers-are-in-charge

16. accusations of 'land hoarding'... at local governments: Christophers, Brett. *The New Enclosure: The Appropriation of Public Land in Neoliberal Britain* (London: Verso, 2018), p. 133

17. As Josh Ryan-Collins et. al. highlight... during market slumps: Ryan-Collins, Josh, Lloyd, Toby, Macfarlane, Laurie. *Rethinking the Economics of Land and Housing*, (London: Zed Books Ltd, 2017), p. 97, pp. 214-215

18. When the property development industry imploded... shortage of bricks: *Bricks Campaign: A report for NAEA Propertymark*, Centre for Economics and Business Research, accessible at: https://www.naea. co.uk/media/1044993/bricks-report.pdf

19. private housebuilding... peak in council housebuilding: *How Macmillan built 300,000 houses a year*, Conservative Home, accessible at: https:// www.conservativehome.com/thetorydiary/2013/10/how-macmillan-built-300000-houses-a-year.html

20. Government must no longer be... politically controversial: *May's housing adviser backs campaign to force landowners to offer huge discount on their land, The Telegraph*, accessible at: https://www.telegraph.co.uk/ politics/2018/08/26/mays-housing-adviser-backs-campaign-force-landowners-offer-huge/

21. Prime Minister... accessing finance to build homes: *'My time at Number 10': an interview with former government housing advisor Toby Lloyd, Inside Housing*, accessible at: https://www.insidehousing.co.uk/insight/insight/ my-time-at-number-10-an-interview-with-former-government-housing-advisor-toby-lloyd-63073

22. Ditto for housing sold as 'freehold'... endless fees and management charges: As government wises up to the abuses of leasehold, developers and estate management firms are devising alternative ways to sustain their revenue streams. See: *'Fleecehold' property trap returns to parliamentary agenda with new private member's bill*, LKP, accessible at: https://www.leaseholdknowledge.com/fleecehold-property-trap-retu rns-to-parliamentary-agenda-with-new-private-members-bill/

23. 'Stray away from mainstream living'... 'a great stinking recycling yard': Tweet by @BagelFactoryE9, Sep 4, 2018, accessible at: https://twitter. com/BagelFactoryE9/status/1037014525025890304

24. According to the BBC... stood at 1,200: *Dozens of London council estates earmarked for demolition, BBC News*, accessible at: https://www.bbc.co.uk/ news/uk-england-london-45196994

1. In 1879, George published... *and Poverty*: George, Henry. *Progress and Poverty* (CreateSpace Independent Publishing Platform, 2017)

35. Time for a land value tax

2. *Progress and Poverty*... except the Bible: *The time may be right for land-value taxes, The Economist*, accessible at: https://www.economist.com/briefing/2018/08/09/the-time-may-be-right-for-land-value-taxes

3. It's the latter component... in the last 20 years: *Where's all the money gone?* Shelter, accessible at: https://blog.shelter.org.uk/2017/12/wheres-all-the-money-gone/

4. many economists... fairest form of tax: *Why Henry George had a point, The Economist*, accessible at: https://www.economist.com/free-exchange/2015/04/01/why-henry-george-had-a-point

5. According to a *Financial Times* article... recommended a land value tax: *Fairer fixes for the public purse lost in a chancellor's drawer, The Financial Times*, accessible at: https://www.ft.com/content/251ddb24-1d5b-11e4-b927-00144feabdc0

6. The Stern cover-up... 'neither confirm nor deny' the report's existence: Harrison, Fred. *As Evil Does* (Teddington: Geophilos, 2016), pp. 63-64

7. Theresa May... 'homes and gardens': *Land Value (or Garden) Tax – more Adam Smith than Marx, British Politics and Policy Blog*, LSE, accessible at: https://blogs.lse.ac.uk/politicsandpolicy/land-value-tax-history/

8. Sections of the press... came to pass: *Labour's Land Value Tax: will you have to sell your garden?* Full Fact, accessible at: https://fullfact.org/economy/labours-land-value-tax-will-you-have-sell-your-garden/

9. A 'Georgist' economist... 'single tax propaganda': Gaffney, Mason. 'Neoclassical Economics as a Stratagem against Henry George,' in Gaffney, Mason and Harrison, Fred, *The Corruption of Economics*, (London: Shepheard-Walwyn, 1994), pp. 29-145, accessible at: https://masongaffney.org/publications/K1Neo-classical_Stratagem.CV.pdf

10. The housing policy with the most damage potential... 'cost of deposits': *The Conservative and Unionist Party Manifesto 2019*, p. 29, accessible at: https://assets-global.website-files.com/5da42e2cae7ebd3f8bde353c/5dda924905da587992a064ba_Conservative%202019%20Manifesto.pdf

11. The solution proposed... afford a mortgage: *Resentful Renters: How Britain's housing market went wrong, and what we can do to fix it*, CPS, accessible at: https://www.cps.org.uk/files/reports/original/191222122235-ResentfulRentersFINAL.pdf

12. I tweeted about... 'a point we address thoroughly': Tweet by @rcolvile, Dec 23, 2019, accessible at: https://twitter.com/rcolvile/status/1208932161300107265

13. the report openly accepts... further tax changes: *Resentful Renters: How Britain's housing market went wrong, and what we can do to fix it*, CPS, pp. 30-31, accessible at: [see above]

14. Banks pump roughly... grow the economy: In 2018, secured lending to individuals accounted for £1.2 trillion of the £2.2 trillion total UK debt outstanding (approx. 55 per cent), while 'productive lending,' i.e. loans to sectors which contribute to GDP, constituted £226.5 billion – just 10.4 per cent. See: *HOW HAS BANK LENDING FARED SINCE THE CRISIS?* Positive Money, accessible at: https://positivemoney.org/2018/06/how-has-bank-lending-fared-since-the-crisis/

15. The Shadow Housing Secretary... annual house price inflation target: *Labour considers house price inflation target for Bank of England, The Guardian*, accessible at: https://www.theguardian.com/business/2019/apr/10/labour-considers-house-price-inflation-target-for-bank-of-england

16. Council tax reform... pay just 1.3 per cent: *A POOR TAX: COUNCIL TAX IN LONDON: TIME FOR REFORM*, IPPR, accessible at: https://www.ippr.org/files/2018-03/a-poor-tax-council-tax-in-london.pdf

17. a report on land-use reform... not domiciled in the UK for tax purposes: *LAND FOR THE MANY*, accessible at: https://landforthemany.uk/wp-content/uploads/2019/06/land-for-the-many.pdf

18. Homeownership nationwide... forecast to dwindle over the next 20 years: *UK set to become a nation of renters in next 20 years, Property Wire*, accessible at: https://www.propertywire.com/news/uk/uk-set-to-become-a-nation-of-renters-in-next-20-years/

19. NatWest bank has predicted that... than mortgagees: *More People will Rent than Own their Homes in 8 Years, Economist Believes, Landlordnewsco.uk*, accessible at: https://www.landlordnews.co.uk/people-will-rent-homes-8-years/

20. In London... owning as of 2016: *In London, Renters Now Outnumber Homeowners, CITYLAB*, accessible at: https://www.citylab.com/equity/2016/02/londons-renters-now-outnumber-homeowners/470946/

21. Tenants now save more... pensions of their own: The average pension contribution in 2017/18 was £2,700, while the average private rent in the same year was £908 per month (£10,896 for the year). *See Average pension contributions fall, FT Adviser*, and *HomeLet Rental Index*, HomeLet, accessible at: https://www.ftadviser.com/pensions/2019/09/26/average-pension-contributions-fall/ and https://homelet.co.uk/assets/documents/HomeLet-Rental-Index-June-2018.pdf

22. Mortgaged homeowners... own outright: *UK private rented sector: 2018*, ONS, accessible at: https://www.ons.gov.uk/economy/inflationand riceindices/articles/ukprivaterentedsector/2018

23. The value of private rented sector... in 2018 alone: *UK housing stock gains £190 billion and hits a record £7.3 trillion valuation*, Savills, accessible at: https://www.savills.co.uk/insight-and-opinion/savills-news/273857/uk-housing-stock-gains-%C2%A3190-billion-and-hits-a-record-%C2%A37.3-

trillion-valuation

24. about £22,000... in the UK: Assuming a UK population of 66.44 million (2018). See: *Population (United Kingdom),* accessible at: https://www.google.com/publicdata/explore?ds=jqd8iprpslrch_&met_y=pop&idim=country:GB&hl=en&dl=en

INDEX

Telling the real story since 2013

www.canburypress.com